Odd Man Out

A Memoir of the Hollywood Ten

Edward Dmytryk

**Southern Illinois
University Press**

Carbondale and
Edwardsville

Designed by Hillside Studio, Inc.
Production supervised by Natalia Nadraga
03 02 01 00   5 4 3 2

Library of Congress
Cataloging-in-Publication Data

Dmytryk, Edward.
   Odd man out: a memoir of the
   Hollywood Ten/Edward Dmytryk.
        p.   cm.
   Includes index.
   1. Dmytryk, Edward. 2. Motion picture
producers and directors—United States—
Biography. 3. Communism and motion
pictures—United States. I. Title.
PN1998.3.D6A3   1996
809'.916—dc20   —dc20
[791.43'0233'092]
[B]   94-39958
                             CIP

ISBN 0-8093-1998-5 (cloth).—
ISBN 0-8093-1999-3 (paper)

The paper used in this publication meets
the minimum requirements of American
National Standard for Information
Sciences—Permanence of Paper for Printed
Library Materials, ANSI Z39.48-1984. ∞

I allowed myself to be forced into a position of feeling guilty ... about the very virtues of love and pity and a passion for individual freedom which had brought me close to Communism. The Communists told me those feelings were "bourgeois." The Communist, having joined the Party, has to castrate himself of the reasons which have made him one.

—Stephen Spender, *The God That Failed*

Contents

Illustrations   *ix*

    1. *Mr. Tavenner.* What is your
name, please?   *1*

    2. For a short time during the
thirties   *10*

    3. In 1944   *18*

    4. "Time is but the stream I go
a-fishing in"   *24*

    5. This book is not   *27*

    6. In the fall of 1947,
Joe McCarthy   *33*

    7. "Hollywood Accused"   *39*

    8. The honorable J. Parnell
Thomas   *50*

    9. *Mr. Crum.* May I request the
right of cross-examination?   *57*

  10. The hearings were now
history   *72*

  11. We had departed   *89*

  12. The next day   *96*

  13. Our return to our country's
capital   *102*

  14. On Sunset Boulevard   *111*

  15. On June 9, 1950   *118*

Contents

16. West Virginia   *127*

17. "It's a *beautiful* morning"   *135*

18. The one certain thing   *143*

19. After a long, slow trip   *150*

20. *Mr. Tavenner.* What is your
name, please?   *156*

21. The FBI   *170*

22. The Menjou anecdote   *178*

23. Once again   *186*

24. In 1926   *193*

25. The July 20, 1988 issue   *197*

26. It is odd, but amusing   *201*

Index   *205*

Illustrations

Directing Ginger Rogers in *Tender Comrade*, 1943   77

Directing Dick Powell and Claire Trevor in *Murder, My Sweet*, 1944   77

With John Wayne and Paul Fix on the set of *Back to Bataan*, 1944   78

Portrait photo, 1944   78

Communist Political Association membership card, 1944   79

Preamble to the Constitution of the Communist Party of the United States   79

Subpoena to appear before HUAC, Sept. 18, 1947   80

With Bartley Crum and Adrian Scott, Washington, D.C., Oct. 1947   81

Crossfire nominated for five Academy Awards, 1948   82–83

On garage duty in prison, Mill Point, West Va., 1950   84

Letter from prison denying Communist Party affiliation, Sept. 9, 1950   85

With Spencer Tracy on the set of *The Broken Lance*, Arizona, 1953   86

On the set of *The Caine Mutiny*, 1953   87

On the set of *Raintree County*, 1956   88

Odd
Man
Out

1

Mr. Tavenner.	**What is your name, please?**
Mr. Dmytryk.	Edward Dmytryk.
Mr. Tavenner.	And the spelling is D-m-y-t-r-y-k?
Mr. Dmytryk.	That is right.
Mr. Tavenner.	When and where were you born, Mr. Dmytryk?
Mr. Dmytryk.	I was born in Canada, Grand Forks, British Columbia, September 4, 1908.
Mr. Tavenner.	Are you a naturalized American citizen?
Mr. Dmytryk.	I am . . .
Mr. Tavenner.	What is your profession?
Mr. Dmytryk.	I am a screen director . . .
Mr. Tavenner.	And you are one of those commonly referred to as the "Hollywood Ten"?
Mr. Dmytryk.	I was.
Mr. Tavenner.	I notice you say you "was", rather than "are."
Mr. Dmytryk.	I don't think I will be considered so much longer.
Mr. Tavenner.	Your testimony today will throw considerable light on the subject?
Mr. Dmytryk.	I imagine so, yes.
Mr. Tavenner.	I believe you are one of the group who were prosecuted for contempt of Congress, and that you received a sentence, and that you have served that sentence?
Mr. Dmytryk.	I have, yes.[1]

Saint John quoted Christ as saying, "And the truth shall make you free." Well, I was willing to give it a try. Not that I had lied the first time. I had, in effect, said nothing, and I had been sorry for it ever since. Now I was trying to make amends: to Congress, to my wife and family, and to others who had been hurt in the process. After nearly four years of navi-

---

1. House Committee on Un-American Activities, April 25, 1951. All of the hearing material in this book is excerpted from the official transcripts of the Hearings before the Committee on Un-American Activities of the House of Representatives.

gating a storm-driven sea, where each impossibly dark cloud was blacker than its predecessor, and which had included two years in exile and six months in prison, I was steering for a harbor that might furnish some peace and stability. But I had still to negotiate a most-difficult passage—I had to exorcise the past, and I knew even then that the rite of purgation heals old wounds only at the cost of new ones that would affect the remaining years of my life. I had to make a second appearance before the House Committee on Un-American Activities (HUAC). And I was sworn to tell the truth, the whole truth, and nothing but the truth, and to tell it in public.

I was going to name names.

But jumping into the middle of this story is no way to relate a tragedy that actually began in California on a fateful day in 1947.

That was a great year for clarets; it was also a great year for me, at least for the first nine months. September in southern California is usually a month of beautiful days, and this particular late September day was perfect. Thirty years later, I wrote in my memoirs: "I was on top of the world and confident of the future. The way things were going I could be rich in a few years. Jean and I were more in love than ever. We had bought a hundred acres near Agoura, were drilling water wells, and planning our house and horse farm. One Sunday afternoon, after a day spent in pruning some of the great oak trees on our land, Jean and I sat on a hill looking out over a lovely landscape. We could see forever, and there wasn't a cloud in the sky. The next day I was handed a pink subpoena."

For me, and for Jean, that hot pink subpoena marked the beginning of a new and difficult life, though I didn't know it then. Like many dire documents, it had a totally unexpected cause, fathered by misunderstanding and born of fear. Its distressing aftereffects brought outrageous fortune to scores of other lives and still affects, in a number of ways, not the license but the freedom of too many Hollywood filmmakers.

Something as intimidating as a congressional subpoena is, by its very nature, never the beginning of an investigation; it is a culmination of earlier sleuthing of which the recipient of the subpoena is quite ignorant. And sifting through the past years for a clue to the real start of this unwelcome situation led me back to a short time after the Japanese attack on Pearl Harbor, another date that changed millions of lives but affected mine only indirectly.

Despite my age, thirty-three, my marital and parental status, I was

1-A in the draft (clue number one). I wondered about that but dismissed it as an example of bureaucratic thinking. However, I anticipated an eventual participation in the war, and I prepared for it. I brushed up on my math and the science of navigation, sold my home in Sherman Oaks to my old friend, Dick Arlen, and bought an income-producing apartment building in Beverly Hills that would take care of the mortgage payments with enough left over to keep my wife and eighteen-month-old son, Michael, in relative comfort for the duration of the war.

Somewhere around that time, I heard that Colonel Frank Capra was putting together a Signal corps unit to record the war on film. I visited his temporary headquarters at the old Fox lot at Sunset Boulevard and Western Avenue and volunteered my services—not as a director, since I assumed that Capra was quite capable of handling that job, but as a film editor, a craft in which I had an industry-wide reputation. My offer was warmly accepted, and I was told to sit tight and wait for the word. I waited. And waited. But the word never came. Nor did I ever receive an explanation from Capra or any of his assistants. (If I had, I may have stopped to think—and that was clue number two.) It was some ten years later that I learned the Signal Corps had turned me down as a security risk: I had been a premature antifascist.

That term, which may sound like double-talk to our younger generations, was used before, during, and long after the war as one of the leading loyalty-check guides. It meant that anyone who was *currently* against Franco's Spain, Mussolini's Italy, or Hitler's Germany was OK; obviously, we were at war with them. But anyone who had been against the same regimes *before* December 7, 1941, was just as obviously an extreme and dangerous leftist, since only the communists officially resisted the spread of fascism at that time. Of course, most premature antifascists were not communists, but that was an issue that attracted many, including me, to the Party.

While I waited for the call that never came, I made several films, one of which, *Hitler's Children*, became my passport to fame and fortune (a phrase difficult to write with a straight face), and A pictures. The film was one of the great sleepers of Hollywood history; costing about $100,000, it reaped, by some accounts, a harvest of seventy-five times that amount. And all of this only in that part of the world not yet under the domination of the Axis.

My first A film was *Tender Comrade*, a mild propaganda picture aimed at the wives and women workers of our wartime economy. It would function as a mild wavemaker during the HUAC hearings in 1947. (It may be hard to believe, but I have just realized that the word *comrade* in the title could set off an alarm that would frighten a large number of sensitive patriots. But in 1943, when the film was shot, it was simply half of a title derived from a poet's encomium to his beloved wife.)

I was now in the big league, walking the high road. I had a script written by Dalton Trumbo, Hollywood's most successful writer (later identified as a communist); a cast spilling over with talent, headed by Oscar winner Ginger Rogers; a sixty-day shooting schedule; and a ball of lead in my stomach. I was scared stiff—not of the project, but of Ginger Rogers, RKO's biggest star.

Ginger turned out to be a pleasant and highly disciplined professional who, far from throwing her weight around, treated me as if I were a seasoned director. Possibly taking their cues from Ginger, so did the rest of the cast and crew, and in a few days, my stomach returned to its usual gastritic state. Today I consider *Tender Comrade* an overly sentimental, even mawkish film, but it suited the times and was something more than a modest success. It told the stories of four working wives who pool their resources while their husbands are at the front. They share a house, a housekeeper, a car, and their fears, hopes, disappointments, and triumphs. Their relationship is based on the motto "Share and share alike," which, at a time of sacrifice for all Americans, sounded unequivocally democratic, even to Ginger's mother, Lela. But four years later, during the hearings, this unselfish phrase colored me red.

Tender Comrade was followed by *Murder, My Sweet*, an all-out critical and financial success for RKO, and when the cinema theorists of Europe hailed it as a classic and the genesis of film noire, it was a gold mine for me. I was airborne—and so was my wife. She decided to establish a separate residence in New York while suing for divorce, leaving Michael with me in Beverly Hills. I could now afford the separate status, as well as a housekeeper-governess for my son, and this presented no problem; in fact, it eliminated a few.

I am a Canadian-born Ukrainian whose parents had left their corner of the Austro-Hungarian Empire to escape the exploitation of the Slavic peoples who lived inside the eastern border of that decaying realm. My parents settled in Grand Forks, British Columbia, a few miles above the American border. My father farmed in the spring and summer and worked in the local copper smelter in the fall and winter. With the help of my mother, who worked all hours, all days, in all seasons, he was doing well, even sending money to the Old Country to buy property against our eventual return. Then World War I erupted.

Once more my father had to run, but now with four sons as well as his wife. The Canadian government was interning all immigrants who had been citizens of Austria, and that meant primarily the Ruthinian Ukrainians. My father slipped the few miles across the border to Northport, Washington, where, as luck would have it, there was a lead smelter. He built a small house with a well pump in the kitchen instead of the backyard, and there we lived until my mother succumbed to a ruptured appendix early in 1917. (We were Catholics, and we consoled ourselves by noting that she died at thirty-three, the age at which Christ was crucified.) My father picked up his four sons and headed for the land of sunshine and oranges—a dream he must have dreamed all along. Our first stop was San Francisco in 1917; then two years later, my father married a woman of Pennsylvania Dutch extraction, and we all moved to a Los Angeles suburb called Sherman, later renamed West Hollywood.

Mike Dmytryk was a superb survivor but a cruel father, and to escape my own mistreatment and exploitation, I ran away from home at the age of fourteen. But not too far. Through the good graces of an older friend, I fell into a job at Famous Players Lasky Studio at Sunset and Vine. Starting at $6.00 a week, I made just enough money to work my way through high school. Suddenly, no longer a child, I was on my way to a filmmaking career, though I didn't know it.

You have been subjected to this thumbnail sketch of my childhood because it may contain a few clues to an understanding of my later feelings about the downtrodden and the socially handicapped, feelings that have a great deal to do with communism's appeal to the socially aware. After all, how can you understand why I turned against the Party unless you understand why I first turned toward it?

In 1944, just three years before the hearings, I held no deep or binding feeling about politics. I felt no great pity for the afflicted; I had grown up in the same world, and if I could get out, so could they. Anyway, I was too busy making a place for myself in American society. My father had taken out his "first papers" but had neglected the final step. My own concern for civic responsibilities was so vague that I did not become a citizen until 1939, the year I became a full-fledged film director, with a one-year contract to make B films for Paramount, the studio where I had grown up. All in all, it was a good year and I had no reason and felt no

Odd Man Out

urge to change the system. I was against fascism on humanitarian rather than political grounds, and having matured during the Great Depression, I believed that one could be concerned with the problems of the wretched of the world while leaning neither right nor left. I certainly did not tolerate the idea of armed revolution, but I believed that social progress could be made through persuasion leading to legislation. Of course, I was only partly right; with the advent of World War II, my perceptions began to change.

It wasn't the fighting that changed them; it was the emergence of Hollywood as a temporary world center of culture. The influx of European intellectuals had started earlier as men like Aldous Huxley, and the two Christophers, Frye and Isherwood, became permanent residents; later, the war in Europe spouted exiles like an anthropomorphic Vesuvius. Many of those displaced persons were artists working in different fields, but whether they were writers like Thomas Mann or Lion Feuchtwanger, playwrights like Bertholdt Brecht, filmmakers like Fritz Lang or Franz Murnau, composers like Arnold Shoenberg or Hans Eisler, they came and settled in Hollywood. (After the war, HUAC's demonstration of the congressional concept of democracy caused many of them, even some who had become American citizens, to return to their more democratic native countries. This was probably the Committee's worst legacy, and Hollywood and the United States are much poorer for it.)

It was probably pure coincidence, but the beginning of the war also marked the theatrical world's recognition of the unmatched influence of Hollywood's product. Easterners, primarily men and women from New York, including such theatrical idols as Harold Clurman and Clifford Odets, invaded Hollywood in noticeable numbers. To us natives, they were definitely a political breed, activists of a type we had rarely seen. They seemed to live much closer to reality, and whatever their political affiliations, their dramatic theories were based on Marxist philosophy. Their ideas flooded our arid community, and some of us began to realize how unsophisticated we really were. In the main, the old guard ignored them, but many of the town's younger filmmakers who were at odds with Louis B. Mayer's vision of the world embraced the new ideas and eagerly explored the avenues that had opened up in the development of story, background, and especially character and social concerns. It was a new frontier, and what curious mind could ignore it?

Ideas alone are never enough; action is necessary. And action followed quickly. First came the Actors' Lab, a spin-off of the Actors' Studio. It was there I met Larry Parks. The lab was soon joined by the People's Educational Center (I will let you guess the dangerous word in that title), which held classes in several private homes. I was occasionally invited to lecture on film editing and directing. Before long, the school was endowed with enough money to allow it to move into an abandoned school building on Vine Street, just north of Hollywood Boulevard. Few of us wondered about the identity of the donor, and once the school was centralized, I accepted, at no salary, the chairmanship of an orientation course in filmmaking. My guest lecturers included such film greats as Lewis Milestone, George Cukor, William Cameron Menzies, and James Wong Howe.

Under the auspices of a number of leading writers, the Writers Mobilization not only supplied material to be presented at the front by the USO, it also organized seminars to inform Hollywood workers about the political background and causes of the war. As this work went on, I was informed, quite casually, that both the Writers Mobilization and the Educational Center had been created and financed by the communist members of the industry.

I found this information interesting and by no means a deterrent. On the face of it, both these activities and others that soon came to my attention were generous and high-minded enterprises—a benefit to all. I considered the work of the Educational Center irreplaceable—a high mark for whoever had financed the school. Few universities of the time offered courses in filmmaking, and those available were crude and unsatisfactory. The Writers Mobilization was the only group in town that concerned itself with the causes and the purposes of the war against fascism. At the same time, study groups were organized to help young war wives fill their lonely hours while they waited for their husbands' return. The Hollywood Citizens Committee of the Arts, Sciences, and Professions was also active in its support of the war effort.

And all of these activities were created, organized, and sustained in large part by the Communist Party of America.

While I was involved in these movements, I had looked around, wanting to do more. But neither the Democrats nor the Republicans were taking any organized action to mobilize American youth. It suddenly seemed quite clear that only the communists cared. And though I had previously given no thought to becoming a party member, when I was approached, sometime in 1944, I was ready to be had.

The procedure: I was invited to a gathering of some twenty-odd men and women at the home of Frank Tuttle, a prominent film director. Some of those present were undoubtedly communists, though none advertised it. But some, like myself, were there to learn what it was really all about. The chief salesman was Alvah Bessie, later one of the Hollywood Ten. I had not met him before. He had been an active member of the Lincoln Brigade in the Spanish civil war, which was another plus for the Party. Although that made him a very premature antifascist, most Americans had sympathized with the Spanish Republicans, and Bessie had become a small celebrity in local liberal circles. His tale of the communist effort in the war was quite impressive (although, as I learned later, not entirely true) and only a little self-serving.

By the end of the evening, the air was filled with excitement, tinged with a seductive undercurrent of secretiveness, and when the membership applications were handed out, I signed without a qualm. Both the secrecy, which, at the moment I did not question, and the inner excitement were augmented by my membership book, number 84961, issued on May 6, 1944, in the name of Michael Edwards (hardly a difficult alias for the FBI to decode, which shows how little I thought of the secretiveness). The book further included the preamble of the consistitution of the Communist Party of the U.S.A., and that was an added excitement. It read, in part: "The Communist Party of the U.S.A. is a . . . political party carrying forward . . . the traditions of Jefferson, Paine, Jackson and Lincoln . . . it upholds and defends the United States Constitution . . . through a government of the people, by the people, and for the people; its abolition of all exploitation of man by man, nation by nation, and race by race . . . striving toward a world without oppression and war, a world of brotherhood of man." Now I ask you, what collection of rhetoric (borrowed though it was) could be more uplifting or more American in spirit?

There was no word there of revolution, violence, or terrorism; nothing but pious promises of reliance on the constitutional rights of citizens to create a perfect world. And when Bessie warned us that party discipline was difficult and rigid, we related that warning to the efforts we were expected to expend in pursuit of that perfection, and we were all the more eager to prove our mettle. What novitiate would suspect that the rigid discipline referred to was to be applied to the control of creative thought?

My initiation fee was 50 cents. I paid $2.00 in dues in June and $2.50 more in July, and that was my only financial contribution to Communism. Shortly after I had become a member, the Party changed its name to the Political Association to signify its war-born rapprochement with the American political system. I received my Political Association card, number 46859, on July 6, 1944, and my membership in the Party was considered a thing of the past. Although many of us were elated by the seeming progress in our country's relationship with the Soviet Union, the new name did nothing to change the underlying organization or its spirit. Soon after the end of the war, the name change was reversed. Once more we were members of the CPA, and the excitement generated by the will-o'-the-wisp rapprochement quickly faded, as did my esteem for party discipline. But disillusionment developed slowly; dreams die hard.

2

For a short time during the thirties, Ernst Lubitsch, one of Hollywood's greatest directors, took over the reins as vice president of production at Paramount—nobody knew why. But everybody waited for the inevitable. As expected, he suffered through a few weeks in the gigantic office, then resigned in disgust. He was an artist, not a businessman; organization on that scale was not for him. Lubitsch was no communist, but his dilemma was only a slight variation of one of the least-understood contradictions of the communist movement in the theatrical fields. It is a given that a real artist must be free to break the rules, to experiment with those still unacknowledged, and to search for those unknown; creativity finds it difficult to flourish when circumscribed by an index, whether religious or political. Yet a number of artists willingly joined an organization whose very existence depended on a fixed structure and on the restrictive discipline that made that structure impregnable. And impregnable it was—until Gorbachev.

I had always had some distaste for organizations beyond those of the movie set and the guilds I necessarily belonged to, and now I found myself bemused by the processes I encountered as a member of the CPA. At this late date, I can't remember what a "section" was, or a "fraction," but I believe the various groups I visited over the next few months were all fractions. I was bounced from one group to another; I was never with any one of them (about four) long enough to pay more than a few dollars in dues, but I believe that what mattered most to the Party was not some miniscule monthly payments but large donations and, especially, the work extracted from its members. This was definitely true in Hollywood, where a number of personalities carried a good deal of influence with the general public. I soon learned that the head of the local section had not yet decided where I would best fit in, where I could function most effectively. So far, I was the biggest fish they had hooked from the Directors Guild, and they wanted to make the most of their catch.

Each fraction I attended had a different agenda, and since I never met the same group twice, I didn't get to know the people in attendance. This mattered little; they were all similar types, especially the women—stern-faced, dedicated, masculine in manner, dress, and appearance, and with a few exceptions, quite humorless. Eventually, I was dropped into a group that was focusing on a carefully conceived exploitation of the local racial conflict, which in the mid-forties, was beginning to simmer in Watts. At this meeting I met, for the first time, two or three local party heavyweights and an attorney, Ben Margolis, who two years later became a spark plug of the Hollywood Ten's defense corps. The group's plans were well developed, and I felt that here at last was a cause I could enthusiastically support. But if I had any idea that I was the master of my fate, I was dead wrong.

A message was sent through Adrian Scott, and we knew that something was in the works; for the first time, he and I were to attend a group meeting together. (Scott and I made four of RKO's most successful films, he as producer and I as director. I admired him for his skill at working with screenwriters and appreciated his support when production problems arose, but though we obviously respected each other's talents, we had never been close friends. If memory serves, this meeting and two or three relating to *Cornered*, which will be discussed later, were the only evenings I ever spent with Adrian. In fact, despite two years of collaboration, I had only recently learned that he was also a member of the Party.)

The message to Scott had given us a date, a time, and an address—nothing more. What followed could have been the start of a Philip Marlowe mystery. Early one evening, we took my car to the place of rendezvous. One thing of importance we already knew—the address belonged to one of the Party's most sequestered members. I had been astonished to learn his identity since I new him only as an influential associate of Gary Cooper, one of Hollywood's most conservative stars.

We pulled into a parking area in front of a small, neat house in the hill country above Beverly Hills. There was no sign of life; the place was eerily dark. However, following instructions, we rang the bell, waited, then knocked on the door. No response. But just as we were starting back to the car, wondering what to do next, the door was pulled slightly ajar and a black man in a white butler's jacket appeared in the narrow opening. A brief conversation followed, and we learned that the meeting place had been changed. We climbed back into my car and headed for an address in the San Fernando Valley. We were going to Sidney Buchman's house.

(Sometime later I learned that such misdirection was often a deliberate ploy to avoid possible tailing by FBI infiltrators, of whom there were many.)

Odd Man Out

Buchman was not at home; neither was the man whose instructions had led us here. But ten or twelve guests were assembled in the living room. I knew only a couple of those present, and though the aura of a small, upper-class Hollywood affair was something I had rarely encountered, there was no mistaking the underlying conspiratorial atmosphere of a party fraction. That titillation was present at all party meetings, which should have rung a bell, but I always enjoyed the exhilaration. Over tea and cookies, we learned that this was indeed a newly formed group of men and women whom the "brass" felt might be of special importance to the Party's activities. They were not all film people; several held sensitive posts in some of the city's important enterprises. One woman we had not met before was an executive for a leading department store chain; her husband was a man of influence in city government circles.

Since this was only a get-together, a preview to determine whether the "gears meshed," the discussions were purely exploratory, with no plans made and no future meeting set. But later that night, completely unaware that we would soon be leaving the Party, Adrian and I drove home with a scarcely suppressed sense of excitement, wondering aloud about the possible goals of such a supersecret group.

It must be remembered that in spite of the clamorous right-wing propaganda to the contrary, the number of living and breathing communists was always exceedingly small—about one in five thousand. Working alone, their impact would hardly have been felt. To realize its ambitious programs, the Party needed the willing cooperation of a large number of outsiders, and at this stage of the class struggle, the unaware liberals were its greatest asset. Since no one enjoys being a cat's paw, these men and women could never be allowed to learn they were being manipulated by one or two, rarely more, members of the Communist Party. So, like the cuckoo, the CPA organizers laid their eggs in other birds' nests and depended on those birds to hatch their chicks and nourish their fledglings. This was one of the chief sources of the Party's suprising power, and exposure was the greatest danger it faced. It suffered a deep blow whenever an influential man or woman was exposed as a Party member, for the anonymous Communist who lost his or her cover immediately lost control of the unwitting outside helpers he or she had been able to bring to the aid of the Party's cryptonymous projects. And that was the reason for their tight membership secrecy, and why naming names was the ultimate sin.

A somewhat more obscure reason for the uncompromising opposition to any sort of membership disclosure by entertainment industry communists was that such a disclosure would render them vulnerable to punitive action by their employers, thus cutting short their enjoyment of the perks furnished by the capitalistic system they were plotting to destroy. Some may have suffered occasional twinges of conscience, but few were eager to rush the day of their triumph—they were in no hurry to sacrifice their Beverly Hills life-styles for an egalitarian existence. They wanted it both ways. It is an irony of history that wealthy right-wing extremists and well-to-do Hollywood communists faced a common threat—the loss of their goods and chattels if the Party was ultimately victorious. For the Hollywood communist, the juxtaposition of selfish material interests and altruistic political ideals was a mind-boggling problem indeed, and some sort of psychocatharsis or emotional safety valve was essential; a psychotic dread of exposure was balanced, though inadequately, by a self-destroying hatred of those who exposed them.

Inevitably, however, they sometimes exposed themselves. In 1944, shortly after I had joined the Party, Paul Robeson, the great black singer and actor (also member of Phi Beta Kappa, an all-American lineman at Rutgers, and a law school graduate) came to Hollywood to speak at a meeting of the Hollywood Citizens Committee of the Arts, Sciences, and Professions (HICCASP). He was met at the station by the committee's executive secretary who presented Paul a huge bouquet of flowers. Robeson had always denied being a communist, but when has truth ever conquered rumor?[2] Since HICCASP was composed overwhelmingly of men and women who were liberal, but by no means extremist, there was a great uproar in town. A considerable number of members resigned. But what very few of those members knew, and others could only suspect, was that the executive secretary of HICCASP was the party member. Of course, no committee VIP could take the rap without being exposed, so the bouquet fiasco was palmed off as the secretary's

2. "Adolfe Menjou was permitted to cloak thousands of innocent Americans with Communism by the astounding statement that 'anyone who witnesses Paul Robeson and applauds is a Communist' " (from a speech by Congressman Emmanuel Cellar, Chairman of the House Judiciary Committee, Nov. 24, 1947, qtd. in Gordon Kahn, *Hollywood on Trial*, 170).

unauthorized boo-boo, which benefitted neither Robeson, HICCASP, nor the CPA.

More or less coincidentally, Robeson discovered that Hollywood hotels had miraculously filled up overnight; there was no room at the inns. I had a spare bedroom in my apartment, and he stayed with me for the duration of his visit. Paul was a remarkable artist and an even more remarkable man. Political power plays meant nothing to him unless they could advance the causes of his people first, then those of humanity at large. He was the kind of man who made liberalism attractive to the public-spirited citizen, but like many other good men, he was naive in his perception of the extremists' ultimate aims. He did not enjoy complete freedom of movement in L.A. and that caused him some pain. I still remember one of his ironic comments: "I truly believe," he said, "that the deep South will accept us as brothers long before the North drops its hypocritical attitudes." But we also laughed a lot and talked a good deal during his stay. I always considered the inns' loss was my great gain.

Rather than an outsider who was being used, I had become an insider who wasn't. The new super-secret group was not yet activated, and while I was marking time, I tried to learn more about the CPA. As far as I could see its goals were idealistic; many of them embraced by Ronald Reagan, who was then a Democrat. And Robert Montgomery, later a strong conservative, once sneaked in that radical unionist, Harry Bridges, for a secret meeting with some of the more daring Hollywood leftists. I never knew whether Montgomery was sincerely interested or whether he was gathering information for the opposition.

Other strange incidents occasionally perplexed me, though I thought them quite unbelievable—fantasies within a fantasy. For instance: Some time after I had joined the party, Scott and I were walking across the lot at RKO when I happened to mention that I was reading an extremely interesting book.

"What book," asked Scott.

"Koestler's *Darkness at Noon*," I replied.

Adrian stopped short, and as I turned to face him, he spoke in a subdued voice. "Good God!" he said. "Don't ever mention that to anyone in the group!"

"Why not?" I was honestly puzzled.

"It's on the *list*!" he breathed, looking a little embarrassed. "Koestler is corrupt—a liar. He is an *ex*-communist, and no member of the Party is allowed to read him."

I wanted to ask, "Allowed by whom?" But I was too flabbergasted to speak. We never discussed the matter again, but I had been given something to think about.

I had not known the Party maintained an index of its own. I was naive, but not totally stupid. I learned two things from that brief, half-whispered exchange; first, that Scott was also a member of the Party and, second, that to a communist, nobody is as low as an excommunist —nobody! Defection cannot be forgiven nor forgotten. This, as much as naming names, generates implacable hatred. It seemed paradoxical, but in the twinkling of an eye, defection transformed a Galahad of the Party, a model of virtue and integrity, into the most vile and corrupt of villains.

On those thankfully rare occasions when my thoughts return to that period of my life, I sometimes wonder why it took me over a year to recognize the Party's duplicity, but incidents such as the one just mentioned seemed too absurd to be believed. In the United States, one grows up in a societal atmosphere created by the doctrines of separation of state and religion and freedom of speech. It is an example of beneficial brainwashing, though not all Americans succumb to its ministrations. There are citizens who try to circumvent both of these political imperatives; some, like the fanatical right-to-lifers, by stretching them past a sane and reasonable limit, while others, like those who object to fairy tales in our schools, narrow them down to their own norms. But the average intelligent American refuses to believe that "it can happen here" and ignores the efforts of the bigoted minorities to undermine these principles. As a former Catholic, I had known about the Index, and like many Catholics, I had ignored it. I considered it a purely religious concern. But I was to learn from experience that communism is functionally much closer to a dogmatic religion than it is to a people's political party. Question: "Who created the modern world?" Answer: "Lenin and Stalin created the modern world." So went the catechism of that rock-hard party, a party which considered apostasy the greatest of mortal sins.

In truth, there was a much more important reason to ignore Scott's warning and to minimize its significance; the Party was a distant second on my list of immediate concerns. First was filmmaking. In 1944, the war in the Pacific was our major involvement, and we had no clear idea when it would end. (The atom bomb was still a deep military secret.) I had one more propaganda film to make, and it was to be with John Wayne.

At the time, the Philippines were still occupied by the Japanese, and our story dealt with the actions of the Filipino guerrillas, a field not yet touched by Hollywood studios. Screenwriter Ben Barzman (later identified as a communist) and I created a running script out of news stories and bits and pieces of underground information that had been trickling out of the Philippines since the beginning of the war and, as our invasion began, out of developments that were actually occurring on the Philippine front. The army gave us no advance notice of their intentions, and our script changed from day to day. For instance, near the end of our open-ended schedule, Allied survivors were freed from Cabanatuan, the infamous prison camp, and many of them were returning to the States. Obviously, such historical incidents had to be incorporated into our film.

Our technical adviser was a Colonel Clark of the U.S. Army. He had served most of his career in the Philippines, but because of serious wounds received in the fighting on Bataan, he had been one of the few evacuated from Corregidor just before its surrender to the Japanese. His accounts of the fighting in the Islands were fascinating; his loyalty to, and love for, the native troops were touching; his hatred for General MacArthur was unending. One of his most bitter stories concerned MacArthur's departure from Corregidor by submarine, accompanied by another sub full of his furniture rather than fighting men.

Except for Wayne, whose faith in the general was unshakeable, we in the company were puzzled by the colonel's tales. We didn't know what to believe. Then, as some of the Americans who had fought with the guerrillas started coming through Hollywood on their way home, we heard their stories, and our sympathies shifted in the colonel's favor. One experience of a U.S. Navy chief petty officer who had spent the entire war fighting in the mountains of Luzon was typical. His group had been in frequent touch with American submarines. The bushfighters' most pressing needs were guns and ammunition. At last, they got the word that a supply sub would rendezvous with them on a particular night. They made their way down to the beach, and the meeting went off without incident as rubber rafts and other makeshift craft ferried a number of crates ashore. The first crate was torn open in great anticipation—it contained no guns, no bullets, nothing but cartons of cigarettes. Each carton was embalzoned with the words: ''I shall return—Douglas Mac-

Arthur." Crate after crate contained similarly useless cargo. The shock was great, and the guerrillas were so angry that if they had had the means, they would have blown the sub out of the water. Instead, they sat down and cried.

Although we heard a number of similar stories at first hand, we could use none of them in our film, whose chief purpose was to keep the workers on the home front inspired and at their lathes. As should be expected, films like *Tender Comrade, Behind The Rising Sun,* and *Back to Bataan* were necessarily oversentimental and chauvinistic. But I am still proud that at a time when most American films showed English-speaking heroes single-handedly winning battles in which they were not only outnumbered by the enemy, but handicapped by the presence of non-white allies, we presented "the Duke" in the role of adviser and contact man (although he did play an important part in the climactic battle), while the Filipinos themselves did most of the fighting and occasional dying. For a man who considered the whole world kin, it was nice to feel that one could love and respect our allies—even if they were Russian.

This film was my only working experience with John Wayne, truly an amazing man—in many ways. He threw his 6-foot, 4½-inch, 245-pound body around like a lightweight gymnast. His acting was honest, which is a good deal better than clever; he lived life with gusto; and he was alreading beginning to think of himself as some kind of political pundit, but we all make mistakes. Due to the undercover work set up by the Motion Picture Alliance for the Preservation of American Ideals, of which he was a charter member, Wayne probably knew more about me than I could have suspected. But at that time, the undeclared armistice within the United States was still in effect, or so I thought, and we got along extremely well during the shooting. Once, in a charitable mood, he told me that though our methods were different, our political aims were the same. It was the most truly democratic sentiment I ever heard him utter and, in light of later events, very interesting.

One hundred thirty days of shooting produced a film that did well in the United States, despite the sudden end of the war, and sensationally in the Philippines. But long before I had finished postproduction on the picture, I was preparing another film with Adrian Scott; the film that would really open my eyes and mind. It was to star my good friend, Dick Powell. The film was *Cornered.*

3

In 1944, RKO acquired a new head for its story department: William Dozier. He looked around for an opportunity to establish his presence as quickly as possible and found it in a twenty-page treatment by Ben Hecht—a steal at $50,000. It was a hard-boiled mystery yarn, and Scott and Dmytryk, who had made *Murder, My Sweet*, were the logical team to bring it to life. However, there was a hitch in the project: the treatment was so incredibly bad and the plot so incredibly trite that Adrian and I decided that any attempt to salvage it would be a waste of time. (Scott and I agreed that Hecht had probably needed some ready cash, not an unusual state of affairs for a writer, and he had lent his name to someone else's treatment for a share of the loot.) Years later, I spent two weeks with Ben at his Nyack home working on the script of *A Walk on the Wild Side*. He was as pleasant a man as I have ever known. But it was common knowledge that he delighted in outwitting the establishment, an art form he had polished to perfection. In the end, we used only the treatment's title, *Cornered*. What other writer has ever received $50,000 per word?

At that time, I could only guess why our third partner, John Paxton, had not been asked to write our new script. The apparent reason, which I could not completely accept, was that Dozier insisted we use a writer to whom the studio was committed, a man who happened to be one of Hollywood's most dedicated right-wingers. This bothered me not at all; whatever his political bent, he had a solid reputation as a writer of mystery and suspense. Scott, however, blew a fuse; he had many strong objections to the man, all of them political. He also had an instinct for circuitous strategy.

"Never mind," he said, when I suggested a team attack on Dozier, "I'll handle it." And so he did. But as one strange development led to another, I had a feeling that someone behind Adrian was pulling the strings. I had always respected Scott as a person of integrity, but his present behavior was quite out of character for the man I thought I knew.

We spent some time with the writer, discussing our new concept, which was quite simple and straightforward (and fresh at the time). A Canadian fighter pilot, wounded and out of the service, searches for the hideout of an SS officer who had brutally murdered the pilot's young French bride. He trails the Nazi to Buenos Aires, runs him to earth, and beats him to death with his fists. Simple and straightforward.

Scott waited patiently until the writer handed in his first completed sequence. Without bothering to read it, he hurried off to Dozier and declared the material unusable. There was no debate. The writer was off the project, and Scott's choice, John Wexley, was on. Scott's moves were beginning to make a certain kind of sense, but I was very busy with *Back to Bataan*; I had little time to decipher his motives, and no desire to question his actions. Wexley was the author of *The Last Mile*, and a man of extreme leftist leanings. He had apparently been Scott's choice in the first place, and I wondered if he had been ordered to use him. *The Last Mile* was good theater, but Wexley's screen credits were not impressive.

Wexley was half-finished when Scott had to admit that we were in deep trouble. However, ensnared by his own machinations, he couldn't make a change without having to answer too many embarrassing questions. Once again, we had to wait it out. The trouble was that Wexley engaged in agitprop. At every opportunity, he wrote long speeches loaded with thinly disguised communist propaganda. Expressed in classical antifascist rhetoric, there were manifestos by the dozen, or so it seemed. Major surgery was in order, and as soon as Wexley was finished, thanked, and sent on his way, reliable, nonpolitical John Paxton was called in to undertake the operation. The final rewritten script still contained a strong antifascist point of view, but it presented nothing that any good Republican moderate could question.

In the meantime, I finished my chores on *Back to Bataan* and flew to Buenos Aires to research the town and its people. The film was to be made in Hollywood, but I wanted to minimize the possibility of errors of ignorance by absorbing the feeling, the color, of this great city. The plot of our film was there, but not the smells, the tastes, the dark places our pilot would haunt during his search for the killer. What was even more important was my need to flesh out the characters he would encounter in this strange and distant environment. The Argentineans have always been a hospitable people, but at this time, I experienced an emotional outpouring I shall never forget.

I arrived in Buenos Aires on April 11, 1945. The death of Franklin Roosevelt was announced on April 12, and the city came to a halt. Argentina had been officially pro-Axis throughout the war (a war that was not yet finished), and I was not prepared for the mass demonstration of sorrow by the people of Buenos Aires. My president had just died, and here, in a foreign country five thousand miles from home, well over one hundred thousand men and women filled the great Square of Obelisk, and all were openly weeping with me. Long after that unforgettable day, I felt that I was not a Yankee in South America, but one of millions of people throughout the world joined together in our mutual appreciation of a great leader.

I was soon back home, the rewrite was finished, and with some minor exceptions, we assembled a good cast. To help Dick Powell, we had two excellent actors: Walter Slezak as a conniving intermediary and Luther Adler as the Nazi. The script had never been inspiring, the beating it took didn't help, and the shooting was more or less routine. As is true of most contrived stories, the film was not completely satisfactory. Some good scenes were scattered throughout the film, but only the last reel and a half were worthwhile; a good example of what cinematic suspense ought to be. However, once in release, it rode the coattails of *Murder, My Sweet* to an even better gross than its predecessor. But long before that release, Scott and I faced an unbelievable situation, one that precipitated our break with the Communist Party of America.

In the late summer of 1945, when postproduction on *Cornered* had been completed, the negative cut, and release printing about to start, we got a sudden surprise. I was already deep into preparation for my next film, *Till the End of Time,* a Dore Schary production, when Scott and I received a summons from John Howard Lawson (a man later called the Gauleiter of the Hollywood section of the Communist Party). At Wexley's request, we were to meet him and Lawson. Naturally, we agreed. We thought it might be a complaint concerning screen credit, and that was nothing unusual.

To our astonishment we were confronted by a committee of four men (including Lawson, Wexley, and Dick Collins—the fourth name escapes me). They were all communists, of course, who had been picked to hear Wexley's complaint. We quickly learned that the meeting would have nothing to do with the film's credits, but with content. Wexley charged that our severe editing had emasculated his work, that is was now pro- rather than antifascist, and he demanded that we shoot the eliminated scenes and insert them in the film. Shades of *Alice in Wonderland.* The situation was incredible. Scott and I would have needed the studio's permission to recall the film, and such permission could not have been obtained without a complete disclosure of our reasons. Very obviously, that would have been impossible, and I knew that everyone at this meeting was fully aware that Wexley's request was unrealistic beyond belief. I couldn't imagine on what grounds it was being made. Aesthetically and commercially, Wexley's scenes were pure trash, and though our film was by no means great, Scott and I had earned a reputation for a certain standard of excellence, and we weren't about to throw it away on scenes that would ruin both it and us. I was ready to blow, but Scott understood party procedure much better than I. He asked for another meeting. Now that the nature of the problem was clear, he said, we could discuss it in greater depth.

The final meeting took place in the rumpus room of my apartment, which seemed most appropriate. The same four writers spoke for Wexley, but this time we had two writers, also communists, since this was obviously a party affair, to balance the scales. Scott had recruited Albert Maltz, whom I had never met, for our side, and I had pulled in Ben Barzman. Maltz became our strongest defender. He was also shocked by Wexley's silly demands, but being a more seasoned party member than either Scott or I, he recognized the reasons behind the action. He realized that the issue was not the salvaging of a writer's ego, but the savaging of two recalcitrant members. It was a question of the Party's control over its artists. After a long Kafkaesque meeting in which Wexley took his lumps, nothing had changed.

I was angered by the masquerade, but Scott was anxious to pursue the matter in the hope of arriving at a reconciliation with the Party. He arranged a luncheon meeting with Lawson at the Gotham Deli. It was cold, unpleasant, and unsatisfactory. Lawson was unfriendly and uncommunicative, offering no explanation for his behavior. For him, there was no possible compromise on the matter or, more particularly, on the principles involved. His final words were, "For the time being consider yourselves out of the Party. When you decide that you can accept Party discipline, we'll explore the situation further." Wearing his usual mirthless smile, he left us.

Almost in disbelief, Adrian and I looked at each other, exchanged a few words, and went our separate ways. It seemed so easy. After a little more than a year as a Party member, I was free! But I had no way of knowing that real freedom was still six years in the future. I was to learn that neither the communists nor the witch-hunters were about to accept my exit from the CPA.

For the time being, I lived in blissful ignorance of coming events. Representing the Party, Lawson had attempted to chastise Scott and me, but it was Maltz who suffered the most immediate indignities; Albert, who never had the courage of his excellent convictions. It was probable that he had harbored misgivings concerning party efforts to curb artistic freedom before our meetings with the "thought control" committee; he may even have contemplated a critical dissertation on that aspect of Party discipline. But now he recognized that issue as the real purpose behind the inquisition, and he was incensed. In the heat of his anger, he wrote one of his better essays on the absolute necessity for creative freedom. The article was published in the February 1946 issue of the *New Masses*. In it, Maltz strongly attacked the narrow Comintern concept of "art is a weapon in the class struggle" (qtd. in Elia Kazan, *A Life*, 399). He felt it placed him and his "comrades" in a straitjacket. "It has become necessary for me to repudiate the idea," he wrote. And the muck hit the fan.

It seemed as if every member with a gift for vilification, invective, and scurrility was asked to join the mob. Howard Fast, Alvah Bessie, Joseph North, Samuel Sillen, Michael Gold, and John Howard Lawson each took his best shot as Albert, like the clown with his head thrust through the canvas hole at the county fair, stood defenseless. But that was only the beginning. The whole top echelon from the East descended on Maltz in two party meetings held in Hollywood. As usual, the two men with the most bitter tongues, Alvah Bessie and Herbert Biberman, both future members of the Hollywood Ten, led the pack. "With," as Leopold Atlas put it in his statement before HUAC, "a snarl of triumph [they] made him crawl and recant." In his autobiography, *A Life*, Elia Kazan suggests that after this "star chamber" had beaten Maltz to the ground, they sent him off to Europe to "clear his mind" (399).

Later, Maltz said that he wanted to remain a Communist and not become a renegade. Since my defection I have heard the word *principle* bandied about a good deal. It seems to me there is a choice here. Is belief in the Communist Party a higher principle than the people's right to freedom of thought and expression? Maltz chose the answer that led to nothing but years of ignominy.

I had known and admired Albert's writing for some time, and I felt ashamed and embarrassed for this man of talent. But years later, damned if he didn't do it again! When Boris Pasternak's *Doctor Zhivago* was published in 1958, Khrushchev had eased the censor's touch a bit, and Maltz wrote a favorable review. A few years later, there was a new

Kremlin regime and an old Kremlin attitude. Pasternak was in disgrace, and throughout the world, communist intellectuals once more faced a change and a choice: does one beg forgiveness for "sins" committed during a relaxation of the rules, or does one take the opportunity to get out? As has happened at every new party crisis, many got out. But Maltz was still frightened, still oblivious to the fact that to be a renegade under such circumstances was a distinct honor. He wrote a second review of *Doctor Zhivago*; apparently, the passage of time and the passing of Khrushchev had changed the meaning of the printed words, and Maltz confessed that, once again, he had been wrong. A second reading of the book, he said, enabled him to recognize that it was shallow in substance and inferior in quality—really not worth reading at all.

But that was fifteen years in the future. In 1945, free of all political pressure, I could not have imagined that within five years Albert and I would both be members of a unique group called the Hollywood Ten, or that, shackled side by side in leg irons and wrist chains, we would be taking a communal leak in the bushes just off the highway that led to the prison camp at Mill Point, West Virginia.

4

"**Time is but the stream I go a-fishing in,**" wrote Thoreau, and before I wade into the clamor, the deviousness, the idiocy of the HUAC hearings, and the occasional terror that followed, I would like to pause for a moment to drop my line into more placid waters and snag a rainbow.

After the dour and ominous figure of John Howard Lawson had exited my world—I thought forever—life was much more serene. My wife was enjoying MacDougall Alley in New York while our attorneys were taking their time composing a property settlement preparatory to the divorce. But outside of that, the stream flowed smoothly, and my next film was nearly ready to go into production.

Till the End of Time, an adaption of Niven Busch's novel, *They Dream of Home*, was a dramatic study of the problems of returning veterans, a subject of vital concern immediately after the war. Its preparation was an exercise in studio subterfuge. Dore Schary, the producer, had come to RKO from Selznick, but the silver cord had not yet been cut. RKO and Selznick frequently made deals with each other; the one involving our production was as abstruse as North's Iran-Contra arms deal, and nearly as covert. Selznick "owned" some of the most important stars in the business, but he made few pictures; RKO made fifty or sixty films a year but had very few stars. A trade-off was mutually advantageous.

From Selznick, we got a fine actress, Dorothy McGuire—but at a price beyond her salary. I didn't realize I was being conned when I was encouraged to test a number of young actors for the male lead; some of them were quite good. The last candidate was a Selznick contractee who had just been demobbed from the U.S. Navy. His name was Guy Madison. I found the test had been a waste of time; without my knowledge, Guy had been written in as part of the deal some time ago, even though he was a completely inexperienced non-actor. But I was in too deep to walk, and the addition of Robert Mitchum, Bill Williams, and a fine supporting cast somewhat assuaged my disappointment and anger. Then, too, there was Shirley Temple to play the girl next door, the one who has always loved our boy, but who is destined to lose him.

Shirley was also a Selznick property, but a very acceptable one. Suddenly, however, she exercised a woman's prerogative and did me the greatest favor of my life: she decided to marry John Agar and withdrew from the film. I started another search, this time for a girl who could re-place Shirley Temple as the teenager. It wasn't easy, and the schedule soon forced me to stop testing. Within a few days, I was to begin filming at the Marine boot camp in San Diego. We still had no girl next door, but Dore had a brainstorm. "Once bitten, twice shy," runs the old saw, and I was on my guard.

"There's a girl at MGM," said Schary, "who always comes through when it gets down to the nitty-gritty. She's not a teenager, but she looks like one. Her name is Jean Porter."

I had never heard of her, but at least she didn't belong to Selznick.

"She's been doing leads and second leads at Metro," Dore continued, "and there's a lot of film on her. I'll have them send some over."

What I saw on the screen called for a closer look. Fortunately, she was not working at the moment, and MGM agreed to an interview. She bounced in, all five beautifully proportioned feet of her, dark brown eyes flashing. On her cheek was a small bandaid. I couldn't take my eyes off her while Dore made the introductions.

"Every week Dore does something especially nice for me," I said. "This week you're it." I wasn't being charming. It's against my nature.

Much later, Jean told me she had misheard my name, which is not unusual, and she thought she was being asked to see Dieterle. He had interviewed her some time before, and she had never forgotten it. (Teu-tonic directors can be very trying.) So she had used every possible ruse to avoid our appointment—even caught a quick cold—but MGM's cast-ing director could be most persistent when he saw an opportunity to make a little profit on an investment. Jean's relief at seeing a stranger was so overwhelming, she was licked before she knew it. She agreed to play the part and headed for home. I left the next day for San Diego.

A week or two later, I arrived back at the studio—and found a picket line. The "Painters" were targeting RKO. Herbert Sorels's union was thought to be dominated by communists (which was probably true), and they were staging their first tentative attack against the AFL, the studios, and the status of the International Association of Theatrical and Stage Employees (IATSE). Outside of the painters, only a few workers favored the walkout, but the Screen Directors Guild had decided to honor the picket lines.

I chatted with the pickets until they disappeared for lunch, then en-tered the gates. First, I checked the set. It was ready for action, but the crew was in the commissary. I headed in that direction, and walked into

a madhouse. The waitresses had arrived earlier, encountered a belliger-
ent picket line, and retired. There was no table service, but the counter
was being manned by volunteers. I elbowed my way through the mob
to pick up a sandwich and found myself face-to-face with the world's
loveliest waitress, all made up and dressed to look like the girl next
door. Only over fifty years have I discovered the myriad reasons that
made my snap reaction the best move of my life.

In the trying years after the hearings, the memory of that moment in
the crowded commissary often swept my mind clean of the bleakest
emotions, but the almost unbelievable wonder has been the constant
love and faith of that girl-woman who gave up her own career to walk
beside me through the years of pain and misery, who believed in me despite the calumny of my enemies and the advice of her "friends," and
who even now is my constant inspiration. Indeed, indeed! When He
made this one, He knew he had topped Himself and He broke the mold.

5

This book is not meant to be a filmography, but since certain of my films were hauled, willy-nilly, into this complex controversy, I feel that the two or three that were found to be suspect by the Committee, or useful to the Ten, are historically pertinent to this account. And since this will entail only a few brief words of description, I beg you to bear with me. The two films I made in the year preceding the 1947 hearings were *So Well Remembered* and *Crossfire*.

I finished *Till the End of Time*, and Jean and I had been together for about eight months when we suffered our first separation. Immediately after the war, Hollywood studios found it advantageous to exploit the low cost of labor abroad and the freshness of foreign locales. RKO and J. Arthur Rank undertook the production of a joint venture, a film version of James Hilton's novel, *So Well Remembered*. Adrian Scott and John Paxton had been working on the script for some time, and I was now asked to take over its direction. This film was to be shot in England, and we were to fly over in early June. Leaving the States was no problem—leaving Jean was. However, we decided the advantages outweighed the disadvantages, and I accepted the assignment.

I had not been in Europe since before World War I, when I was two or three years old, and never in England. I arrived there with all my stereotypical attitudes intact. To my astonishment, the English I met were by no means arrogant, distant, or aloof. On the contrary, they were extremely friendly and hospitable, and the range and quality of their humor was decidedly to my taste. Our first meeting with J. Arthur Rank and his associates was typical of a running pattern that surprised and pleased us. The great industrialist and revitalizer of the British film industry was a very down-to-earth man. He had made several trips to the United States immediately after the war and could have outfitted himself completely. Instead, he wore shirts with tattered collars and cuffs and frayed ties similar to those that adorned his less-fortunate countrymen who were still practicing austerity at home.

London was an extremely overcrowded city, and it took a few days for us to settle in, but once we were established in proper housing at Denham, where the film's interiors were to be shot, things ran smoothly enough, except, of course, for the occasional difference in point of view.

Odd Man Out

We had been at Denham only a few days when Rank welcomed his domestic exhibitors to a studio convention. He had spent a couple of month's worth of ration stamps to lay out a few finger sandwiches for a cocktail party on one of the stages. Though we were in sympathy with England's austerity program, Adrian and I had seen the spread and thought it rather pitiful. However, a couple of shop stewards, whose living experience over the last few years had been quite different from ours, had also visited the stage, and a short time later a two-day strike was called in protest. Rank, the union, and the workers had lost far more than the sad sandwiches were worth, but some odd sense of order had been satisfied.

As preparations got underway, we scouted the Midlands, looking for the right location—Birmingham, Leeds, Manchester, and even Ashby de la Zouch. Our search finally led us to Macclesfield, just south of Manchester, and one of England's leading mill towns. It was new to us, and in order to save time, we pulled up beside the first bobby we saw and asked for directions.

"We're looking for a slum section," I said, after some introductory remarks. The bobby looked at me with the slightest smile on his face.

"I don't think you'll find anything else in Macclesfield," he said. So much for civic pride.

But he was right. And that made it the town we were looking for. The packed-together houses were small, and the mills looked like maximum-security prisons. But the unfailing good nature of the townspeople, many of whom worked for us as extras, was extraordinary. Every Englishman will tell you soon after you meet him that summers in England are either the hottest on record or the wettest on record; the summer of 1946 was unquestionably one of the soggiest. But our people worked with a will under conditions that would have sent the average Hollywood extra screaming to his guild for adjustments—danger money, rain money, bonus money—money.

The film, which included John Mills, Martha Scott, and Trevor Howard in the cast, was a story of a socially mismated couple. The wife, a Tory, was the daughter of a wealthy mill tycoon; with his death, she became the owner and manager of the family mill. Her husband, a socialist and a Labourite, was the editor of the local newspaper, a man whose lifetime career was devoted to fighting for the rights of the working class, and especially of the mill workers. As one would expect, their marriage was an interesting conflict, filled with surprises.

The surprises continued long after the picture was completed. Howard Hughes bought RKO before the picture was released, and looking over his newly acquired merchandise, he saw an imagined communist touch in nearly every sequence of the film. He hacked it down until it was not even a shadow of the picture that James Hilton had characterized as the film that most closely resembled the substance and the spirit of any one of his novels. When one considers that Hilton was not a communist and that J. Arthur Rank was one of the wealthiest mill owners in England, and that neither of these men had discovered anything undemocratic in the film, one must either stand in awe of the remarkable acuity of Howard Hughes or agree that the contrast between political thinking in England, the mother of modern democracy, and in the United States, the land of the free, is striking and hardly defensible. Incidentally, our faithful cut did quite well in England, while in the United States, Hughes's monstrosity sank in the studio-created muck.

(Some years later, when I was once again working in Hollywood, and under contract to Twentieth Century–Fox, a publicity woman at the studio arranged a meeting between me and Hedda Hopper. The Lady in the Hat rarely wrote a column without castigating me. It didn't bother me—much—but it did bother Zanuck, and he wanted her off my back. Over tea, I was suprised to learn that the irritating bone in her craw was *So Well Remembered*. Hughes, or his publicists, must have done a job on her. For those who care, Hopper and I reached an understanding. She agreed never to mention my name again in any context, which made her columns shorter and made Zanuck and me happier.)

If I've spoken well of England, it is purely hindsight. In spite of the weekend bicycle rides through idyllic countryside and some very good new friends, I hated England for every minute it kept me away from Jean. Letters just aren't enough, and the long-distance phone in 1946 was an instrument of torture. But at last, I was going home, though ever so slowly.

Sailing alone across the Atlantic on the "Queen" was like being interned in a luxury hotel for five days. The same turns around the deck, the same meals, the same daily routine. However, there was a break or two in the monotony; the Duke of Windsor was on board. We took our constitutionals at the same time each day but, like English versus American race courses, in the opposite directions. I noticed he never avoided a gaze, and he looked me squarely in the eyes each time he passed by. I could feel his sense of personal pride, and I wondered why some of our

Odd Man Out

Hollywood royalty couldn't learn to do that. We also had the same daily schedule in the steam room, where he was always accompanied by his equerry. They spoke of nothing but the restaurants they had frequented and the chefs they had known, which led me to ruminate on the proposition that a kingdom is a sometime thing, but a good meal is forever.

My last film before my world flipped on its axis was *Crossfire*. It was, and still is, an expectional film, a film that set important precedents and won a greater variety of awards than any other film in RKO's history. It was a milestone in my career, which, in spite of my continuing good fortune, was a puzzle for me. I was unchallenged as the studio's number one director and invited to speak each year at the national sales convention. The exhibitors, here and abroad, were most complimentary. But why? Why had all this happened? I had made a couple of sleepers, one better-than-average suspense film, *Murder My Sweet*, for which I had been presented and Edgar, the Mystery Writers of America annual award, and all my films had made money, some even a lot of money. But there wasn't an outstanding film in the lot. And I knew it. However, I accepted all the industry seemed anxious to give me, happily riding the crest of a beautiful wave. I didn't know it would turn out to be a sand-buster.

Adrian had optioned Richard Brooks's novel *The Brick Foxhole* earlier in 1946. It was a loose, rambling story of the frustrations of stateside soldiers at the end of the war. The book had an unusual number of subplots, one of which concerned the murder of a homosexual by a sadistic bigot. At that time censorship still ruled, and any mention of homosexuality, whether the noun or the life-style, was strictly taboo, but Adrian had an inspiration. What if the murder was the main spine of the story, and what if the victim was a heterosexual Jew? We could then tell the story of bigotry as it relates to anti-Semitism and, by analogy and implication, the story of all racial hatred as well. Nothing like this had ever been attempted in Hollywood before.

John Paxton was with us in England to polish the script of *So Well Remembered*, and at odd times, we discussed and worked on *The Brick Foxhole*. By the time we returned to Hollywood, at the end of 1946, we had a full treatment but not yet a complete script. Our option was running out, and the studio's interim production head, N. Peter Rathvon, planned to drop it. Scott and I hurried to his office and launched into a fervent sales talk. After a few minutes, Rathvon was overwhelmed.

"I'll gamble a thousand dollars on your enthusiasm," he told us. A thousand bucks! Even then! Good Lord! Rathvon never placed a better bet; it was the high point of his career.

First, *The Brick Foxhole* became *Crossfire*, a change for the better. Neither Scott, Paxton, nor I was Jewish, which was an advantage, but also a problem. The advantage was that no one could accuse us of self-serving or religious bias. The problem was that we had to learn about the sources of anti-Semitism as well as the techniques for combatting such bigotry. This was largely new ground for us. How does one keep a movie viewer entertained while disclosing that WASPs, rather than Jews, are in control of the financial structure of the United States, or ensure that he or she stays awake long enough to learn that Jews *don't* control the film industry, that those same WASP financiers do.

We had a lot of serious things to say, but how were we going to get people to listen? Simple. Our message was buried within a murder mystery to make it palatable. (Could that be considered a comment on public taste?) Still we approached the film as an experiment, a risk, and we determined to make it at a price, somewhere in the vicinity of $500,000. Even if the film turned out to be a bust, it could hardly lose money at that cost, and the cause of experimental films would remain relatively undamaged. However, to strengthen its box-office appeal, we put most of our money *above* the line (reserved for talent) and hired a strong cast. That meant B picture expenditure *below* the line, and a schedule of only twenty-two days.

Dore Schary had just taken over as production head, and he facilitated our start. He postponed a couple of B productions so we could use their sets, and he helped us assemble an A film cast, which included Robert Young, Robert Mitchum, and Robert Ryan, supported by Sam Levene, Gloria Graham, Paul Kelly, and half of RKO's stock department.

We also selected a great veteran photographer, J. Roy Hunt, an expert in high-contrast texture, my preferred style of lighting. He was also known for his quick, though accurate, work, which assured me the extra time I needed to work on the set with the actors, thus allowing them to give super-A performances.

I finished the film in twenty days. It cut together more easily and smoothly than any other film I had ever directed or edited, but one tiny change was made. In referring to the killing of Irish immigrants in the 1840s and 1850s, Robert Young says, "They may not teach it in school, but it's good American history just the same." Dore was afraid the word *good* might be misinterpreted to mean we favored lynching of the immigrants, so the line was redubbed to read, ". . . it's *real* American history . . ." This was a small thing, really, but what a large problem it indicates: the continued underestimation of the public's ability to understand.

And yet, I could be wrong. After our fine-cut was shown to the post-production crew, one of the young assistant sound cutters, an Argentinean, complimented the film.

"It's such a fine suspense story," he said. "Why did you have to bring in that stuff about anti-Semitism?"

"That was our chief reason for making the picture," I answered.

"But there's no anti-Semitism in the United States," he protested. "If there was why is all the money in America controlled by Jewish bankers?"

I stared at him in astonishment. Obviously, someone had gotten to him before we did. I worried that we might have that problem all the way down the line. For that reason, and because *Crossfire* was the first film on anti-Semitism to be released—the first to use the word *Jew* openly (and pejoratively, when used by the murderer)—we were all apprehensive and held a good many more than the usual number of previews. They were all great, however, and the film was released to fine response and rave reviews. New York's leading film critic, Archer Winston of the *New York Post*, wrote: "RKO . . . [has now] got *Crossfire*, a film which is not merely a step forward. It's a step into another world of thinking and doing . . . a film to be praised, praised again, and seen by all" (June 25, 1947). In 1948, *Crossfire* garnered five Oscar nominations; for a twenty-day film, that was unique—and not bad for *any* film.

I was so high, so completely confident in the future, that I willingly gave my wife everything when she finally sued for divorce. I felt indestructible, and Jean and I could see nothing but roses ahead. But just around the corner was September 23, 1947, and the pink subpoena. In one brief moment, my whole world changed.

6

In the fall of 1947, Joe McCarthy was not even on the horizon, certainly not on the national scene. When he did strut into the limelight, he had bigger game on his mind, and he so dominated the public's attention in the early 1950s that his name became the everlasting symbol of everything evil in the first postwar decade. Today, most people believe he was responsible for all the many witch-hunts of that period. (I say "that period" because there have been several other such periods in our history, and there will undoubtedly be more in years to come; in the ongoing fight to preserve democracy, there are no lasting armistices.) Actually, HUAC came into being as a result of a hunt for subversives following World War I, long before McCarthy was a member of Congress. After a number of administrations and their accompanying changes, the particular committee that pursued the Hollywood hearings was chaired by the Honorable J. Parnell Thomas. The subpoena that bore his signature instructed me to appear before the House Un-American Activities Committee (HUAC) on October 23, 1947.

Adrian Scott and I received our separate summons in Dore Schary's office at RKO on September 23. Our first shared emotion was one of elation; the confrontation had been brewing for some time, but since I was no longer a party man, I took little notice of it. In early spring, a subcommittee of HUAC had invaded our peaceful town seeking information and interviews with a number of potential friendly witnesses in preparation for the later hearings of the full committee. We weren't quite sure of HUAC's ultimate intentions, but we welcomed the opportunity to have *our* say. Unfortunately, we couldn't anticipate that within three years, we and the honorable chairman would be guests of the Federal Prison Administration—he for malfeasance in office, we for contempt of him and his committee.

What is generally forgotten, or overlooked, is that Thomas was not the real instigator of the investigation. The Committee's previous targets had been labor unions and other workers' organizations. Show business was well off the beaten path, and Thomas had yet to realize the truth of the old adage, "Nothing is as scared as a million dollars," and to become aware of the full potential of Hollywood as a fresh source of self-aggrandizement and world attention. Enter the Motion Picture Alliance for the Preservation of American Ideals (MPAPAI, for short, which really doesn't help that much.)

This organization was formed early in 1944. Senator Robert R. Reynolds, on March 7 of the same year, inserted a communication in the *Congresstional Record* that announced the principles of the Motion Picture Alliance: "Because of the flagrant manner in which the motion picture industrialists of Hollywood have been coddling Communists and cooperating with the so-called intellectual superiors they have helped import from Europe and Asia, there has been organized in Hollywood, the Motion Picture Alliance."

A few books on that period note that the MPAPAI was responsible for supplying HUAC with a number of friendly witnesses, but its germinal role in *initiating* the Hollywood hearings, and the fact that nearly *all* the "friendlies" were members of the Motion Picture Alliance, is rarely, if ever, mentioned. Among the charter members of the organization were directors Sam Wood (also its first president), George Marshall, Leo McCarey, Mike Curtiz, and Cecil B. DeMille (who should get top billing); actors John Wayne, Robert Montgomery, Adolphe Menjou, and Ward Bond; union leader Roy Brewer; Ginger Rogers's mother, Lela; Hollywood columnist Hedda Hopper; and a host of lesser lights. Industrialist Howard Hughes joined the organization later in the proceedings. With great zeal, this group importuned HUAC for its intervention into the Hollywood scene.

As early as July 9, 1945, the Committee's senior member, Congressman John Rankin of Mississippi, was quoted in the *Congressional Record* as saying: "But I want to say to the gentleman from California that these appeals are coming to us from the best people in California, some of the best producers in California are very much disturbed because they are having to take responsibility for some of the loathsome, filthy, insinuating, un-American currents that are running through various pictures sent throughout the country to be shown to the children of the nation."

California's "best people" finally succeeded, and in October of 1947, they were able to bask in the light of a fait accompli.

Adrian and I accepted our subpoenas and wasted no time in getting under way. After we left Schary's office, we walked to the tiny park in the center of the studio lot and discussed the alternatives. The Committee had established a record for bias—John Rankin admitted his racism with pride—and we knew legal representation was mandatory. But who? Hollywood attorneys specialized in contracts (making and breaking) divorces, occasional slander suits, and similar matters; we knew of none with Washington experience.

Fortunately, Adrian had just finished reading *Behind the Silken Curtain* by Bartley Crum, a noted San Francisco attorney. Scott had been impressed. Crum was a Catholic, a Republican, and a man of great intelligence and broad vision. He had been one of the leaders of the Young Turks who had bandwagoned Wendell Willkie to the 1940 Republican presidential nomination. More recently, he had been President Truman's representative on an international committee investigating the political and military situations in Palestine (still a British protectorate). Crum's book presented his own broad-minded view of the investigation.

I liked what Adrian told me; we could afford the best (what god-awful optimism!); so we called San Francisco. Crum was free to talk, already knew our situation, which had hit all the nation's news outlets, and was aware of the Committee's activities. He suggested we fly up as soon as possible. We met him at his offices on the following day; he was a small, trim, good-looking, and socially pleasant man, with a liberal Republican attitude toward HUAC and its attempts to censor by intimidation: he was appalled. He agreed to represent us in Washington, and we flew back to L.A. in a state of euphoria. Neither of us could realize that, with his unwitting cooperation, we were putting the quietus on an extremely outstanding career.

Scott and I returned to Hollywood that same evening to find that a good deal of activity had been going on during our short absence. We were advised that seventeen other potentially unfriendly witnesses had also received subpoenas and had tentatively agreed to pool their mental and financial resources in the interests of a common defense, that there would be a meeting of the group within two or three days, and that we and our attorney were invited to attend and participate with the rest. We were not surprised. Since the list included John Howard Lawson and Albert Maltz, as well as other party members, it was obvious that organized action would be the order of the day. Although I fully realized it only after group discussions got underway in Washington, the greatest danger to the Party resided in the presence of loose cannons, like Scott and me, who might be inclined to go our separate ways. For the communists, it was much safer to have us in than out.

Although we were aware the group had a strong pink tinge, we were lulled by the knowledge that the nineteen witnesses counted a few other men who were not, and never had been, members of the Party. Yet that fine writer, Howard Koch, was already threatening the group's plans. He proposed to take out ads and give interviews to deny holding extreme leftist leanings. He was strongly advised to cool it, but that wasn't the end of the matter. Director Irving Pichel, as nice a man as one could find in Hollywood, was a strong liberal, who went along for the promised excitement. But the wild card on the list was Lewis Milestone, one of Hollywood's top filmmakers, the director of *All Quiet on the Western Front, Front Page,* and many other fine films. His summons was a shock to most of us, since he had been politically inactive for years, but it provided Lawson and his advisers with the opening they needed—a new cuckoo's nest. What could be less ominous to those of us who might refuse to carry the banner of the Party than a meeting at Millie's home in Beverly Hills?

But first, a preliminary get-together, apparently ecumenical, which did little more than introduce us to the few we didn't already know, was held at the home of Edward G. Robinson. He was not a communist, nor had he gotten a subpoena, and he probably had not the faintist idea that the group was anything more than a batch of persecuted liberals. (Incidentally, he was not at home that evening.) A few days later, we got down to business. If memory serves me right, there were at least two meetings at Milestone's house, but to my knowledge no records were kept. So I shall try to combine the substance of both sessions into one summation, while trying to maintain some logical progression.

The meetings were attended by all nineteen potential witnesses and their attorneys. Two of the lawyers, Bartley Crum and Robert Kenny, were as pure as new-fallen snow. Kenny had been attorney general of California, where he had earned an excellent reputation as an honest adminstrator and prosecutor. He was highly respected by everyone, and though inclined to imbibe a touch too much, he was clear-headed and fast on his feet when it counted. It was clear from the start that if the gathered individuals agreed to act as a unit, Kenny and Crum, because of their blameless characters and established reputations, would be the front men.

I had met one of the other lawyers, Ben Margolis, at a fraction, so I knew him to be a Red. Charles Katz I suspected, but I had never met him before. In any case, it soon was easy to see that these two would be the power; of that there was little question. If any reader wonders why that knowledge aroused no suspicion or doubt among the noncommunists in the group, he can credit naïveté. Although none of us knew exactly how many of those present were party members, we were quite sure that at least a few were not. Each of us had worked with, or known, most of those men at some time in the past; nearly all had excellent reputations as artists, citizens, and persons of integrity, and none had shown any sign of malignant antigovernment activity. Among the nineteen potential witnesses, political dissatisfaction was abundant, but find me one person with an active conscience who is not unhappy with one thing or another in any political system or three persons who can agree on all elements of an utopian regime. We are all aware of the inevitability of such differences, and we are willing to tolerate them, each for his own sake, but at least some of us were unaware that this group would not actually function as a unit, or that there would be a group within the group that would be fed advice and direction from an unacknowledged source. However, at the meetings in late September and early October of 1947, Margolis and Katz, while taking an active part in the group's discussions, were especially careful to keep any mention of the Party or party principles out of the conversation, and to establish an aura of nonpartisanship—even Jean was allowed to accompany me to some of these meetings.

There was some very tentative discussion of strategy, and tea or coffee and cookies were supplied by the gracious Mrs. Milestone. But the preliminary purposes of the meetings were realized; the Nineteen agreed to work together and to share all costs, which included ads, transportation to, and lodging in Washington, D.C., plus expenses and fees of our four legal representatives. An indication of the success of the Party's laissez-faire camouflage was that Bartley Crum had agreed to join the team.

Procedural rules for our more formal meetings were established, one of which was to limit each member's freedom of choice and action completely and eventually cause painful disaffection. Although my own disenchantment came late, it cured me of any and all partiality for the words *unanimous* and *unanimity*. At this point, when at least some readers will start to wonder why an intelligent excommunist could not see the probable dangers of such strictures, I will take refuge in another man's words.

In his autobiography, *A Life*, Elia Kazan has written words that may puzzle some "straight" people who are inclined to favor a simplistic solution. But his words will instantaneously revive in every excommunist memories of what was perhaps the most singular and confusing period of his life. Kazan writes that after his resignation from the Party, "my relations with my old comrades did not change. . . . I was glad to be *out* and glad to still be *in*. . . . In othe words, I continued to think like a Communist. . . . Only I and those like me had the answers. . . . In fact, I still believe a good part of what I believed then" (131–32). And that's the glue.

Only some three years later, while I was in jail and largely isolated from contact with my former associates, was I able to realize the inconsistency of that long-lasting state of mind, but I wondered how noninfected men such as Kenny and Crum could have failed to recognize the tactics of the group's communist members—until it was too late, for them and for me.

Larry Parks was one of the Nineteen. Throughout our first meeting, he had seemed tentative; reluctant to cooperate with the group. He was the image of the skittish nonjoiner, and I couldn't imagine him as a communist. I am now inclined to think it was a clever act, but since Larry was known to seek frequent advice and to consider all facets of a problem with care, those of us who were his friends tended to believe him in his misgivings. When, late in the evening, he took the floor with a proposal, we were ready to support almost anything he asked for.

He was concerned, he said, with the possibility that the Nineteen might succumb to the indecision and lack of unity that plagued many small political groups. He would join the other eighteen only if we agreed that all decisions would be affirmed unanimously, a rule that we had to promise to honor absolutely. If this suggestion had come from John Howard Lawson or Ben Margolis, the noncommunists among us would have been on guard, but Larry Parks? Good fellowship reigned that early in the game, as well as high hopes, and it seemed an easy way to extinguish Larry's apprehensions; we voted to adopt the resolution unanimously.

Years later, Larry told me that he had been urged to press the proposal during a premeeting conversation with Dalton Trumbo, whom he idolized. But I also learned from another member of the group that Lawson and Margolis had initiated the scenario. Perhaps it was too late in the evening for a morning mentality like mine, but I was not aware of the full consequences of our decision at that time; I was soon to learn that with it, we lost any pretense of functioning according to the old democratic principle of accommodation of differences. I had pledged myself to march in lockstep with the communist majority, no matter where it led me.

7

"**Hollywood Accused:** Red Issue Splits Film Industry." So shouted the headlines of the *Los Angeles Daily News* on October 20, 1947. The third, and smaller subhead squeaked, "Vishinsky in Bitter Tirade Against the U.S." Forty-one years later, not one college student in a thousand can identify Vishinsky, but a surprisingly large percentage of those same students are aware of the existence of the Hollywood Ten.

Like a troupe of mummers, the unfriendly witnesses invaded the nation's capital shortly before the hearings began. The group of nineteen writers, actors, and directors—enough to make a number of excellent films or start a small revolution—plus their stable of lawyers and a few wives, holed up at the Sheraton.

The curtain was about to go up on the hottest show in town. Solidly, for the next three weeks and intermittently for the next five or six years, the proceedings that created the Hollywood Ten captured the headlines of the leading newspapers and periodicals, not only in the United States but throughout the world. A public that had grown accustomed to daily reports of world crises during World War II had suffered boring reading for two years. They were hungry for something sensational and eager to lap it up. On opening day, the *Los Angeles Herald Express* plastered its entire front page with headlines, photos, and stories of the testimony being heard in the old House office building in Washington, D.C. With some of Hollywood's best producers taking the stand to be grilled and verbally mauled by members of the committee, even the cold war and Vishinsky had to be content with a story on page two.

The Caucus Room was the largest hall on hand in the Capitol complex for public hearings. Well over four hundred persons waited in line for over an hour to snatch the seats available when the doors were opened. (Throughout the hearings all sessions were "standing room only.") To add to the crush, a battalion of Capitol police was strategically scattered about the room. According to *Hollywood Variety* (Oct. 21, 1947), which called the hearings a "Red Quiz Barnum Show," ninety seats were reserved for the journalists at the press table. Ninety-four showed up, and eight or nine newsreel cameras covered the chamber's various centers of interest. The four major radio networks were also present in force, and crouched at the foot of the crescent-shaped dais, which spanned the width of one end of the room, twenty-four or twenty-five news photographers faced the witnesses' table, cameras at the ready, waiting to snap the performers of the day in their most awkward poses. All who had been subpoenaed or had volunteered to testify, occupied the choice seats immediately behind the scene of action.

The interrogators would soon take their places. We sat with the curious onlookers, but we were really the actors who had to face an unpredictable audience. "Confidence!" I thought. But how could I be sure? I didn't even have a God to fall back on. Palms sweating, heart beating a ragged tattoo, butterflies trying to escape my stomach, I waited for the show to begin.

Shortly after 10:00 A.M., J. Parnell Thomas sat down on his chair, which was supplemented by a red cushion atop a District of Columbia telephone directory, and gaveled the meeting to order. Three other members of the Committee had already taken their seats; they were John Mc-Dowell of Pennsylvania, Richard B. Vail of Illinois, and Richard M. Nixon, the freshman congressman from California. Their chief investigator was Robert E. Stripling.

Hot on the heels of the chairman's opening remarks, Kenny and Crum claimed the floor. As the *Los Angeles Daily News* put it on October 21:

> Chairman J. Parnell Thomas banged his gavel mightily when attorneys Robert W. Kenny and Bartley Crum tried to snatch the ball and run with it.
>
> The attorneys asked permission to present their previously announced motion to quash the subpoenas issued to 19 Hollywood actors, writers, and producers on grounds that the Committee and the investigation are unconstitutional and illegal ... Thomas silenced Kenny and Crum with repeated blows from his gavel, but not before Crum, a San Francisco Republican, had said sarcastically, "This is certainly an un-American procedure."

The chairman held his gavel like a scepter, but wielded it like an axe. He reminded me of an assistant director I had known who fell in love with a bullhorn. It gave him a sense of superiority and power over a mob of extras. For Thomas, the rod of his office was his gavel. Without it, he was a short, dumpy, very average human being.

Scheduled first was the testimony of the cooperating witnesses. The more I review it now the sillier it seems, although *silly* is hardly the appropriate word when one considers that lives, families, and careers of hundreds of men and women in all branches of the entertainment business were irreparably damaged by the allegations and opinions that followed. An abstraction of the friendly witnesses' performances would paint only an abstract picture, so a brief review of some of the questions and answers are in order.

The first to testify was J. L. (Jack) Warner, the vice president in charge of production for the Warner Brothers studio, in Burbank, California. At the spring subcommittee rehearsals in Hollywood in May of 1947, he had been asked: "Don't you think the most effective way of removing these Communist influences is the pay-roll route? In other words, if the owners and producers cut these people off the pay-roll it would eliminate it much quicker than a Congressional committee on a crusade and so forth."

"Well," Warner had answered, "that definitely would be."

Now, in October, the committee hoped to extract a sworn admission of the desirability of a blacklist. But the knowledge that the world was listening (or some older brother's advice) had had a sobering effect, and this indiscriminately rambling man had reconsidered his position. As usual, he was more than free with his rhetoric (to the tune of about 57,000 words), but he resisted having the onus of a blacklist shifted from the Committee's narrow mind onto his shoulders.

And though he testified he had "never seen a Communist," he was more than willing to identify a few men who had aroused his suspicions.

Mr. Warner.	In New York I saw *All of* [sic] *My Sons*, written by Arthur Miller. . . . the play is a good play, but it has all of this stuff in it. In fact, it won the Critics' Award in New York, and was directed by a chap named Elia Kazan who is now at Twentieth Century-Fox as a director. . . . Can I say something off the record?
Mr. Thomas.	Put it on the record.
Mr. Warner.	This fellow is also one of the mob. . . . I pass him by but won't talk to him.

While testifying about his efforts to "clean" the studio's scripts of communist propaganda, Warner mentioned Clifford Odets and his script for *Humoresque*, from the novel by Fannie Hurst.

Mr. Warner.	John Garfield played the part of the boy and he was mad at Joan Crawford for romantic reasons and said, "Your father is a banker." He was alluding to the fact that she was rich and had all of the money. He said, "My father lives over a grocery store." That is very, very subtle. . . . But it is not in the film. I eliminated it from the script. Sometimes you eliminate these things and they leave them in because it plays good and everybody is trying to be a Voltaire. All these writers and actors want to "Voltaire" about freedom of press and freedom of speech.

Later in the morning, Congressman McDowell, trying to lead Warner, made an interesting statement and asked an interesting question. He got an interesting answer.

Mr. McDowell.	You know, during Hitler's regime they passed a law in Germany outlawing communism and the Communists went to jail. Would you advocate the same thing here?
Mr. Warner.	Everyone in this room and everyone in the world knows the consequences of that type of law.

This should have stopped that line of questioning. But a bit later, Thomas slid in more smoothly:

The Chairman.	If we passed a law that would be a proper legal procedure, wouldn't it?
Mr. Warner.	I, as an individual citizen, naturally am in favor of anything that is good for all Americans.
The Chairman.	Are you in favor of outlawing the Communist Party?
Mr. Warner.	You mean from the ballot?
The Chairman.	Yes; making it an illegal organization.
Mr. Warner.	I am in favor of making it an illegal organization.

At the end of the long session, Vail ventured into the scene.

A Memoir of the Hollywood Ten

Mr. Vail.	It would seem to me that this organization [Motion Picture Producers Association] should concern itself with cleaning house . . . through the elimination of the writers and the actors to whom definite communistic leanings can be traced. . . .
Mr. Warner.	I agree to it personally, Mr. Congressman, but . . . I can't, for the life of me, figure where men could get together . . . to deprive a man of his livelihood because of his political beliefs.

And for the moment, things looked promising. If Jack Warner, who disliked unions and studio liberals more than anyone in Hollywood, could take such a stand, and if the testimony of Eric Johnson (president of the Motion Picture Producers Association) to our attorneys—"As long as I live I will never be a party to anything as un-American as a blacklist . . . Tell the boys not to worry. We're not going totalitarian to please the Committee"—were indeed meant as an honest promise, the danger of a blacklist seemed to have diminished.

By an odd coincidence, the next two friendly witnesses were both Russian-born. The first of these was Louis B. Mayer, the head of MGM. Mayer was the highest paid executive in the land and certainly the boss with the greatest clout in Hollywood. That meant nothing to the congressman; he was bullied and harried by them and their investigators as if he were the movie capital's buffoon. No doubt some of our group were delighted at the lack of class distinction. But their high spirits were squelched when Mayer made the following statement: "It is my earnest hope that this committee will perform a public service by recommending to Congress legislation establishing a national policy regulating employment of Communists in private industry. It is my belief they should be denied the sanctuary of the freedom they seek to destroy." So much for the lift we had gotten from Jack Warner not too many minutes before.

However, the Committee now had before them the head of the studio that had produced *Song of Russia*. In their zeal to find a modicum of Red propaganda in films, they locked onto the film whose title implied the downtrodden Russians dared to sing. H. A. Smith, who spelled a weary Stripling as inquisitor, was eager to learn if the MGM film, starring Robert Taylor, had included scenes that might mislead its viewers concern-

ing conditions in the USSR. Mayer wanted to know what scenes Smith
was referring to.

Mr. Smith.	Do you recall scenes in there at the night club where everybody was drinking?
Mr. Mayer.	They do in Moscow.
Mr. Smith.	Do you feel that that represents Russia as it is today?
Mr. Mayer.	I didn't make it as it is today. I made it when they were our ally in 1943.

Since the studio heads had insisted that no "stuff" had infiltrated
their films, the Committee called Ayn Rand, who was also an émigré
from Russia. She had no doubts about the presence of propaganda in
Hollywood films and stronger feelings about viewers' susceptibilities.
As a guest of the Committee, she had viewed *Song of Russia* and noted
that the Russians occasionally smiled. In her opinion, the portrayal of
such unusual emotion was "one of the stock propaganda tricks of the
Communists, to show these people smiling," or, for that matter, to show
them living in clean cottages.

Sam Wood, the president of the Motion Picture Alliance, also appeared on opening day. Throughout the hearings, the Committee was
hard on studio executives past the point of common rudeness, but they
were excessively polite to witnesses from the MPAPAI. Wood's complaint was not that Hollywood portrayed Russian peasants as smiling,
but that they showed American bankers and senators as villains. In his
own words: "I think it is particularly bad if that is constantly shown.
Every night you go to the pictures you see a dishonest banker, or senator, you begin to think that the whole system is wrong." (I wonder what
he would think if he were alive today.) And who is responsible for such
a state of affairs?

Mr. Stripling.	What group in the industry must be watched more carefully than the rest?
Mr. Wood.	The writers.

Most of the friendly witnesses felt confident in naming a number of
writers as communists, but their identification, based on suspicions,
would hardly be considered permissible evidence outside the chambers of

Congress. When asked if there was any question in his mind whether Lawson was a communist, Wood replied, "If there is, then I haven't any mind."

In typical Hollywood fashion, later witnesses tried to top him. Two days later when questioned about Lester Cale, Morrie Ryskind said that if he "isn't a Communist, I don't think Mahatma Gandhi is an Indian." This gave Fred Niblo Jr. a cue when he referred to Gordon Kahn during testimony the following day: "I cannot prove it [that Kahn is a Communist] any more than Custer can prove that the people who were massacring him were Indians."

Although the witnesses had no valid proof for their identifications, the Committee did. They could have ended the hearings in a hurry, especially since their efforts were creating more amusement and grounds for criticism than public heat. But they had not yet called on their first-line troops, and they decided to let Hollywood names carry the ball a little longer. The headlines in the *Los Angeles Examiner* of October 21, 1947, stated in bold letters, "Film Leaders Tell Red Menace to Hollywood" and "Military Experts Urge U.S. Start Training Now." The juxtaposition of the headlines were indeed food for thought.

On October 21, 1947, the second day of the hearings, the MPAPAI witnesses were Adolphe Menjou, Rupert Hughes, and John Moffit. Moffit, a screenwriter, reported on a communist undercover man who posed as a literary agent. He succeeded, Moffit said, in obtaining the secret of the military's latest supersonic plane from one of its test pilots, but the FBI could find no evidence of such a Communist Party coup.

Rupert Hughes, the uncle of Howard Hughes, wrote short stories for ladies' magazines. He also wrote the first biography debunking George Washington, which seemed an odd accomplishment for a man sworn to preserve American ideals. At the preliminary hearings in May, Hughes had come out against the "Four Freedoms" on the grounds that "they would rob the American people of the stimulus of fear and poverty." But he went a little too far, even for the chairman. The *Los Angeles Examiner*, on October 22, 1947, reported: "The author clashed with Chairman Thomas . . . when the witness called the University of California at Los Angeles a 'Communist dominated' institution. Thomas ordered the testimony stricken from the record."

That suave, fastidiously dressed actor, Adolphe Menjou, proved to be one of the most loquacious and well-informed witnesses of the week. Under oath, he said he had read over four hundred books on Russia and over one hundred fifty books on communism. He recommended a read-

Odd Man Out

ing list of thirty-five books to all who really wanted to understand the Red menace, and he instructed anyone who cared to listen on the methods of recognizing party members and "pinkos," although he admitted he could not positively identify any of Hollywood's Reds. Suspicions, however, he had in plenty, but his most telling contribution was his disclosure of the methods by which communist actors could insinuate party propaganda into films: "I believe that under certain circumstances a communistic director, a communistic writer, or a communistic actor, even if he were under orders from the head of the studio not to inject communism or un-Americanism or subversion into pictures, could easily subvert that order, under the proper circumstances, by a look, by an inflection, by a change in the voice. I think it could be easily done. I have never seen it done, but I think it could be done."

Testimony of this kind was offered and accepted with gratitude throughout the week. My mind was in a continuous haze. I had only to close my eyes and picture myself as a masculine Alice in Wonderland—it was just as ridiculous and almost as funny. But it was also humiliating. I had never realized Hollywood's bigwigs (whom I never knew socially) could be so unwittingly stupid in their defense of the American way of life. For a few days, I could almost accept *Time* magazine's supercilious attitude about the town I lived in and the people I worked with. But, apparently unheeding of reactions such as mine, the friendly witnesses carried on regardless.

During the May rehearsals in Hollywood, Lela Rogers had testified that the phrase "Share and share alike—that's democracy," which was spoken by her daughter in my film *Tender Comrade*, was subversive, dangerous, and clearly communist propaganda. But at the time the film was made, Ginger was a powerhouse at RKO, and although apparently less doctrinaire than her mother, she was never bashful about expressing an opinion or voicing an objection. Yet neither Ginger, Lela, nor anyone else at the studio objected to that line of dialogue when the film was shot or when it was released, which is perhaps why Lela did not repeat the charge in October. But to add zest to her testimony, she did identify Clifford Odets as a communist. When questioned about her source of information, she replied she had read it in O. O. McIntyre's column, which appeared on January 8, 1936.

I knew one of the witnesses who testified on October 23 quite well. I had edited several films for Leo McCarey in the 1930s, and we had become good friends. Two eminently successful classics, *Going My*

Way and *Bells of St. Mary's*, had made him a wealthy man, and though I understood that one must be forgiven for defending one's property against the most visible enemy, I was not happy to see him take the stand. Leo now hated the IRS, and like Sam Wood, he resented the way bankers and the rich were portrayed in films. He warned that leftist directors "can cast a character so repulsive when you take one look at him you don't like that man who is portrayed as a capitalist, a banker, or whatever part he is portraying." Perhaps he had forgotten, but Leo failed to mention that he, no leftist, had cast the ugly, greedy scoundrel who had tried to repossess Bing Crosby's church in *Going My Way*.

The testimony of two of Hollywood's leading actors was hardly earthshaking, but it is probably worth a brief mention. The first, on October 22, was Robert Taylor.

Mr. Stripling.	You would refuse to act in a picture in which a person whom you considered to be a Communist was also cast; is that correct?
Mr. Taylor.	. . . if I were even suspicious of a person being a Communist with whom I was scheduled to work, I am afraid it would have to be him or me, because life is a little too short to be around people who annoy me as much as these fellow travelers and Communists do.

Actors may have been apprehensive, but not one writer felt endangered by Taylor's watchful eye. He had just finished playing in *The High Wall*, written by Sidney Boehm and Lester Cole. Almost anyone interested in politics considered Cole a communist, and Cole would have been the last to deny it.

On the following day, October 23, Gary Cooper foreshadowed the future with a statement that was echoed frequently in the next few years. When asked whether he thought communism was on the increase or on the decrease, he gave a considered answer: "It is very difficult to say right now, within these last few months, because it has become unpopular and a little risky to say too much. You notice the difference. People who were quite easy to express their thoughts before begin to clam up more that they used to."

The fourth day of the hearings was coming to a close. The statements of Ronald Reagan, president of the Screen Actors Guild, and two ex-presidents, Robert Montgomery and George Murphy, were nearly carbon copies of each other. None had seen any sign of propaganda in his scripts, none felt the communists were a menace to the guild. Although they engaged in no bitter attacks on Hollywood writers, all three were congratulated as good and articulate witnesses. But there was one slight hitch in Reagan's testimony; as was his wont, he quoted Thomas Jefferson as saying the American people, if acquainted with the facts, would not make a mistake. Chairman Thomas sensed a subtle aspersion on the Committee and attempted to set Reagan straight: "That is just why this committee was created . . . to acquaint the American people with the facts. Once [they] are acquainted with the facts there is no question but what the American people will do a job . . . to make America just as pure as we can possibly make it." Mr. Reagan was not cowed; he still thought that "democracy can do it."

On that high note, four days of testimony ended. Besides the testimony of the Hollywood executives and artists, there had been numerous skirmishes with Crum and Kenny, as well as with Paul V. McNutt, Eric Johnson, and Maurice Benjamin, the high-powered representatives of the studio heads and the Motion Picture Producers Association. Showing no partiality, the chairman shouted and wielded his gavel with great vigor regardless of the lawyers' political coloration. The newspapers made due note of Thomas's near-maniacal behavior. Their sympathies were largely with those who were being so casually and illegally attacked by the Committee, as was the goodwill of the great majority of the audience. Anyone sitting through the first five days in the Caucus Room could easily have prescribed the tactics needed to defeat Thomas and his bullyboys. Unfortunately, as I was to learn the following week, our tactics were being laid down by people who had never seen the Caucus Room, the Committee, or most of the Nineteen.

Will it ever end department: More than four decades ago, MGM placed Robert Taylor's name on one of their white, three-story office buildings in gratitude for the millions of dollars and the untold wealth in prestige he brought to the studio. Early in 1990, two producers for Lorimar, Stan Zimmerman and James Berg, collected about fifty signatures (mostly from writers, who never stop screaming for their right to speak) demanding the removal of Taylor's name from the building because, in 1947, he took advantage of *his* right to speak while cooperating with

the House Committee on Un-American Activities—about two generations ago. And Lorimar (who owned MGM) buckled. ("Who's Blacklisting Now?" asked an editorial by Eric Breindel in the *New York
Post*.) Obviously, the pendulum has swung the other way, and a new
generation, with nothing to write, seeks to perpetuate the age-old preju-
dices and bigotries against people about whom they know little or
nothing at all.

8

The honorable J. Parnell Thomas and his machine-gun gavel were the laughingstock of Washington, and during the first week, the Hollywood brass did its best to keep the laughs rolling. At this point, it didn't look too bad for our side, but there was to be no resting on our oars. Our days were filled with meetings, counseling, interviews, attendance at the friendly hearings, and dining at one of Washington's few good restaurants. (This was 1947.) Our preferred eating place was Harvey's, where lovers of fine seafood could gorge on steamed clams and soft-shell crabs while watching J. Edgar Hoover, paunched and powdered, enjoying his evening meal with one of his cohorts while seated at his usual observation post just inside the establishment's front door.

During the first few days of the hearings, Adrian Scott and I made a feeble attempt at lobbying. Escorted by Bartley Crum, who knew his way around town, we visited a number of friendly congressmen, only to learn that friendship is Washington's most fickle relationship. Our efforts were a complete waste of time. The average Capitol politico had all the instincts of a sea anemone—wide open to the world until he felt the slightest troublesome touch, which always produced an instantaneous reaction of self-protective shrinkage and withdrawal.

One afternoon, we called on Emmanuel Cellar, the chairman of the House Judiciary Committee, and one of the most influential men in Congress. He listened to our story with every sign of sympathy, and a touch of sorrow. Then he leveled with us: "I think you're absolutely in the right," he said, "but it's a political matter. I wouldn't touch it with a ten-foot pole." (Later, during the House debate on our contempt charges, Cellar put up a strong fight for our cause. Unfortunately, he was one of the very few.)

While not very original, the message was clear. We gave up haunting the halls of Congress. Much of the time we were being approached by friends whom we had never met, assailed by the press, and advised by those who claimed to be in the know. We were cautious and noncommittal with our self-proclaimed friends, and we were purposely ambiguous with the press, but we listened carefully to the initiated. One bit of information on everyone's tongue was that Hoover had bugged every office and hotel room in the District, and it was probably true. Certainly, the clicks that emanated from every lifted hotel phone indicated that these instruments, as well as the rooms at large, were on a party line. We were also told, and chose to believe, that the best technique for foiling eavesdroppers was to keep snapping our fingers, which we did enthusiastically whenever a private conversation took place. It was hard to believe that Yankee know-how had fashioned no filters to cancel out the sound of snapping fingers, but the activity always furnished a few moments of comic relief from the grimness that surrounded us. Probably a more effective, though less-amusing, ploy was the choice of milieu; a bathroom with all the faucets and the toilet running at full flow was the preferred meeting place. (This practice continued after our return to Hollywood.)

The opening week's hearings were completed, and our number was up. But first we had a free weekend for conferences, planning, and a bit of relaxation for Scott and me. That Saturday, the first warning flag went up—Albert Maltz invited us to join him for a visit to the war museum. I wondered about Albert's choice for an afternoon's diversion and why, in a city that was a sightseer's delight, this man of peace had chosen to subject us to an exhibition of articles of mass murder. But what appeared to be the museum's chief exhibit on that day had nothing to do with war.

There were rooms full of large, liquid-filled jars containing fetal monstrosities—well-developed embryos with eyes in the middle of their foreheads, heads extruded from bellies, small dessicated cadavers comingled with their larger, more normal-appearing siblings, and scores of other attractions too horrible to mention. To this day, the riddle of such a display within the confines of a *war* museum continues to mystify me. Even as a child, I could not tolerate the sight of geeks at the circus sideshows, and at my request, we cut short our tour and returned to the hotel. There I found a possible explanation for the why of our cultural pilgrimage, if not the where.

A meeting was underway in our main conference room; some rather loud voices could be heard. At Albert's suggestion, we chose not to intrude. Only after two or three similar episodes did I realize that these meetings were for communists only, and those who were not currently members of the Party were sidetracked in the most convenient ways. Maltz had been chosen to take us on a tour because his presence was not essential to the meeting; he could be counted on to follow the line no matter how labyrinthine it might be. But Scott and I were not too stable, and our attendance at such meetings was not desirable.

The discussion taking place that afternoon was especially one at which our presence might have been troublesome. It might have resulted in a change of mind. Howard Koch had never been able to rid himself of his early apprehensions, and the witch-hunting atmosphere of the week's hearings had driven him over the edge. Quite sensibly, he wondered why he, a naïf who didn't know a communist from an Eskimo (he was unaware that one of his best friends was a Red) should be asked to risk his freedom in our defense. He was now determined to testify openly, and among other considerations, the leaders and lawyers of the Nineteen were concerned that his decision might sway Scott and me, who knew much more about the group than he did.

That possibility was never realized. As we heard the story later that night, Koch had been bombarded with every possible argument, but he remained unconvinced. The communists were left with one resource— Koch's wife (or possibly girlfriend). I never knew whether or not she was a member of the Party, but at this meeting, so we were told, she threatened to leave Koch if he deserted the Nineteen. Howard had no choice but to reconsider. (Koch's immediate problem was eliminated when the Committee failed to call him to the stand, but his future remained bleak. In 1951, he was blacklisted at HUAC's request. He did not work in Hollywood again for over seven years. It may also interest readers to know that, to my knowledge, there were at least three other instances in which strong-willed wives were used to influence their husband's loyalties.)

We had come to Washington naively secure in our belief that, whatever happened in Congress, the current liberal Supreme Court would bail us out. But our high hopes had been deflated by our interview with Cellar. Immediately after that meeting, Scott, Crum and I had discussed the possibility of testifying to our past membership in the Party, while making it clear that we were now free of its entanglements. Crum was enthusiastic about the idea and agreed to discuss it with the other attorneys. The answer, of course, was an emphatic, "No!" We were asked to adhere to our pledge of unanimity, and with some misgivings, at least on my part, we agreed.

The meetings of the Nineteen's inner circle were almost a daily affair, although they never again dealt with family matters. But following what every politically aware person now understands is standard practice whenever communism worms its way into a coalition, all procedural and positional decisions were made by the fraction. These decisions were then circulated as attorney's advice, with little or no opposition. Most of us noncommunists were unaware that we were on a one-way track with no sidings available, or that we were committed to a trip with an undesirable destination. Crum was deeply concerned, but the weight of four party lawyers (we had been joined by two party attorneys from New York) plus Robert Kenny's inclination to go with the flow, left him outnumbered, outvoted, and, without any solid determination from Scott or me, completely helpless. As a man of great integrity, he could not bring himself to urge us to break our pledge.

Some time later I learned from one of the Nineteen who had defected after the hearings that the inner group's crucial decision in defense strategy was channeled through one of these meetings. It was commonly assumed by experienced party members that no action of national significance could be taken without the agreement of the Party's national leaders. It was further assumed that, since the Party's existence was under constant threat from a hostile citizenry, major decisions or positions on questions of vital importance to the Party's well-being could be taken by the Communist Party of America only with the advice and permission of the Communist International, or Comintern. Its headquarters were in Moscow.

As I have previously indicated, there had been some discussion concerning our choice of plea; a few of the Nineteen, especially the noncommunists, were by no means certain of the legal validity of the First Amendment defense. With the exception of certain traditional relationships of privilege, such as those between priest and confessor, or a lawyer and client, it has never been established that the right to remain silent is protected by the amendment that guarantees us all the right to speak. The Fifth Amendment, which protects a witness from self-incrimination, was by long odds the safer alternative, but in the average person's mind "taking the Fifth" always implies guilt. The leaders of the Party felt that public backing, influenced by the group's use of ingenious evasion, which would cast doubt on the persecution of at least some members of the Nineteen, would force the Committee to retreat and serve to strengthen the resolve of a few of the industry's executives who, like Dore Schary and Harry Cohn, disapproved of HUAC and its current activity. And indeed, if the Party's tactics had been half as clever as its strategy, that might have happened.

Odd Man Out

It had been judged that this was a major battle of the cold war, and as I learned later, our defense strategy, without possibility of appeal, came from abroad. Ignoring the inherent contradictions, the Nineteen were to march as the champions of free speech, a revered idea in the United States and one with which the press would certainly sympathize. Of course, it was understood that the ploy might not work, that the Supreme Court's liberal majority could retire or die or simply refuse to endorse our point of view. It was also understood that we were guinea pigs, the possible sacrifices, the honorable martyrs, but the crisis had to be met head on. (It must be clearly noted here that after the Supreme Court refused to hear our First Amendment defense, every communist forced to face the Committee "took the Fifth" to avoid going to jail. The highly respected First Amendment continued to function as a cloak of purity, but it was never again offered as a strategy of defense.)

Perhaps our greatest, though not most important, activity was the preparation of position papers. Each of the Nineteen was expected to write a three- or four-page statement disclosing his political beliefs, his faith in basic American principles, his attitude toward the Committee's unjustified and illegal procedures, and his reasons for refusing to cooperate with its witch-hunt, which included the defendant's guess as to why the Committee was out for his particular scalp. During the course of the first week in Washington, party attorneys met with each of the Nineteen, usually in the early evening after the hearings had adjourned for the day. Unlike our purely organizational meetings in Hollywood, there was always the present danger of an indictment for conspiracy, a felony that called for much more severe penalties than did the misdemeanor of contempt, and the lawyers were careful to discuss statements with each man separately. But since the same lawyers were moving from one man to another, a definite coordination of purpose was achieved. Because of this, many of us felt our legal positions in the matter of conspiracy were quite weak, and to the last, we expected the Committee's counsel to institute such a charge. I have always believed that their failure to do so indicated that HUAC was actually out to expose a movement rather than nail a tiny group of individuals, and in that, however illegal, unethical, and un-American it was, they obviously succeeded.

Then the big show came to town—a happening that set Washington and the world agog. At the beginning of the second week, the capital was invaded by a group of stars far greater and more impressive than most of those who had appeared as friendly witnesses. And these stars were here to root for the underdogs, the members of the Nineteen. The presence of this large group of actors, directors, and writers from Hollywood and from Broadway was the end result of a movement that had begun as early as September, a few days after we had received our subpoenas.

Under the leadership of directors John Huston and Willie Wyler, writer Philip Dunne, and actor Alexander Knox, a small group of Hollywood artists met and formed the Committee for the First Amendment. Even the Screen Directors Guild, normally the most conservative of Hollywood's unions, issued a statement in October in which, among other idealistic sentiments, they said: "Any attempt on the part of an official body to set up arbitrary standards of Americanism is in itself disloyal to both the spirit and the letter of our Constitution. . . . As Americans, . . . we hereby resolve to defend the reputation of the industry in which we work against attack by the House Committee on UnAmerican Activities, whose chosen weapon is the cowardly one of inference and whose apparent aim is to silence opposition to their extremist views, in the free medium of motion pictures" (Gordon Kahn, *Hollywood on Trial*, 137). (I offer this as a perfect example that talk is cheap.)

Meanwhile, through the use of ads and personal contacts, the Committee for the First Amendment had grown until hundreds of Hollywood's most important artists were lending their names to protests against the hearings. A brief listing of just a few of these men and women says a great deal about Hollywood's support for the Nineteen at that stage of the fight and the strength of our position before our appearances.

There were Lauren Bacall and Humphrey Bogart, Richard Brooks, Eddie Cantor, Norman Corwin (who later wrote and produced two radio broadcasts about the hearings), and Agnes DeMille. I. A. L. Diamond and his collaborator, Billy Wilder, Kirk Douglas, Henry Fonda, Benny Goodman, Ava Gardner, Moss Hart, and Katharine Hepburn joined John and Walter Huston, George Kaufman, Gene Kelly, Danny Kaye, Burt Lancaster, and Myrna Loy. There were also Dorothy McGuire, Vincent Price, Jean Porter, John Paxton, Gregory Peck, Robert Ryan, Irwin Shaw, and Cornel Wilde. These were only a few of the personalities who signed the Hollywood Committee's ads.

And now, a sizable percentage of these people were, at their own expense, arriving on a chartered plane to root for our side. They might have done our cause a great deal of good; it could be assumed that with such an army of powerhouse personalities to aid them, victory for the Nineteen was in the bag. The phrase was probably not yet in the common language at the time, but the first unfriendly witnesses to take the stand promptly gave a new meaning to the words *self-destruct*.

9

Mr. Crum.	**May I request the right of cross-examination?** I ask you to bring back and permit us to cross-examine the witnesses, Adolphe Menjou, Fred Niblo, John Charles Moffit, Richard Macauley, Rupert Hughes, Sam Wood, Ayn Rand, James McGuinness—

It took a sharp-eared court clerk to winnow the last few names out of the "dread-bolted thunder" of the pounding gavel.

The Chairman.	The request—
Mr. Crum.	Howard Rushmore—[*The chairman pounding gavel.*]
Mr. Crum.	Morrie Ryskind, Oliver Carlson—
The Chairman.	The request is denied.
Mr. Crum.	In order to show that these witnesses lied.
The Chairman.	That request is denied. Mr. Stripling, the first witness.
Mr. Stripling.	John Howard Lawson.

The Committee had its own effective sense of theater, and it was dramatically correct that John Howard Lawson should be the first of the unfriendly witnesses to be called. He was widely considered by Hollywood's politically aware to be the Party's number one man in the film industry. Many of the first week's witnesses had identified him as that on the basis of hearsay—which is nearly as dependable as the truth—and the communists in Hollywood knew of his position in the section on the basis of experience.

On the morning of October 27, 1947, I was a very nervous man. It was our red-letter day. The crowd that had been waiting for hours to get into the Caucus Room was larger than ever. It would still be SRO, though more so, but it could not be said that the presence of the VIPs representing the Hollywood Committee for the First Amendment was the only reason for the greater than usual show of interest. Those of the Nineteen who were to testify were also important performers on that day's playbill.

I had taken my usual place in the second row; the Hollywood observers occupied a fair-sized section of the seats behind me, and Dore

Schary, RKO's production chief, was seated at my right. Both of us were so tense we had barely said "Good morning." *Good* seemed hardly the word to characterize this day of the year.

At the first swing of the chairman's gavel, Robert Kenny and Bartley Crum had once again taken the floor to present more evidence of the hearing's illegality and, failing that, to ask for the right to cross-examine earlier witnesses. We all knew this was not a judicial trial, but a congressional hearing at which court precedents did not apply. Nevertheless, it had been decided to fight the Committee to the end, and (as the French warned Lyndon Johnson when he escalated the war in Vietnam) in an unequal battle, the end can be bitter indeed.

Those of us who had watched the members of the Committee take their places on the dais that morning noticed that it was one man short. Richard M. Nixon had been the producers' sympathetic ear while sitting through the first week's hearings. Whenever the going got rough for Hollywood's befuddled and intimidated executives, Nixon could be counted on to ask a question or two that could be answered in a self-serving fashion and that would give the respondents time to collect their wits and realign their defenses. It would be uncharitable, but not unjust, to suggest that he did so because they were, or could be, a source of support in his future campaigns. It was not often that Nixon failed to look ahead, and he had returned to California at this appropriate time to touch base with his constituents in Whittier. After all, he had little to gain and much to lose in being identified, if only geographically, with the unfriendly Nineteen.

Many of the previous week's witnesses had offered, and had been allowed to read, prepared position statements. John Howard Lawson now requested the same privilege. There was a brief hiatus as his statement was handed up to the chairman. With his colleagues on either side looking over his shoulders, Thomas flicked a quick peek at the typewritten sheets, then threw them down in disgust.

"I don't care to read any more of the statement," he said. "The statement will not be read."

Naturally, Lawson protested. But Thomas remained unshakable.

"I refuse you to make the statement [that's what he said], because of the first sentence in your statement." And that was that. With one surprising exception, Thomas refused to hear the statements of any of the nine men who followed.

Lawson's screed was not recorded in the Committee's proceedings, but like those of the rest of the Hollywood Ten, it was released to the press. The first sentence, which had elicited such a painful reaction from the chairman, read as follows: "For a week, this Committee has conducted an illegal and indecent trial of American citizens whom the Committee has selected to be publicly pilloried and smeared."

Had Thomas found the patience to read further, he would have seen that the first sentence was mild compared to much of what followed. But, while not especially scurrilous, it was important in one way; it was the keynote of the raucous defense that came in its wake. The First Amendment, advertised as the basis for our contention that we need not answer the questions asked, was not evoked as often as the words, *illegal*, *indecent*, and *smeared*. Whenever the Committee's counsel asked one or both of the following questions

(1) Are you a member of the Writers Guild?
(2) Are you now or have you ever been a member of the Communist Party of the United States?[3]

the answer was usually some version of the first sentence of Lawson's statement. Although Thomas did not know that when he peeked at the paper, he would soon get more of it tossed his way than he could amiably support.

Before chronicling the more violent exchanges between the chairman and the members of the Hollywood Ten (the rest of the Nineteen were later excused from testifying but never forgiven for their sins), I would like to analyze the statements of some of the group, especially the statement of Lawson, which served as a model for most of the others, to further my contention that even if, as some apologists have claimed, we were forced to give tit for tat, our responses were, on the whole, dishon-

3. Since many people are unaware of the evolution of the phraseology of the Committee's main question, a short explanation will, I hope, be welcomed. In the early days of the Martin Dies Committee, a precursor of HUAC, the question had simply been, Are you a member of the Communist Party of the United States? As a countermeasure, the Party adopted a rule that automatically cancelled a Communist's membership the moment the question was asked. He could then answer "No" without perjuring himself. The final wording of what came to be called "the $64 question" was adopted to circumvent the Party's tactic.

est and reproachable. And though I will always maintain that the Committee's behavior was more reprehensible than ours, the adage "Two wrongs don't make a right" allows no room for weighing the inequity of the iniquities.

In his statement, Lawson wrote in part: "The socalled 'evidence' comes from a parade of stool pigeons, neurotics, publicity-seeking clowns, Gestapo agents, paid informers, and a few ignorant and frightened Hollywood artists." Now that was more like it! Anyone who has ever read *The Daily Worker* will immediately recognize such vituperation as the hallmark of the doctrinaire communist's attitude toward anyone who might disagree with his or her vision.

Lawson further wrote: "They [the Committee] want to muzzle the great Voice of Democracy. Because they're conspiring against the American way of life. They want to cut living standards, introduce an economy of poverty, wipe out labor's rights, attack Negroes, Jews, and other minorities, drive us into a disastrous and unnecessary war." That, of course, is crude demagoguery, but it is interesting that Lawson implied that *some* wars are necessary.

As one can see, the strategy Lawson used was one at which the communists were past masters: construct your own straw man, then proceed to knock him down. Even a second-rank journalist could recognize that such arbitrary charges against the Committee, dealing with subjects not mentioned by anyone during the hearings, was a clear expression of the communist mode of attack. It was unnecessary for Lawson to identify himself as a communist; the answer was implicit in his position paper, not only to members of the press and the politically sophisticated but, sadly, to many of the representatives of the Hollywood Committee for the First Amendment.

In another section of his statement, Lawson wrote: "The writer has a special responsibility . . . to further the free exchange of ideas. I am proud to be singled out for attack by men who are obviously . . . out to stifle ideas and censor communication." This from the man who tried to stifle Budd Schulberg, to censor Adrian Scott and me and to control our film, *Cornered*, who crucified Albert Maltz, and who would shortly use the same tactics to try to discipline Robert Rossen is about as unprincipled, shameless, and devious as writing can be.

But there was enough chutzpah left over to more than go around. "I am not going to touch," he wrote, "on the gross violations of the Constitution of the United States, and especially of its First and Fifth

A Memoir of the Hollywood Ten

Amendments, that is taking place here." In the aftermath of the hearings, neither Congress, the federal bench, nor the Supreme Court found that any of the Committee's actions had violated the Constitution. Legal purists may argue the correctness of the decisions, as do I, but even though justices often disagree, the Supreme Court's *majority* interpretation is still the "word" on what is or isn't a violation of the Constitution.

Finally, this statement of principle from the man who took orders from Moscow: "I am like most Americans in feeling that loyalty to the United States and pride in its traditions are the guiding principles of my life. I am like most Americans in believing that divided loyalty—which is another word for treason—is the most despicable crime of which any man or woman can be accused."

The second unfriendly witness to take the stand was Dalton Trumbo. Stacked under his chair at the witness table were some twenty scripts, each from 115 to 170 pages long; roughly 2,800 pages of difficult reading. Trumbo's stated purpose was to prove to the Committee that his work in no way attempted to impress un-American ideas on American moviegoers' minds. With a curt, "Too many pages," Thomas refused to accept the scripts as evidence, which surprised neither Trumbo nor any other occupant of the Caucus Room.

Dalton Trumbo was a puzzle—at least to me. Considered one of the most literate and articulate minds in Hollywood, his manner, understanding of people and situations, as well as his ultra-dry humor made him one of the town's most likable personalities. He had a fiercely independent intellect, and although he could wither an opponent in an ideological debate, he had an extremely broad tolerance for the other view (as his "only victims" speech at the Writers Guild after the fiasco dramatically illustrates).

Until the hearings, I had never considered him a communist, and to this day, I have not been able to understand how such an inner-directed and unfanatical man could have maintained a loyalty to an organization as doctrinaire as the Communist Party.

I must explain that I have no problem with his *joining* the Party. His very qualities made him, and many other brilliant persons, an easy mark for the Party's recruiters. As Stephen Spender put it, "The very virtues of love and pity and a passion for individual freedom which had brought me close to Communism" (*The God That Failed*, 272) were shared by many men and women of goodwill. But, though the times of awakening varied, men like Arthur Koestler, André Gide, Richard

Wright, Stephen Spender, and hundreds of other intellectuals opened their eyes to the Party's duplicity and got out.

But Trumbo, although mentally and morally the equal of these men, was apparently blinded by a long-held dream and an ideal that never was. And his loyalty to the Party is still a puzzle.

Trumbo asked to read his statement and was refused. As might be expected, it was one of the more reasoned statements of the week. In it, he identified the Committee as an enemy of labor and labor unions and accused it of attempting to establish a favorable climate for the policing of thought (a concept right out of prewar Japan). Here is a sample of an exchange, during the hearings on October 28, between Trumbo and the chairman, after that gentleman had repeatedly tried to elicit a positive "yes" or "no" from Dalton.

Mr. Trumbo.	Mr. Chairman, this question is designed to a specific purpose. First—
The Chairman.	[*pounding gavel*]. Do you—
Mr. Trumbo.	First, to identify me with the Screen Writers Guild; secondly, to seek to identify me with the Communist Party and thereby destroy that guild . . .
The Chairman.	[*pounding gavel*]. Excuse the witness—

Trumbo prepared to leave the stand, but with his usual presence of mind, Stripling stopped him by asking the $64 question. After a bit of sparring, Dalton was excused.

Trumbo was correct when he accused the Committee of trying to establish him as a threat because of his membership in the Party, but his charge of the Screen Writers Guild destruction was simply another version of the straw man that each of the Ten had fabricated. I have always doubted that Dalton seriously believed his own accusation. It is true that, like most right-wing extremists, the chairman feared the iron control the Party exercised when they succeeded in capturing a union, and that fear was justified, but the destruction of the unions, per se, was not one of Thomas's aims, at least not at this time.

In quick rebuttal, Thomas called up Roy Brewer, the head of IATSE, that great conglomerate of film-craft unions. Brewer, a member of the Motion Picture Alliance and one of HUAC's strongest supporters, also feared the threat of communist penetration. In two hours of testimony, which was largely a monologue, he left no doubt concerning the union's cooperative stance in relation to the Committee.

Paul McNutt, a former government VIP and, at the time, a legal representative for the Motion Picture Producers Association, had asked to be heard once more. His testimony, in which he gave the Committee a thorough going-over, served to dampen the procommittee atmosphere created by Brewer. "Insinuation and innuendo are never fair and are not facts," he said. But McNutt's words were water off a duck's back, as evidenced when Thomas called Maltz to the stand. After having been sworn in and identified, Maltz asked permission to read his statement.

The Chairman.	May we see it, please?
Mr. Maltz.	May I ask whether you asked Mr. Gerald L. K. Smith to see his statement before you allowed him to read it?[4]
The Chairman.	I wasn't chairman at that time.
Mr. Maltz.	Nevertheless, you were on the committee, Mr. Thomas, were you not?
The Chairman.	I asked him a great many questions and he had a hard time answering some of them, too.
Mr. Maltz.	I am interested in that, but I still would like to know whether he had his statement read before he was permitted to read it.
The Chairman.	Well, we will look at yours.

And they did. To the complete surprise of Albert and the entire audience, the Committee unanimously agreed to permit Maltz to read his statement.

That statement was more of the same; after excoriating the Committee for its biased behavior, Maltz identified a number of his films, short stories, novels, and the awards they had won. He then accused the Committee of supporting the Ku Klux Klan. Near the end of his statement he wrote: "I insist upon my right to think freely and to speak freely . . . to publish whatever I please; to fix my mind or change my mind, without dictation from anyone; to offer any criticism I think fitting of any public official or policy."

4. Gerald L. K. Smith was a notorious American fascist at the time.

The sentiments are admirable, if not new or surprising. All statements of the Ten proclaimed the same ideals, so have such statements and speeches since the beginning of democracy. In truth, however, they are more often the refuge of demagogues than of honest men, and a demagogue of the extreme left is no more to be taken seriously, or at face value, than a demagogue of the right.

Maltz's words were straightforward, but to those of us who remembered how he buckled under the weight of the Party's undemocratic and censorious discipline, his defiant stance seemed merely the blowing of an arrant wind. We who were, or had been, party members, knew how easily honorable statements could be used to distort actuality. And we all knew we were doing just that in our statements and in our evasive speeches to the Committee. The old question "Do two wrongs make a right?" passed often through my mind that week; I found it impossible to deceive myself into a favorable response.

Soon after Maltz finished reading his statement, Stripling asked him the obligatory two questions, and we were back on familiar ground.

The fourth unfriendly witness, writer Alvah Bessie, was known in Hollywood film circles less as a screenwriter than as a veteran of the Abraham Lincoln Brigade, which fought at the side of the Republican troops in the Spanish civil war. What the heroes of the brigade refused to remember was that, in 1947, there was a body of evidence indicating that some of them, along with Spanish and Iron Curtain comrades, were more intent on killing Republican Socialists than Franco's fascist rebels. In the era of Stalin, that was not to be wondered at. Most Americans who have only a popular knowledge of Marxist political philosophy assume that socialism and communism are cut from the same cloth. That is by no means true; the mirror image of communism is fascism. To the Comintern, socialism was a far greater threat than capitalism, and it had to be eliminated.

It seemed the Committee was trying to make a record when, following the Maltz surprise, they allowed Bessie to read the first two paragraphs of his statement. It was, in essence, the by now familiar attack on the legality and activity of HUAC. However, Bessie carried it a couple of steps further by charging that the Committee's objective was to change or abolish *every* democratic element in our society, and that was the end of our position papers.

A short portion of Bessie's tussle with Stripling effectively demonstrates the unfriendly witnesses' strategy of evasive response. The counsel had asked Bessie if he belonged to the Writers Guild.

Mr. Bessie.   This is the same sort of question that was asked of other witnesses. It involves a question of my association.

Mr. Stripling.   Do you refuse to answer the question?

Mr. Bessie.   I have not refused ... but I must answer the question in the only way in which I know how, and that is, that I believe that such a question violates my right of association and is not properly falling—I do not believe it falls properly within the scope of this committee's inquiry.

Mr. Stripling.   We will move on to the $64 question, Mr. Bessie. Are you now or have you ever been a member of the Communist Party?

Bessie's answer to that question invoked the right to a secret ballot and the propriety of General Eisenhower's right to secrecy of his voting procedures; a strictly modern version of Mom and apple pie.

On the morning of the eighth day, October 29, the Committee called Samuel Ornitz. But first, Thomas once more made it clear that "prominent Americans ... all from the industry, are the ones who leveled the charges; it wasn't the committee." For a few hopeful minutes, it seemed that Thomas was trying to get out from under. Nobody wanted to put the onus of these particular hearings where it belonged and HUAC, which, God knows, had enough knavery to answer for, found itself stuck with this bit of villainy as well. It seemed for a moment as if the Committee were looking for a way out, but the Ten's behavior would help it get off the hook.

I had never heard of Sam Ornitz before the birth of the Nineteen. Later, I learned that he was a communist, but of so little importance in films that I still don't understand why he was selected as one of the Committee's targets. But there he was, the fifth unfriendly witness of the week. According to Ornitz, what kept him from cooperating with the Committee was his conscience. That struck Mr. Thomas as being irrelevant.

Odd Man Out

The Chairman.   Conscience?
Mr. Ornitz.   Conscience, sir, conscience.

Sam's statement, which he was not allowed to read, stressed what he called the anti-Semitic record of HUAC, and its position parallel to that of prewar Germany, Italy, and Japan. Stripling asked Ornitz the familiar questions, received the familiar replies, and Sam was summarily excused, his brief moment in the eye of the world wiped out.

Herbert Biberman came next. When asked his place of birth during the identification formality, he leaped at the opportunity.

"I was born," he said, "within a stone's throw of Independence Hall in Philadelphia, on the day when Mr. McKinley was inaugurated as President of the United States . . . on the second floor of a building at Sixth and South, over a grocery store."

Obviously, Herbert had the necessary credentials for an all-American patriot, but although he remained a loud and persistent adversary to the end, that first sentence was by far the longest he was to complete that day.

In his position paper, Biberman wrote at one point: "I have never been a stand patter." When read later by some of the Nineteen, that sentence brought smiles to a few faces. Among Hollywood's party members, Herbert had a reputation as a man who stood very pat when the party policy stood pat, but who changed with incredible speed and political agility when party policy took a new direction. His straw man was the Bill of Rights and Committee's "attempt to crush . . . the calm and security" of the country's citizens. His performance was the most obstreperous of the week. His statement, which, fortunately, he was not allowed to read, ended with a transcription of our old national anthem, "America," including verses that even its poet-author had forgotten. And when Thomas finally screamed, "Take him away!" he was giving a life-saving order.

The seventh and eighth unfriendlies were Adrian Scott and I. The two of us were so closely linked that Stripling, at one point, called Scott, "Mr. Dmytryk." That verbal slip impelled Gordon Kahn to write in *Hollywood on Trial* that "Scott and Dmytryk were subpoenaed *because* they produced and directed *Crossfire*. That now celebrated film attacked anti-Semitism in particular and racial hatred and intolerance generally" (105).

It is true that *Crossfire* was breaking box-office records, garnering unusually high praise from critics, and winning a variety of awards, but all that makes it more logical to assume the reason for the Committee's harassment was not the film's message but the fact that its success had advanced our prestige in the industry and, coincidently, our worth to the Party. In the Committee's eyes, this must have seemed a clear and present danger. Of course, its undercover operatives should have informed committee members that we were no longer members of the Party, and they should have left well enough alone. But fanatical zeal is a cataract of the mind that blinds reason and logical thought, and HUAC's sense of selection was correspondingly dim. Besides, were Thomas really intelligent, he wouldn't have been keeping Lester Cole and Ring Lardner company in a federal correction facility three years down the line.

Probably because we were no longer members, the Party's tactics repelled us, and neither Scott nor I spent much time or energy opposing Thomas or Stripling. Neither of us was allowed to read his statement, which paraded our straw men of choice. Scott's argument was that we were being persecuted because of *Crossfire* and our stand against racial prejudice. Mine was a brief but broad attack on what I considered to be HUAC's desire to blacklist all who disagreed with its narrow interpretation of Americanism. In a remarkably short time, each of us in turn was asked the usual question, the evasion of which brought the usual dismissals.

On October 30, 1947, a date that would unexpectedly turn out to be the last day of the hearings, the first witness, and the ninth of the group to testify, was Ring Lardner Jr. Ring, who stammered slightly when he talked, and who was rarely seen without a mildly cynical smile on his face, was a writer whose work helped people to laugh their way past some of life's afflictions and annoyances.

Thomas seemed in a good mood that morning, and he agreed to let Ring read his statement after he had concluded his testimony. But, when questioned about his membership in the Writers Guild, Ring's evasive answers were not to Thomas's taste.

The Chairman.   Now, Mr. Lardner, don't do like the others, if I were you, or you will never read your statement. . . .
Mr. Lardner.   But I understood you to say that I would be permitted to read the statement, Mr. Chairman.
The Chairman.   Yes; after you are finished with the questions and answers . . . but you certainly haven't answered the questions.

Odd Man Out

Mr. Lardner.	. . . I don't think you qualified in any way your statement that I would be allowed to read this statement.
The Chairman.	Then I will qualify it now. If you refuse to answer the questions then you will not read your statement.

The puerile trap had been sprung, but the mouse had not been caught. Lardner, without apparent pain, sacrificed the reading of his paper. But he won the consolation prize; he got the biggest honest laugh of the hearings with a reply that captured the world's attention. When Thomas, no longer jovial, sneeringly suggested that a "real American" would be proud to answer the $64 question, Lardner replied: "It depends on the circumstances. I could answer it, but if I did I would hate myself in the morning." A cliché's effectiveness also depends on the circumstances, and Ring chose just the right time to eloquently revive the power of one of the most hackneyed bromides in the book.

At least one of the Committee smiled, but Thomas did not join in the fun. Banging his gavel, he shouted, "Sergeant, take the witness away." And one of the hearing's most placid witnesses was ushered off the stand.

"Will Mr. Larry Parks please come forward!"

Bodies straightened and necks were craned as Larry's name was called, but he was not to be seen. He had just left for the men's room. A few quick whispered words from Crum to Stripling, then Stripling to Thomas, and a substitute was promptly summoned to the stand.

Lester Cole, who, after John Howard Lawson, was probably the most dedicated communist of the group, was run through the Committee's wringer in a hurry. On hearing Cole's evasive responses to the question about his membership in the Writers Guild, Thomas erupted.

The Chairman.	No, No, No, No, No.
Mr. Cole.	I hear you, Mr. Chairman. I hear you. . . .
The Chairman.	You will hear some more. . . . It is a very simple question.
Mr. Cole.	What I have to say is a very simple answer.
The Chairman.	Yes; but answer it "Yes" or "No."
Mr. Cole.	It isn't necessarily that simple.

Cole was not permitted to read his statement, which, like most of the others, attacked the Committee as an enemy of Hollywood and its guilds and unions. Cole was dismissed, but it was still early in the day. There was time before the clock struck lunch for one more witness. This time the expression "unfriendly witness" turned out to be a complete misnomer.

In the morning press, Thomas had promised the world a "revelation," an all-star surprise witness. In his book, *Hollywood on Trial*, Gordon Kahn wrote that "even the 'unfriendly witnesses' were caught in the mounting tension of excitement. Who, indeed, was the Committee's Mystery Witness, and what earth-heaving disclosures would he make?" (121). Those sentences must be regarded as literary license. All of the Nineteen, including Kahn, knew quite well who the mystery witness was to be and what earth-heaving disclosures he would make.

He was a small, shy man who displayed little of the energy that lends so much vitality to his plays. He spoke English with difficulty, and like most people with a language problem, he preferred to say little and listen a lot. But Bertholdt Brecht's appearance on the stand gave Thomas his only victory of the hearings, though the extent of the victory was debatable. I considered it a large win for the Nineteen.

Brecht was sworn in with some difficulty. He was offered, and accepted, the help of an interpreter who, as it developed, had as much trouble pronouncing English words as Brecht did, but who probably understood them better. It made for a halting but often amusing session. The world-famous playwright was not allowed to read his statement, which deprived the *Congressional Record* of a rare touch of class. It was rejected on the grounds that it dealt largely with Brecht's career in Germany, and his troubles with the Nazis. Instead, Stripling immediately went for the jugular.

Mr. Stripling.　Mr. Brecht, are you a member of the Communist Party or have you ever been a member of the Communist Party? . . .

Mr. Brecht.　Mr. Chairman, I have heard my colleagues when they considered this question not as proper, but I am a guest in this country and do not want to enter into any legal arguments, so I will answer your question fully as well as I can. I was not a member or am not a member of any Communist Party.

The Chairman.　Your answer is, then, that you have never been a member of the Communist Party?

Mr. Brecht.	That is correct.
Mr. Stripling.	You were not a member of the Communist Party in Germany?
Mr. Brecht.	No; I was not.

Stripling had been disarmed. Since his main line of questioning showed little promise, he took a detour. He quoted, and misquoted, a number of Brecht's poems about Nazism, which had nothing to do with the United States. Then, hoping to trap him into guilt by association, Stripling questioned Brecht about his friends. This elicited a startling admission. Yes, Brecht said, he did know Hanns and Gerhardt Eisler (who were well-known communists); in fact, they were very close friends; often they played chess and talked politics. That made the members of the Committee sit up, but this detour soon reached a dead end, and Stripling got back to the main line.

| Mr. Stripling. | Mr. Brecht, did you ever make application to join the Communist Party? . . . |
| Mr. Brecht. | No, no, no, no, no, never. |

And though the sparrows pecked at the hawk for an inexcusable length of time, Brecht finally received the chairman's benediction.

| Mr. Thomas. | Thank you very much, Mr. Brecht. You are a good example to the witnesses of Mr. Kenny and Mr. Crum. |

Those of us who knew how Brecht had got there smiled at Thomas's remark. With a tired sigh, Bertholdt Brecht left the witness table, escaped from Washington, and was soon on his way to East Germany, a democracy he must have admired. But to the Nineteen and their lawyers, the scene played out in the Caucus Room was purely an anticlimax.

Like Howard Koch, Brecht knew he had no American record, and he saw no harm to the Nineteen in cooperating with the Committee. At this particular time, he cared little what happened to free speech in the United States. Like the alien in the movie *E.T.*, he wanted to go h-o-o-me! And since home was outside the limits of this country, he couldn't do that with a contempt charge hanging over his head. Brecht knew that every decision of the Nineteen had to be unanimously approved, so he asked for a meeting of the group as a whole.

Eighteen film men and six lawyers listened to Brecht's plea. I will never forget the touching climax. "I had attacked war and the people's enemies who now marched under the swastika of Adolf Hitler," he said. "Practically overnight my writings had become treasonable, so the day after the Reichstag fire I left Germany. First, I went to Denmark, but there were many Nazi sympathizers there, and I fled to Sweden. Within a year I had to leave Sweden, and I went to Finland, where I waited for a United States visa. When I left Finland, the Nazis were swarming over the land. By train, I crossed Russia and Siberia to Vladivostok, then by ship to Manila. Finally I reached the United States—*and here they caught me.*"

To this great man, even the party hard-liners dared not say no. Unanimously, Brecht received our permission to appear and testify before the Committee. But later, when the force of Brecht's rhetoric had dissipated, some of us wondered if he had told Thomas the truth, the *whole* truth, and nothing but the truth.

In the late afternoon, on October 30, 1947, without any previous notice to our attorneys, Thomas brought the hearings to a halt. In his final speech to those assembled, he said:

> Ten prominent figures in Hollywood whom the Committee had evidence were members of the Communist Party were brought before us and refused to deny that they were Communists. It is not necessary for the Chair to emphasize the harm which the motion-picture industry suffers from the presence within its ranks of known Communists who do not have the best interests of the United States at heart. The industry should set about immediately to clear its own house and not wait for public opinion to force it to do so.
>
> The hearings are adjourned.

10

The hearings were now history. But, as Henry Ford so aptly put it, "History is bunk!" The past few pages have documented some of the words of witnesses and interrogators. As literature, the scenes make an interesting record that strongly favors the Hollywood Ten. However, when heard, they made a truly sickening impression. It is only when the clamor, the relentless hammering of the gavel, the arrogant voices of the "champions of free speech," the sneering from the dais, the shouting of the witnesses, the shouting of the chairman, the shouting, the hammering, the anger, the palpable hate—only when these are sensed and heard can the virulence that drenched the Caucus Room be understood.

To use a film expression, the scenes must be viewed from a different angle. So, to repeat on that fateful morning of October 27, the room was packed to overflowing. I was in my usual seat in the second row, with Dore Schary on my right, when John Howard Lawson, as pompous of carriage as he was of speech, marched up to the witness table and planted himself squarely in the witness chair.

The motif of our defense had been carefully designed, but the manner of its presentation had never been discussed, at least not in my presence, and I wondered how Lawson would deal with the chairman. I soon found out.

The swearing-in and self-identification rites were hardly over when Lawson, in the words of party member Gordon Kahn, made it clear that he "was not going to be a push-over" (*Hollywood on Trial*, 70).

"I am an American," Lawson said, "and I am not at all easy to intimidate, and don't think I am."

I was shocked! This was not the time for hubris. I could smell the stink of ultimate defeat. I believed it absolutely necessary that we, individually and as a group, create an image that was in complete contrast to the personality and behavior of the Committee. Although some of what I have written, and will write, is hindsight, on this matter, I felt strongly at the time of the hearings. Our behavior should have been that of underdogs, polite but grievously put-upon, reasonable even though attacked on questionable legal grounds, and above all, composed in the face of vulgarity and harassment. In situations such as these, a symbolic turning of the cheek makes a better impression than trying to extract an eye for an eye. At this point, the members of the media were our main source of influence over the general public (a Gallup Poll of November 29, 1947 indicated that eight out of ten peole had heard or read about the hearings), and they were fully aware of the Committee's shabby behavior. HUAC had a few right-wing supporters, but the greater part of the American and world press was on our side. Although Crum and Kenny had made a few legal stabs at the Committee, none of the Nineteen had yet uttered a word, and that worked to our benefit, for the truth was there was little we could say, or do, except equivocate, obscure, sidestep, and misdirect, all of which exposed the negative aspects of our position. We could attack the Committee, but unless we were willing to testify openly, we could say little in our own defense. Now was the time for modest restraint and a minimum of rhetoric. Some version of a simple "No comment" in answer to the $64 question might have hung Thomas out to dry. But to engage in a war of words and retaliatory behavior was to play the Committee's game on their home court.

It seemed only logical to assume that Lawson's demeanor should have been geared to achieve the most favorable reaction possible, especially from the press; instead, he was achieving exactly the opposite. As the chairman's voice became more strident, so did Lawson's; he matched Thomas shout for shout, bellowing out his demagogic affirmations of loyalty and love for the United States, its Constitution, and its Bill of Rights. It was an unholy duet; the louder the chairman banged his gavel and bawled for a simple answer to his questions, the more insistently Lawson shouted.

In a span of a few minutes, the comedy of the past week took the extra steps it needed to convert it to tragedy. In a time of crisis, it is not the heart that falters, it is the stomach that falls away, leaving a painfully felt emptiness. I hadn't felt like this since a car skidded toward me across a wet street many years ago. "This is it!" The same words rang in my mind as I tried to bury myself in my seat. The minutes felt like hours. I didn't dare to look up and around until, to the audible relief of the entire room, Thomas finally begged the police to escort Lawson from the stand. I watched incredulously as he paraded back to his seat with a smug look of triumph on his face. Finally, I pulled myself up and looked at Dore. I wondered if my face was as pale as his.

"What are my chances at the studio now?" I asked.

"You have an ironclad contract," he replied. And that is what made Dore Schary a rather wonderful man, though an uncertain executive; he

Odd Man Out

really believed in corporate integrity. And I wanted to believe him, but I didn't have his guileless faith.

A short spell of relative calm followed while Eric Johnson, the head of the Motion Picture Producers Association, exchanged some acrid words with a member of the Committee, and my taut muscles relaxed a bit. I felt calm enough to turn around and look at our Hollywood brigade. A few gave me a limp victory sign, some smiled weakly, but most avoided my eyes. I tried to bolster my sagging spirits by contemplating the next witness. All is not yet lost, I wanted to say. Dalton Trumbo will go a long way toward ameliorating the situation and restoring your enthusiasm. He is much too bright to emulate Lawson in making a crude and vulgar Thomas his role model, I reasoned. Wrong again! To quote Gordon Kahn once more, "The Thomas Committee . . . discovered in Dalton Trumbo a veritable ring-tailed tiger" (78).

There was no excuse for helping Thomas turn a circus of clowns into a wild animal act, and Trumbo's performance was the greatest disappointment of the week. A ring-tailed tiger is hardly an underdog, and Dalton, normally an unflappable man, flapped like a flag in a gale that day. By the time he had finished, I knew we were dead. Indeed, I lost what little hope I had for a Supreme Court reprieve. I now realized this must have been a planned response, which would be repeated by Albert Maltz, Alvah Bessie, the ailing Samuel Ornitz, and Herbert Biberman. They didn't fail me, especially Biberman.

A short portion of his exchange with the chairman, on October 29, 1947, will be enlightening, but the scene must be read as it played—with a full consciousness of the sound effects. Biberman wants to be heard by the audience, while Thomas wants to be heard by both the audience and Biberman, and during this by no means unique outburst, the two scream totally unrelated strings of words at each other while the constant hammering of the gavel punctuates each syllable of the shouting with an ear-shattering "WHACK!" Even the committe clerk found it difficult to keep the record impartial. In the excerpt, Stripling has just inquired about Biberman's membership in the Writers Guild:

Mr. Biberman.	It has become very clear to me that the real purpose of this investigation—
The Chairman.	(pounding gavel). That is not an answer to the question—
Mr. Biberman.	Is to drive a wedge—

A Memoir of the Hollywood Ten

The Chairman.	(pounding gavel). That is not the question. (Pounding gavel.)
Mr. Biberman.	Into the component parts—
The Chairman.	(pounding gavel). Not the question—
Mr. Biberman.	Of the motion-picture industry.
The Chairman.	(pounding gavel). Ask him the next question.
Mr. Biberman.	And by defending my constitutional rights here I am defending—
The Chairman.	(pounding gavel). Go ahead and ask him the next question.
Mr. Biberman.	The right not only of ourselves—
Mr. Stripling.	Are you a member—
Mr. Biberman.	But of the producers and of the American people.
Mr. Stripling.	Of the Commnist Party?

Such a demonstration was much more devastating on radio and in the newsreels than in the press. It was clear to those who listened that the unfriendly witnesses were behaving as communists could be expected to behave. Of course, a true-blue American could, on occasion, conduct himself as well or as badly as a dedicated party member, but what mattered here was popular perception and public sympathy. And the fact that after such undignified exhibitions Scott, Lardner, and I soft-pedaled our presentations did little to minimize the damage. Even Lester Cole, ordinarily a communist fireball, realized the consequences of the earlier performances and played down his, but to no noticeable effect. It was too late! True to the Party's reputation, the harm had been most efficiently done.

There followed the loneliest week of my life, a nightmare that only a Poe could adequately describe. I was square in the middle of nowhere, with no one to turn to for comfort, no one to confide in, and no one to help me work out my overwhelming doubts. Scott was still too party-oriented to talk to, and Crum was as lost as I was. It was probably only then that he realized how he was being used by the Party, and he must have had misgivings about Adrian and me, but he continued fighting what he hoped was a just fight. I needed Jean, but she was three thousand miles away, and none of the telephoned reports, the radio, or the press could even hint at my private bewilderment and my blighted hopes. I was a gone goose!

By the week's end, I no longer wondered why none of our Hollywood friends had sought my company. All but the most dedicated liberals must have seen the writing on the wall. They could, of course, safely continue to back freedom of speech in principle, but common sense compelled them to avoid any contact with the Party's "tar babies." In his book, *Naming Names*, Victor Navasky quotes from Humphrey Bogart's letter to columnist Sokolsky in which, among a number of disclaimers of pro-Communist sympathies, Bogie writes of his junket to Washington: "That trip was ill-advised, even foolish, I am ready to admit. At the time it seemed like the thing to do" (153).

Bogart had a very sharp mind, and he was the first to recoil, but could others have been far behind? In keeping with his book's bias, Navasky sees Bogie's letter only as an example of the reactionary columnist's crusade on behalf of the Committee's witch-hunt, and he completely ignores its most important implication; that Bogart, who was certainly no coward, showed great sagacity by acting with all possible speed to avoid the Red connection, which was the ineradicable "damned spot" of modern American politics.

The hearings had come to an abrupt halt, and the only thing we had accomplished was the one thing we had plotted so hard to avoid; everyone was now convinced we were all communists. In spite of our double-talk and what could only be described as cute attempts at evasion, few people were deceived. No matter how we equivocated, logic said simply, "If there is nothing to hide, why hide it?" Why, indeed? Too late I awoke to the realization that, since we had gone to great lengths to avoid differentiation, I and the others of the Nineteen who were *not* communists were, in the common mind, lumped with those who were. I had walked into Lawson's cage and locked the door behind me. My refusal to testify had branded me a member of the Party, and however I might protest that such refusal was not an admission of guilt, only friendly relatives, the naive, or the stupid would take me at my word. There was no way out, not even confession; the offer of honest testimony at this stage would have been seen as an act of cowardice.

Just that simply, I had committed myself and, unforgivably, the woman who would soon be my wife, to four years of nearly total hell—because I was a member of the Hollywood Ten.

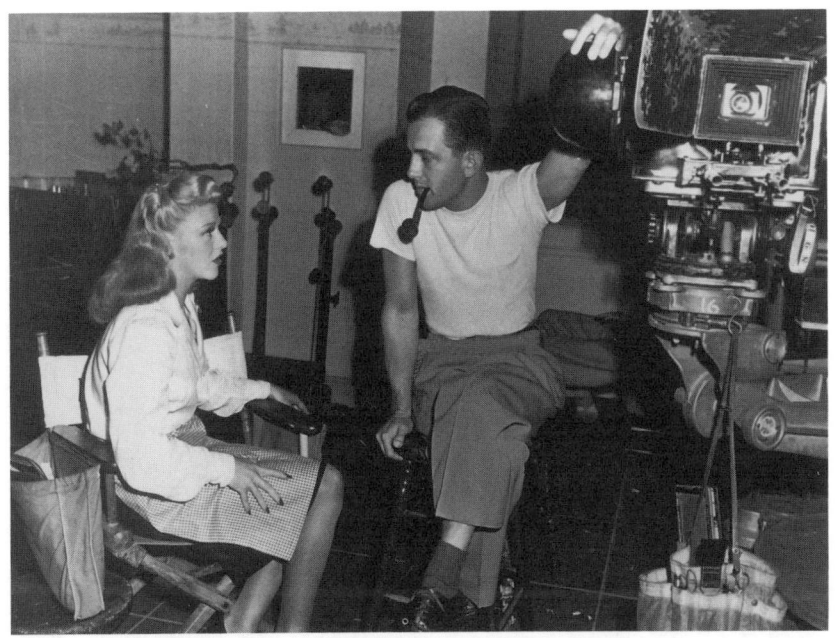

Directing Ginger Rogers in *Tender Comrade*, 1943

Directing Dick Powell and Claire Trevor in
Murder, My Sweet, 1944

With John Wayne *(right)* and Paul Fix *(middle)* on the set of *Back to Bataan*, 1944

Portrait photo, 1944

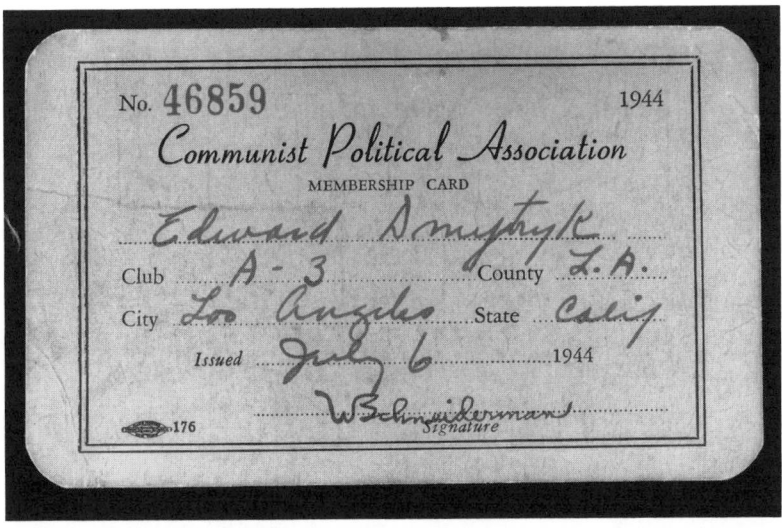

Communist Political Association membership card, 1944

Preamble to the Constitution

of the

Communist Party of the U. S. A.

•

The Communist Party of the United States of America is a working class political party carrying forward today the traditions of Jefferson, Paine, Jackson, and Lincoln, and of the Declaration of Independence; it upholds the achievements of democracy, the right of "life, liberty, and the pursuit of happiness," and defends the United States Constitution against its reactionary enemies who would destroy democracy and all popular liberties; it is devoted to defense of the immediate interests of workers, farmers, and all toilers against capitalist exploitation, and to preparation of the working class for its historic mission to unite and lead the American people to extend these democratic principles to their necessary and logical conclusions:

By establishing common ownership of the national economy, through a government of the people, by the people, and for the people; the abolition of all exploitation of man by man, nation by nation, and race by race, and thereby the abolition of class divisions in society; that is, by the establishment of socialism, according to the scientific principles enunciated by the greatest teachers of mankind, Marx, Engels, Lenin, and Stalin, and the free cooperation of the American people with those of other lands, striving toward a world without oppression and war, a world brotherhood of man.

Preamble to the Constitution of the Communist Party of the United States

BY AUTHORITY OF THE HOUSE OF REPRESENTATIVES OF THE CONGRESS OF THE
UNITED STATES OF AMERICA

To ROBERT E. CLARK, United States Marshal

You are hereby commanded to summon EDWARD DMYTRYK

to be and appear before the UN-AMERICAN ACTIVITIES

Committee of the House of Representatives of the United States, of which the Hon.

J. PARNELL THOMAS of New Jersey is chairman,

in their chamber in the city of Washington, on October 23rd, 1947
, at the hour of 10:30 A.M.

then and there to testify touching matters of inquiry committed to said Committee; and he is
not to depart without leave of said Committee.

Herein fail not, and make return of this summons.

Witness my hand and the seal of the House of Representatives
of the United States, at the city of Washington, this
18th day of September , 19 47

Chairman.

Attest:

Clerk.

Subpoena to appear before HUAC, Sept. 18, 1947

With Bartley Crum *(middle)* and Adrian Scott *(left)*, Washington, D.C., Oct. 1947

THE ACADEMY OF MOTION PICTURE ARTS AND SCIENCES

Invites you to the Series of Screenings

of the

NOMINATIONS

for the

20th ANNUAL AWARDS

SATURDAY, FEBRUARY 21 *through* FRIDAY, MARCH 12, 1948

ADMISSION BY ACADEMY MEMBERSHIP CARD ONLY

ACADEMY AWARD THEATRE
9038 MELROSE AVENUE
HOLLYWOOD 46, CALIFORNIA

ANNUAL AWARDS

FOR ACHIEVEMENTS
DURING 1947

ACADEMY MEMBERSHIP CARDS ARE NOT TRANSFERABLE

This series of Special Screenings of films nominated for final voting in the 20th Annual Awards of Merit is offered to refresh the memories of voters before final balloting closes. The Awards Rules Committee urges that voters make every effort to see nominated pictures which they may not have seen.

Nominated pictures will be shown free to Academy members only as the qualified voters for final selections in each category.

THE PICTURES TO BE SHOWN ARE NOMINATED FOR THE FOLLOWING AWARDS:

BEST PERFORMANCE BY AN ACTOR

Ronald Colman—A DOUBLE LIFE
John Garfield—BODY AND SOUL
Gregory Peck—GENTLEMAN'S AGREEMENT
William Powell—LIFE WITH FATHER
Michael Redgrave—MOURNING BECOMES ELECTRA

BEST PERFORMANCE BY AN ACTOR IN A SUPPORTING ROLE

Charles Bickford—THE FARMER'S DAUGHTER
Thomas Gomez—RIDE THE PINK HORSE
Edmund Gwenn—MIRACLE ON 34TH STREET
Robert Ryan—CROSSFIRE
Richard Widmark—KISS OF DEATH

BEST PERFORMANCE BY AN ACTRESS

Joan Crawford—POSSESSED
Susan Hayward—SMASH UP—THE STORY OF A WOMAN
Dorothy McGuire—GENTLEMAN'S AGREEMENT
Rosalind Russell—MOURNING BECOMES ELECTRA
Loretta Young—THE FARMER'S DAUGHTER

BEST PERFORMANCE BY AN ACTRESS IN A SUPPORTING ROLE

Ethel Barrymore—THE PARADINE CASE
Gloria Grahame—CROSSFIRE
Celeste Holm—GENTLEMAN'S AGREEMENT
Marjorie Main—THE EGG AND I
Anne Revere—GENTLEMAN'S AGREEMENT

BEST ACHIEVEMENT IN BLACK-AND-WHITE ART DIRECTION

THE FOXES OF HARROW
GREAT EXPECTATIONS

BEST ACHIEVEMENT IN COLOR ART DIRECTION

BLACK NARCISSUS
LIFE WITH FATHER

BEST ACHIEVEMENT IN BLACK-AND-WHITE CINEMATOGRAPHY

THE GHOST AND MRS. MUIR
GREAT EXPECTATIONS
GREEN DOLPHIN STREET

BEST ACHIEVEMENT IN COLOR CINEMATOGRAPHY

BLACK NARCISSUS
LIFE WITH FATHER
MOTHER WORE TIGHTS

BEST ACHIEVEMENT IN DIRECTING

THE BISHOP'S WIFE
CROSSFIRE
A DOUBLE LIFE
GENTLEMAN'S AGREEMENT
GREAT EXPECTATIONS

BEST ACHIEVEMENT IN FILM EDITING

THE BISHOP'S WIFE
BODY AND SOUL
GENTLEMAN'S AGREEMENT
GREEN DOLPHIN STREET
ODD MAN OUT

BEST SCORING OF A MUSICAL PICTURE

FIESTA
MOTHER WORE TIGHTS
MY WILD IRISH ROSE
ROAD TO RIO
SONG OF THE SOUTH

BEST SCORING OF A DRAMATIC OR COMEDY PICTURE

THE BISHOP'S WIFE
CAPTAIN FROM CASTILE
A DOUBLE LIFE
FOREVER AMBER
LIFE WITH FATHER

BEST ORIGINAL SONG

"A Gal in Calico"—THE TIME, PLACE AND THE GIRL
"I Wish I Didn't Love You So"—THE PERILS OF PAULINE
"Pass That Peace Pipe"—GOOD NEWS
"You Do"—MOTHER WORE TIGHTS
"Zip-A-Dee-Doo-Dah"—SONG OF THE SOUTH

BEST MOTION PICTURE OF THE YEAR

THE BISHOP'S WIFE
CROSSFIRE
GENTLEMAN'S AGREEMENT
GREAT EXPECTATIONS
MIRACLE ON 34TH STREET

BEST ACHIEVEMENT IN SOUND RECORDING

THE BISHOP'S WIFE
GREEN DOLPHIN STREET
T-MEN

BEST ACHIEVEMENT IN SPECIAL EFFECTS

GREEN DOLPHIN STREET
UNCONQUERED

BEST WRITTEN SCREENPLAY

BOOMERANG!
CROSSFIRE
GENTLEMAN'S AGREEMENT
GREAT EXPECTATIONS
MIRACLE ON 34TH STREET

BEST ORIGINAL SCREENPLAY

THE BACHELOR AND THE BOBBY-SOXER
BODY AND SOUL
A DOUBLE LIFE
MONSIEUR VERDOUX
SHOE-SHINE

BEST ORIGINAL MOTION PICTURE STORY

A CAGE OF NIGHTINGALES
IT HAPPENED ON FIFTH AVENUE
KISS OF DEATH
MIRACLE ON 34TH STREET
SMASH-UP—THE STORY OF A WOMAN

Crossfire nominated for five Academy Awards, 1948

On garage duty in prison, Mill Point, West Va., 1950

STATE OF WEST VIRGINIA)
) SS.:
COUNTY OF POCAHONTAS   )

        EDWARD DMYTRYK, being duly sworn, deposes and says:

        I am one of the ten persons commonly known as the "Hollywood Ten" who was convicted of contempt of Congress for failure to state during the course of a hearing held by the House of Representatives Un-American Committee whether or not I was a member of the Communist Party. I took that position at that time because of a duty which I felt I owed to all Americans to preserve what I believed was a constitutional privilege of substance. I have not foregone that principle and do not do so now. However, in view of the troubled state of current world affairs I find myself in the presence of an even greater duty and that is to declare without equivocation where I stand towards my own country. In the discharge of that duty I want to make it perfectly clear that I am not now nor was I at the time of the hearings above referred to in October, 1947, a member of the Communist Party, that I am not a Communist sympathizer, and that I recognize the United States of America as the only country to which I owe allegiance and loyalty.

                                              Edward Dmytryk

Sworn to before me this
9th day of September, 1950.

K. E. Thiessen

Authorized by Act of February 11, 19..
to Administer Oaths

Letter from prison denying Communist Party affiliation, Sept. 9, 1950

With Spencer Tracy on the set of *The Broken Lance*, Arizona, 1953

On the set of *The Caine Mutiny,* 1953. *Sitting from left to right:* Fred McMurray,
Van Johnson, Humphrey Bogart's stand-in, Bogart, Robert Francis. *Standing
from left to right:* Stanley Kramer, Dmytryk.

On the set of *Raintree County*, 1956. Dmytryk *(standing on left)* with cast *(sitting from left to right):* Rod Taylor, Nigel Patrick, Elizabeth Taylor, Montgomery Clift, Eva Marie Saint, Lee Marvin, Agnes Morehead, Walter Abel.

11

We had departed from LAX as the unfriendly Nineteen, accompanied by the noisy good wishes of a large crowd; three weeks later, we returned to be met by a much smaller and more subdued group. We were now the Hollywood Ten—plus eight. (Brecht, the experienced survivor, was already in East Berlin.) Those of us who faced the Committee were now an entity, with a dubious distinction that included those lucky enough to elude the honorable chairman.[5] Neither our friends nor our enemies could question the political posture of the Ten, but our position as artists was conjectural, to say the least.

Our supporters had welcomed us as young Davids who had slain Goliaths—there was, as yet, no talk of martyrdom or victimization—but for the next four weeks, a subliminal uncertainty nagged at me day and night. I tried to reason it into extinction. I told myself that we had not yet been indicted for contempt, nor was it certain that we would be; that the guilds were supporting us; that jobs were still on hold for the five with studio contracts, and if all else failed, there was the presumably liberal Roosevelt Supreme Court in Washington. Why, then, was there a constant feel of earthquake weather in the air?

Two shocks hit California on November 24 and 25, 1947, but their epicenters were twenty-five hundred miles away. Both the House and the leaders of the film industry met on November 24 with our future as their only business. The House of Representatives struck quickly; in just one day of speeches, of attacks, and of self-justification, it voted contempt indictments for each of the Ten by the overwhelming margin of 346 to 17, a ratio of more than twenty to one, or 95 percent. No matter how the statistics were manipulated, it was a glorious victory for HUAC. The best and most democratic minds of the House blasted the Committee, its behavior, and its dubious aims. Unfortunately, but quite normally, the best and most democratic minds of the House were a tiny minority.

The leadership of the film industry, which convened in New York at the Waldorf-Astoria Hotel, counted a much smaller number of men but, apparently, a much larger percentage of democratic minds; the hot de-

5. However, the eight excused witnesses were not lucky enough to be excluded from the blacklist or from further hounding by HUAC.

bate lasted into the afternoon of the second day. However, its decision matched that of the House, and it was unanimous. The secod paragraph of the Waldorf-Astoria Declaration read: "We will forthwith discharge or suspend without compensation those in our employ, and we will not re-employ any of the ten until such time as he is acquitted, or has purged himself of contempt, and declared under oath that he is not a Communist."

This extinguished the sputtering candle of hope for the five of us with jobs. Paragraph four was shorter, but it was the real killer. It settled the fate of not only the rest of the Ten, but of hundreds more for the next ten or fifteen years: "We will not knowingly employ a Communist or a member of any party or group which advocates the overthrow of the Government of the United States by force, or by any illegal or unconstitutional method."

Paragraph five was perhaps the statement's most interesting assertion; was it naïveté or honest cynicism? "In pursuing this policy, we are not going to be swayed by any hysteria or intimidation from any source" (Gordon Kahn, *Hollywood on Trial*, 184).

The aftershock was inevitable. On the following day, ironclad contracts notwithstanding, Scott and I were called into N. Peter Rathvon's office for the official axing.

And the next day was Thanksgiving.

I have never been able to recall the slightest detail of what Jean and I did on that holiday or the weekend that followed.

As the head of production, Dore Schary should have wielded the hatchet, but he had been a strong opponent of the Waldorf Declaration, and the distasteful deed still stuck in his craw. Understandably, he begged off. I was glad he did; Dore and I had been friends for a long time, and I owed him my eternal gratitude for introducing me to Jean. It would have been difficult for us to face each other unemotionally at a time like this.

Even then, I felt that Dore was a victim of the cold war and the current ascendance of the extreme right. Later, I shifted a good deal of the onus onto an equally extreme left, a blindly dedicated, doctrinaire group to whom the sacrifice and suffering of a few hundred human beings still fell far short of Stalin's triumphant total of twenty million dead. Now that was a worthy example of Lenin's tenet, which most of them believed in: "Terror is an instrument of government."

History is written by men and women who are partisan in their views of the past. Fortunately, if one reads a number of histories, the varied biases usually moderate each other. Occasionally, however, as in the case of Stalinist Russia, only honest and informed revisionism can make good history out of extremist self-service. The story of the HUAC hearings and the years that followed have shown a similar proleft bias, perhaps because only those who admired the Ten and their crusade felt moved to write it. To them, only the Ten were heroes, and since Script Writing 101 teaches us there can be no real heroes without villains, villains had to be created. These were, of course, the Committee and, since they were closer to home, the Hollywood producers. The latter was hardly the truth. The Ten, collectively and individually, did not merit unstinting praise, and the producers did not deserve the beating they got from the liberals.

Although it cannot be denied that for over a decade maintenance of the blacklist was unjust, undoubtedly illegal, and certainly undemocratic, it can be argued that the blame for such a policy does not lie at the producers door. Many of them, notably Dore Schary, Harry Cohn, David Selznick, and Samuel Goldwyn, were openly opposed to the spirit and the letter of the Waldorf Declaration, but the pressures put on them were unquestionably coercive. The myth that the studios' big shots had unlimited power and freedom of action exists to this day, but as can be said of most of Hollywood's myths, there is little truth in it. By the late 1940s, all the studios were involved in interlocking financial relationships with a multitude of banks and corporations, and the executives of these financial entities were, in a crunch, the real bosses of the industry.

In the *New York Times* of December 7, 1947, Bosley Crowther, referring to the Waldorf-Astoria agreement, wrote: "It should be fully realized that this action was engineered by the major New York executives, the industry's overlords, and not by the 'Hollywood producers,' who form a . . . subordinate group."

Historians of the HUAC and McCarthy era have largely ignored another body that had a proud hand in the witch-hunting and blacklisting of that period. The American Legion has rarely been given the well-deserved credit, or blame, for its participation in those activities. With its ranks swollen by veterans of World War II, the Legion became an organization with powerful lobbying and boycotting potentials, potentials it was not reluctant to realize. Its letter-writing campaigns were known and feared by many whose public activities veered ever so slightly from flag-waving conformity. The Legion's heavy hand was also felt by the producers; undoubtedly, it had some influence on their decision. (The only part of the cleansing rites of 1951 that I truly regret is my appearance and soul baring, meager though it was, before the Hollywood chapter of this chauvinistic organization.)

It is impossible to record the events of the next few months in proper chronological order, so I won't try; besides; one crisis at a time will be easier to absorb and understand. Crisis number one: Where did everybody go?

It seemed that I was the only one who considered our HUAC performance suicidal. I didn't know where Scott stood; he was having problems much closer to home at the time, but the rest of the crew basked in the bright spotlight of what they considered a victory. Like a filmmaker scanning his notices, the Ten savored only the good and ignored the bad. They believed they had won because the Party said so. If that seems perverse, even dim-witted, behavior for a bunch of intelligent writers, you must understand that communism rules by revelation. The Party can never be wrong. It is conceded that individuals can make mistakes of interpretation, for which they are punished severely (as was Khrushchev in Russia and Earl Browder in the United States, not to mention the twenty million Soviet citizens who did not survive to tell about it). But, once made, a Communist Party decision is the unassailable word, and contrary opinions are not deemed worthy of notice, much less consideration.

In view of all this, if my continued association with the Ten seems puzzling, I can only say that this is now and that was then. I was blinded by my hatred for HUAC, and dispassionate awareness came slowly. Moreover, short of purging myself, a course of action for which I was not mentally prepared, the group was the only port in a violent storm.

As it was, few of us realized that many of our less-dedicated supporters were quitely retreating into the safety of their Beverly Hills and Bel Air homes. However, a sizable number of friends, led by John Huston and Thomas Mann, who had more faith in the men than in their ideology, were still carrying the ball for our side. And there was always the liberal chic. Fund-raising activities had started almost immediately after our return from Washington, and John Howard Lawson's gurus continued their shortsighted strategies, one of which was to make our hot cause piggyback their martyr of choice. At these affairs, two or three of the Ten usually served as guests of honor, and as magnets for the evening's collection, but the communists could not refrain from squeezing in some of their more obscure causes. Example: For a number of weeks, their martyr of choice was a man convicted of a felonious crime in a southern state. His cause may have been worthy, but it did nothing for ours. One good cause per evening was enough for most donors, even for Thomas Mann. He was willing to lend his name, his prestige, and his presence to a fight for freedom of speech and thought; he was not so willing to front for a convicted criminal about whom he knew nothing.

And so, he dropped off the bandwagon—as did others. In some instances it was the normal attrition of time, in others it was the Party's obtuseness in trying to blend incompatible goals that too often blatantly exposed the ultra-left bias of our group. In the end, we even lost John Huston, and in the eyes of most southern Californians, the Ten became a rather tiresome and uncomfortable story. But anything was better than nothing, and we couldn't afford to give up. One evening, Scott and I invited Charlie Chaplin to dinner. Unlike the Red-baiting columnists who finally drove him out of the country, we knew Chaplin was too self-centered to belong to any party. Still, we hoped to gain his support and maybe a few bucks. We had decided to play it smart, and we merely asked him if we could have a couple of his comedies as bait at an upcoming affair. "Of course," he said. "Just call my office and they'll give you the going rental rates." We left the restaurant poorer by the cost of three dinners and with the knowledge that if Chaplin was truly the fellow traveler his accusers called him, he certainly wasn't going our way.

Money is the lifeblood of an extended court action, and lawyers can spend it faster than a film director. Although our attorneys got precious little in the way of fees, the costs of transcripts, pretrial actions, and trial preparations were gobbling up donations as fast as they came in. There were also the future costs of transportation plus living expenses when we returned to Washington for our trials and the $10,000 that had to be set aside for the fines that would probably be levied along with imprisonment if we were found guilty. All in all, those who wanted to eat had to fend for themselves. And that was crisis number two: How do you get money if you can't work?

Some of the Ten had been insolvent long before the hearings, and none of us was rich. About five months before I was served the pink subpoena, my wife's lawyer had agreed to a settlement, and she filed for divorce in Los Angeles. I was riding high at that time and I felt safe in giving her nearly everything—the apartment complex and all its furnishings, a minimum of $25,000 a year against 25 percent of my salary as alimony, and generous child support for Michael. I kept my car, a small two-seater plane, and an even smaller bank account. It was an inequitable arrangement, to be sure, but it was worth it. However, when my bright world turned dark, I was soon broke. My bank balance had disappeared before I returned from Washington, while the alimony and child support began to pile up. For the fourth or fifth time in my life I was on familiar ground; I was as indigent as you can get.

The other nine were no better off, but they had a small advantage—they were writers. Immediately after the firings, some of their friends came forward, offering to sell their works under pseudonyms or under the table. In a few weeks, it was possible for a producer to buy a first-class script at a fire-sale price. Payment was in peanuts, but a smart producer will never let friendship stand in the way of a good deal, and even at those prices, it was a hit-or-miss operation. Trumbo, Lardner, Cole, and Maltz might receive a tenth of their former salaries, hardly enough to support their former life-styles, but the others were not in much demand even at bargain prices. Retrenchment was the order of the day; homes and furnishings were sold, and households were consolidated. As for me, I had given away my income-producing assets, and worse yet, I was the only director in the group. I couldn't sell my talent under the table. When I worked, I was surrounded by more than a hundred men and women, not including the reporters, who had free access to my sets. I had no place to hide.

There was my union, of course, that well-intentional fellowship that had made such a stout stand for the cause of free speech so early in the hearings, and some time during the hectic postholiday weeks, a group of liberal colleagues called on the Directors Guild to back up their brave words with brave action—action in opposition to HUAC, the Waldorf Declaration, and the blacklist. Quite unexpectedly, what looked like a ray of hope became crisis number three.

A meeting was convened; the interest was great; the hall was crowded. Since I was a second vice president of the organization, I moved through the jostling crowd toward the stand where the members of the board and the executives were taking their places. To my great surprise, I saw C. B. DeMille esconced in an honorary seat at the executives' table. He was not a board member or an officer of the guild. He was, in fact, rabidly antiunion, and he had not attended a guild meeting since his highly publicized fight with the American Federation of Television and Radio Artists (AFTRA) over a one-dollar contribution to some special fund years ago. He did not belong on the dais, but there he was, and I knew at once that I was trapped in another losing battle. I retreated and found a seat in a dim corner of the room.

(Some years later I learned from Perry Lieber, head of publicity at RKO, that he had been in charge of obtaining information on "dangerous left-wingers" at the studio throughout the 1940s and 1950s. This information he relayed periodically to DeMille, Hollywood's chief contact with the FBI. C.B.'s broad definition of *left-winger* suffused even Ike Eisenhower and Adolphe Menjou with a ruddy glow.)

Not long after the meeting was called to order, one of the directors moved that the evening's vote be cast by secret ballot. The chairman called for the motion to be approved by a show of hands. But as the hands came up, Michael Curtiz jumped to his feet, and pointing accusingly in all directions, shouted, "Take their names! Take their names!" It was one of the more astonishing moments in the guild's history. The idea that those who voted for a secret ballot, one of an American citizen's most prized rights, were to be pegged as un-American was mindboggling; the fact that the interdiction was demanded by a foreign-born guest somehow made it worse. In the midst of the hubbub that ensued, DeMille also rose to his feet and screamed at the startled crowd, "This is war! This is war!" And with these words the great C. B. brought his private battle against decency and democracy out into the open.

It has been pointed out that the line that registers political ideologies traces a curve; with Stalin on the left and DeMille on the right, that curve formed a circle as its extreme ends touched each other than night. Never before had I felt as close to giving up as I did when I slipped out of the hall and drove home through the suddenly dismal streets of a bewildering and cheerless Hollywood.

12

The next day, I felt sufficiently detached to analyze the situation. Strange to say, since I had hit a solid rock bottom, I knew exactly where I stood. I had no job, no money, no Directors Guild support, but my feeling of insecurity had vanished. And so had most of my "friends." That ancient cry of disillusionment uttered by a dying Caesar is frequently heard in Hollywood, where sycophantic friendship has been refined to an art, and it still says, "I hurt!" It is as shockingly unexpected as the firefight's chance hit that was never meant for you, and a painful accommodation is required. However, under the developing conditions, it had a forgivable spin. Although a few of those deserting the sinking ship may have been rats, most of them were perfectly decent men and women reacting to the instinct of self-preservation. Only the cleanest people could risk touching the infected, and thank God some of them, like Dick Powell, Charles (Blackie) O'Neal, Harry Gerstad, and, later, Don "Red" Barry, did just that, which took a great deal of courage, because the blight was spreading.

The industry had hired an ex–FBI agent to scrutinize the backgrounds of all employees, and he attacked his duties with zeal. The fallout was frightening. The axe came down not only on dyed-in-the-wool Reds but on a much greater lot of unsuspecting fellow travelers who were largely unaware they had been aiding and abetting party members and party projects until they felt the blade. Almost overnight, writers and actors on both coasts found themselves unemployable. If it is true that misery loves company, it was in seventh heaven.

Rumors thrive on disaster, and Hollywood was overloaded with people whispering "Wolf!" The loudest whispers hinted that suspected Reds were to be rounded up by the FBI and carted off to jail. Considering the corrosion of civil rights and the proliferating blacklist, which had now seeped into radio and the theater, it is understandable that there was some hysteria, even panic, in the entertainment industry. In fear of witch-hunters and in search of freedom, more and more writers fled to Mexico. In time, the fear diminished, money ran out, and the writers drifted back across the border to await the return of sanity in Hollywood. But for a number of months, Cuernavaca was the second largest screenwriters' colony in the Western world.

Four weeks after the Waldorf Declaration, I had not yet reached the edge of panic. I still had faith in my ability to survive, even though my only hope was to trust in blind chance. I waited for something to happen. As improbably as always, luck came my way in the shape of a short, wispy-haired, rather rotund man who spoke with a blend of New York accents. Though physically nondescript, his eyes were alive with intelligence. He was thirty-odd years old, and his name was Rod Geiger.

For the moment, he was in the chips, and he had big dreams. He had been an artist, then a soldier in the Signal Corps. With typical acuity, the military brass had assigned him to designing V.D. posters for toilets reconquered by the armed forces of the United States as they fought their way up the Italian peninsula. In Rome, Lady Luck smiled on him when he met Roberto Rossellini. Rossellini had a film to make, but no film with which to make it. Geiger had access to a great deal of the stuff. He knew the film units of the Signal Corps regularly threw away short-ends and complete rolls of film that might be fogged, scratched, or otherwise deemed unfit for use. Geiger was able to obtain and deliver enough discarded stock to make a feature motion picture. What was dross for the notoriously wasteful American army was pay dirt for Rossellini. The resulting film, *Rome, Open City*, was a classic of the immediate postwar era and helped inspire the surge of Italian neorealism that followed. Before the war, Geiger had worked for an American distributor and exhibitor of foreign films who now helped faciliate the film's release in the United States. In gratitude, Rossellini gave Geiger a coproducer credit, which was all Rod needed.

With a film in hand and Roberto in his pocket, Geiger became a producer in earnest. Back in the States, he promoted a pot of money and some American actors. On his return to Rome, Rossellini turned it all into another hit, *Paisan*. Lightning had struck twice for Roberto, and as he had earned the right to do, Geiger capitalized on those brilliant successes.

Once more in the United States, Geiger was determined to make it on his own. He bought a sprawling first novel written by a Brooklyn bricklayer, Pietro di Donato, and hired a New York playwright to transform it into a screenplay. Then he came to Hollywood. He reached me through a friend, and I called on him in his suite at the Hollywood Plaza Hotel. I had never heard of Geiger, and wildcat producers were a glut in Hollywood; I entertained no false hopes.

I had read di Donato's short story "Christ in Concrete" many years before when it had appeared in the original *Esquire* magazine. It had been a prize winner, and it would make a great sequence, but a sequence doesn't make a picture, and a short story blown up into a novel is often a disaster. Geiger, however, had no qualms. He gave me a short, non-self-serving summary of his background and asked me to make the film. He said he understood my situation, but to be safe, I reviewed it in some detail, stressing that he would find it impossible to raise money in the United States if I were involved. He shrugged off my warning with the casual grace of a true entrepreneur. I knew that independent deals were difficult to put together, and about one in ten achieved actual production, but I said "yes" with some enthusiasm. Having nothing to lose simplifies the decision-making process.

Geiger was easy to get along with, and in a very short time, we established a compatible relationship. Rod and his friend Katya (who has since become a "name" in the world of women's wear) had planned to spend Christmas at Lake Tahoe, and he invited Jean and me to come along. A few days away from Hollywood's poisoned atmosphere was a morale booster, marred only slightly when Katya, caught up by the spirit of Christmas, danced off a curb and broke her leg. I suffered a much more lasting trauma at the time, a psychological wound that would not heal completely for many years to come: Jean and I were living off the generosity of others.

I had been on my own since I was fourteen; the largest amount I had ever borrowed, early in the Great Depression, was $250, and that caused me weeks of anguish both before and after the fact. No matter how small the amount, borrowing money was something I couldn't handle without a great deal of inner turmoil, and now there was no hope of repaying anything to anyone in the foreseeable future. I was a sponger, a grifter. I rationalized the free lunch as a preproduction salary and told myself that the actual production would soon follow to legitimatize my self-justification. But few things happen as quickly as one would wish in Hollywood.

Despite my unequivocal warning, Rod spent some futile weeks testing the local financial waters while I fretted away anxious days awaiting the script from New York. About a hundred pages finally arrived, a hundred pages of total disappointment. Much as I disliked adding the indefinite to an already existing uncertainty by prolonging our waiting period, there was nothing to do but start all over again. Geiger agreed, and

I suggested he hire an old coworker to write the script. Ben Barzman and I had spent many months on *Back to Bataan*, and we had become the best of friends, but friendship had little to do with my recommendation: I thought he could do the job. Ben was blacklisted and available, and Geiger made the deal.

Barzman read the script, from which little could be salvaged, and the novel. It had an abundance of vivid, well-developed characters, the most essential part of any good film, but little plot to support them. Ben spent a day or two thinking; then he, Rod, and I got together. It was perhaps the most fruitful afternoon I have ever spent on a screenplay. We created a step-outline for the plot that, with few changes, saw me through the entire film. The next day, Barzman started to write the script.

The first quarter of the year was an interesting time for our hopeful little company. On February 16, 1948, the Academy of Motion Pictures Arts and Sciences announced its Oscar nominations. *Crossfire* had garnered five, including one for the year's best picture and one for best direction. As expected, the world media took brief notice that a blacklisted director who had been sacked by RKO in November had secured an Oscar nomination. I received a few congratulatory messages from close friends and from my agents, but the mild flurry did nothing to vitalize my career. On the contrary, it increased the Motion Picture Alliance's efforts to ensure that neither I nor my film would embarrass Hollywood by winning an Oscar. (The MPAPAI was surprisingly steadfast in pursuit of its aims and ideals. It was also unforgiving. Their phone campaigns against me continued for many years after my rehabilitation.)

Toward the end of February, I vacated my apartment. I could no longer pay alimony or child support, and my ex-wife (the final decree was due in April) was about to leave McDougall Alley to test the personal and financial security available to an apartment complex landlady in Beverly Hills. Rod and Katya had taken a short lease on a house in Mandeville Canyon, and since it was large and we would all be leaving for Europe in a few days, Jean and I moved in with them.

As I look back over forty-seven years to that depressing period, I am amazed that at no time had I considered asking Jean if she wanted to leave me, at least for the sake of her career. Nor did she, in spite of the urging of many of her studio acquaintances, so much as consider the possibility, at least not to my knowledge. We took great delight in being together and eagerly looked forward to an April marriage in London. I was sure that England with Jean would be a totally different cup 'o tea from my previous sojourn in that country.

And indeed, by the end of the month, we were in London, where austerity still reigned. We settled in, briefly, at the Cumberland, a drummers' hotel on Oxford Street. On the whole, the British suffered austerity with a graceful stoicism, but there are bad apples in every barrel, and thievery in London was becoming endemic. Among its most accomplished practitioners were the hotel's chambermaids; in the first twenty-four hours, they pinched Jean's nylon stockings and her specially made silk lingerie. Salt of the earth, I mused, but Jean was mad as hell. However, we decided it was a waste of time to report the crime.

Within the next few days, I witnessed another, more awe-inspiring kind of expertise. Rod and I were walking down Oxford Street when he touched my arm. "Wait for me," he said, and he bucked the traffic across the avenue. I watched him enter a small "Blue Cars" office, the British equivalent of an Avis or a Hertz rent-a-car establishment. I wondered what he could be doing there, since we had not discussed renting a car. In about fifteen minutes, he came out and crossed over to my side, a smile on his face. With a gesture I would soon know better, he pulled his hand half out of his pocket. In his clenched fist was a wad of British money. *"Five hundred pounds!"* he said. That was worth about $2,000 in 1948 (closer to $20,000 in 1994), and since I knew he had never been in London before, I wondered what kind of magic he had used to make such a touch. At the same time, I realized two things; Geiger was a peerless promoter, and he must have been as broke as I was. What I did not realize then was that in the next sixteen months, I would learn a great deal about how most independent producers are forced to operate.

The £500 delivered us from the mercies of the Cumberland and into the outskirts of London. The Selsden Park was a middle-class residential hotel that catered to pensioners and retired couples, but the hotel's rhododendrons were welcoming an unusually warm spring, and it was pleasing to be awakened by the haunting, plaintive cry of the cuckoo, which seemed to fit my mood. All in all, we weathered the next few weeks rather well.

During this time, Geiger had met an independent producer who had access to high-risk money. He was interested in Rod's project and agreed to help him finance his film on one condition: I had to make a film for his company first. I hadn't felt so wanted in many months.

Christ in Concrete was nearly a year away from takeoff, so I said "Yes," with one condition of my own: First, I had some decks to clear back in the United States.

Plans for Jean and I to marry in England had gone awry when my ex-wife, for reasons of her own, neglected to pick up the final divorce papers, and that had to be dealt with. There were other, less-important matters, like an appearance in court. John Howard Lawson and Dalton Trumbo had been tried separately for contempt of Congress, since charges against them differed somewhat, and two trials had been required. Those covered all eventualities in the other eight cases, and our lawyers had stipulated that we would be bound by the verdicts in the first two trials. Now those verdicts were in—guilty as charged—and we were starting down the long, slow road to the Supreme Court, a journey that would take two years. In the meantime, there were technicalities to dispose of which mandated my presence in Washington, D.C.

13

Our return to our country's capital was not exactly a homecoming, nor will it pain me never to see it again. Since my brush with HUAC, I have not been able to visit the memorials to Washington, Jefferson, and Lincoln; even at a distance, those impressive monuments inspire me only with a feeling of bitter irony. But for those who choose to forget that even idols like Jefferson owned slaves and that it was the *people* of the world's first democracy who condemned Socrates to death for speaking his mind, hope for a return to the mythical nobility of our forefathers lives on. It is that impossible hope, and the ideals that energize it, that brought visionaries into the Communist Party. This is a simple statement of fact that most Americans cannot bring themselves to accept, but *men and women can, and do, join the Communist Party with the purest of motives.* In their haste to improve the system, they are easy pickings for any organization that promises immediate and total perfection. Unfortunately, they cannot foresee that the utopia they idolize is, and always has been, a blighted area. By the time the truth becomes apparent, their ideals and the Party, which are two quite distinct entities, have become so interconnected, so homogenized in the idealist's minds, that it is difficult for them to separate one from the other. This explains their long-lingering relationship and their reluctance to make a clean break even after disillusionment reveals the Party's perfidy. Renouncing the Party seems to be the equivalent of renouncing their own valid and admirable ideals.

It took nearly three years of slow mental reclamation for me to see clearly that the Party and my ideals were *not* related; that I could maintain my beliefs while separating myself completely from a political group that for several decades under Stalin betrayed *all* ideals, including those they originally claimed as their own.

However, in May of 1948, the reasoning process by which I eventually arrived at that liberating conclusion was just beginning to stir, and I had more important matters on my mind. In L.A., my business manager, who no longer had any business of mine to manage, was kind enough to pick up the divorce papers in my name. Jean and I considered our options. The waiting period in Washington was too long to fit our schedule, but the license clerk reminded us that Maryland was right next door, its waiting period was just three days, and Ellicott City was a charming and romantic locale. We thanked the license clerk. At that dreary time in our lives, a little extra romance was more than welcome.

The clerk was right. Ellicott City was a most attractive town. The gilded town-hall cupola was visible from a distance. We spent little time in parking our rental car, finding the registry, and signing the necessary papers. Within thirty minutes, we were on our way back to the capital. We had barely crossed the line into the district when we were flagged by a speed cop, taken to the nearest precinct station, booked for driving five miles over the speed limit, and fined on the spot. Our financial reserve was dwindling fast, and I was beginning to think Washington didn't like me.

On May 12, 1948, we were shaking D.C.'s dust off our feet for good. And we had an extra passenger. Albert Maltz also had an appointment in New York. Along the way, we had to make two stops, the first of which was most important. In Ellicott City, we located a Protestant minister willing to marry us; we set a time for the ceremony and hurried off to pick up our license.

As I braked to a stop at the town hall, I glanced up at the windows that overlooked the parking lot. They were crowded with people staring in our direction. We looked around behind us—nobody. We were the only ones there. They were staring at *us*, waiting for us to get out of the car.

Oh, God! I thought—not again, now now! Apparently the word had gotten out, and the situation might become embarrassing. I had become hardened to this sort of attention; after all, I had, in a sense, asked for it. But Jean was all entertainer, and a political babe in the woods. She was undeserving of animosity that was meant for me. On the other hand, it was more than possible that someone had recognized *her* name; that they weren't interested in me at all. What a humbling thought! Still, it was with some apprehension that we got out of the car and entered the building.

People were regarding us from doorways as we walked down the hall, but most of them were smiling, and as Jean and I approached the license counter, the most beautiful tenor voice I had heard in years started singing "Drink to me only with thine eyes." We turned around. They had crowded into the doorway and short, pleasant, middle-aged man (we learned later he was the town treasurer) was singing his heart out. We almost broke down, but we had business to take care of.

Odd Man Out

We got our license, borrowed the young woman at the desk as a witness, and drove back to the parsonage. There, with Maltz as our second witness, the minister performed a dignified, simple ceremony, and Jean and I exchanged the $15 gold wedding rings we had bought in Washington the day before. Then we drove the young woman back to the town hall. Our welcoming committe was waiting for us, this time to wave good-bye. As we drove away, a lovely rendition of "I Love You Truly" followed us down the road.

We had come into town as strangers and found friendliness, warmth, and a perfect, if unusual, wedding. The good feeling lasted all the way to Philadelphia. There, in the City of Brotherly Love, Paul Robeson, Albert Maltz, two or three other liberals, and I spoke to a hotel auditorium full of cheering supporters. They got what they wanted to hear; we damned the Committee and uttered all the clichés about freedom of speech that they expected. The applause was roof-shaking, but I didn't hear Jean. The bride had gone to bed.

The next few weeks are a blur in my memory—a dream montage vaguely seen through misty oil dissolves, with no sharp focus on any of the events that must have taken place or the people who played parts in them. Except for a few. I know we spent two or three days in New York discussing our extremely obscure future with Bartley Crum. Then we headed for Hollywood. On the way, we stopped for a very short visit with Henry Porter, Jean's father. He was a wonderful man, buried alive in the dreary spaces of Big Spring, Texas. He was always completely supportive of Jean and me, no matter how strange some of our activities must have seemed to him. In a twist that was unusual for the time and place, the vast *openness* of his natural environment surely influenced him far more than its aridity.

In Hollywood, I sold my treasured "woodie," a Chrysler Town and Country convertible, one of the first new cars to appear after the war. Jean had enlisted MGM's most powerful influence in order to surprise me with it. And now, whatever equity I had in it would pay our fare back to Europe. We packed our few belongings in a trunk, which was then shipped to England. When Jean told her mother of our intentions, there was panic in the air. Mrs. Porter, an arch-conservative, was convinced that, once in England, I would take her innocently compliant daughter into exile behind the Iron Curtain. (I have always wondered what went through Mrs. Porter's mind when she found my set of the *Complete Works* of Lenin, which I had stored in her basement.)

Mother was nearly right, but she had the country wrong. The thought of reclaiming my Canadian citizenship and asking for political asylum in England has crossed my mind, but only briefly. Although I had a more promising earning potential in Europe than any of the other black-listed expatriots (and the offers to confirm it), I had never seriously considered living and working in any home base but the United States, not even through the years when there was no hope of anything at home but political and professional rejection.

We flew back to London and holed up at the Atheneum Court Hotel in Piccadilly. Despite its rather impressive name, the seedy inn was the only reasonable accommodation available in war-depleted London. Nat Bronston (nto to be confused with Samuel of the same patronymic), who had asked me to make his film, had bought the rights to an unpublished novel, *Man about a Dog*, written by Alec Coppel. While he worked on the screenplay, we assembled a good English cast, which included Robert Newton, Sally Gray, and Naunton Wayne. The young American lover was played by Phil Brown, perhaps the first Hollywood actor to flee the Hollywood blacklist and make his home in England. The film, retitled *Obsession*, was eventually released to good reviews and decent box-office returns. But it was seven months before the film was in the bag, and in those seven months, Jean and I learned how to triumph over adversity—at least temporarily—kept afloat by a weird mixture of grief and happiness, of love and anxiety, but never hope. Still, it was a period of small victories that permits us to remember it with a certain nostalgia, and when compared to the year and a half that followed, it was a picnic.

While searching for a place we could call home, Jean met an American woman who was completing her tour of duty at the American Embassy in London and returning to the States. The time was right, and so were the vibes; Jean's instant friend agreed to sublease her rented house.

Early in August, we escaped the mustiness of the Atheneum Court and moved into the house that became our home during the rest of our stay in England. Forty-seven Glebe Place, in Chelsea, was just off Kings Road in a historic part of town. Nell Gwyn's seventeenth-century hide-away, now a kindergarten, was four doors down from the street, Carol Reed lived just around the corner, and the Thames was an easy stroll to the south. The house was typically old London in style, one room wide and four rooms high. We had to learn how to bank the coke fire every night if we wanted hot water in the morning and how to lift the sink's drainboard to get out the back door, but such chores were a relative pleasure. It was ours for one year only, but it was the first home of our marriage, and it still occupies a special niche in my memories.

While I spent my days in preproduction, Jean was learning how to cope with everyday living. We were now residents and required ration stamps for all our essential needs: petrol for the rented car, coal for our stove and fireplace, food for our stomachs, and clothes for our bodies—everything except medical care. That was free, even for foreigners. As yet, there were no supermarkets in London, nor small general stores, and shopping was a walking tour. But Jean makes friends more easily than anyone I've ever known, and very soon she was on an "'ello, luv" basis with every shopkeeper on Kings Road. These included the green-grocer, the butcher, the fishmonger, the baker, the grocer, and anyone else who dealt in life's necessities.

For a short while, Jean also found a way to contribute to the "kitty." Early in September, she was asked to star in a musical revue at the Embassy Club on Bond Street. She was an instant success (naturally), but by the end of November, nature put an end to that. Jean was pregnant.

During the war, England had recognized a national emergency that had little to do with military operations. Earlier in 1946, I had criss-crossed a large part of the country seeking locations for *So Well Remembered*. In the poorer areas, most of the prewar children showed signs of rickets, an absolute indication of inadequate diet, but the postwar babies were the healthiest I had ever seen. We soon learned the cause of this remarkable reversal. Jean's pregnancy meant ration stamps for extra food, free orange juice concentrate, and vitamins. There was one more entitlement that grew in importance with each passing month—the privilege of going to the head of any queue in England. And in London, queuing ranked as the third inevitability.

But these small things seemed very important, for tension and anxiety were ever-present conditions of our castaway existence. Even the letters we watched for so eagerly were opened with hesitation. The odds were even that they contained bad news.

On November 8, 1948, the honorable chairman of the House Committe on Un-American Activities, J. Parnell Thomas, was indicted for malfeasance in office. Ironically, he was indicted not for persecuting practitioners of free thought but for staffing his office with freeloading relatives. This in no way ameliorated the situation of the Hollywood Ten, nor did it give me any personal satisfaction. I had spent most of my life in a town that has more than its fair share of people who fatten their egos off others' misfortunes, and I had learned that gloating over someone else's tribulations never served to alleviate my own.

"It's always darkest before the dawn," say incurable optimists. Don't believe it! I don't think anyone ever pinned the lie to that old saw more than Jean and I (except for Job). And, jumping a few months here, one of the blackest times came up in the summer of 1949. Two very liberal justices, Frank Murphy and Wiley Rutledge died, and President Truman effectively buried our hopes for sentence reversals by appointing two relative conservatives, Tom Clark and Sherman Minton. However, immediate problems usually serve to hold off apprehensions of the future, and once preproduction of *Christ in Concrete* got under way, there were immediate problems in plenty. The first, and most important, was money, two kinds of money—pounds and dollars: Bronston had honored his promise to help finance our film after the completion of *Obsession* in December, but his backers could only manage about half the money needed to make the picture. So, my English agent, Jack Dunfee, approached Arthur Rank.

Two and a half years after *So Well Remembered*, Rank's shirt cuffs were no longer frayed, nor was his tie raveling. He was much more than just the richest mill owner in the British Isles, he had extended his interests in a multitude of directions. Besides his more orthodox enterprises, he owned Britain's largest theater chain, a distribution company, two of its busiest studios, and the contracts of nearly all of its stars, directors, and writers. He asked me to see him and John Davis, his second in command.

If ever there was an example of a good capitalist, it was J. Arthur Rank. I have never met an executive with a more open mind. He listened attentively as I explained my situation, then dismissed my communist background as of no real consequence. My political views, he said, were no business of his; he wanted only to know what kind of film I was planning to make. Satisfied with my answer, he agreed to participate; of course, he wanted the distribution rights, and that was another problem solved.

I have never been able to decide whether Rank, a very religious man, was being charitable or so naive as to believe that American exhibitors would ignore boycotts by organizations such as the American Legion. But since he had surrounded himself with unemotional, rock-hard businessmen like John Davis, who would certainly reckon the costs, I am inclined to believe he was being charitable, regardless of mundane considerations. I would like to think he was capable of such generosity, because my "comrades" weren't.

We had the pounds, but now we needed dollars, and that was Rod Geiger's department. I was receiving minimal expenses (in pounds) and no salary, which was legal, but my fellow exiles wanted hard currency, and at that time, only dollars fit the bill. Ben Barzman, in the van of a growing number of blacklisted artists, had moved his family to Paris. He was finishing the screenplay there and insisted on his final payment of $5,000 before he turned it loose. Sam Wanamaker, a fine actor, was also blacklisted and available, so we cast him in the role of Geremio, the male lead in the film. But his agent also insisted on dollars, a large portion of which was to be paid on signing.

That added up to a lot of dollars, and since, with rare exceptions, pounds could not legally be exchanged for greenbacks, Geiger was soon in touch with every black marketeer in London. I had already learned that Rod was a top-level operator (and that label is used in a positive sense); what's more, he seemed to thoroughly relish the operations. On several night trips to darkened houses on badly lit streets, I doubled as his driver, and I always enjoyed the expression of unalloyed pleasure with which he would show me a wad of dollars on the palm of his hand. It was not an expression of greed—never. It was the adrenaline-boosted look of a man who had succeeded against great odds in negotiating a vitally necessary transaction. At all times, Rod was at least as generous as he was cunning, though in the present situation, cunning was more important. Somehow he scraped together the needed hard money. Sam was paid, the script was ransomed, and we started serious work on it and on the preparations for the film.

Christ in Concrete was a somewhat tragic tale of a close group of Italian immigrants in New York and their efforts to survive in the Great Depression. Except for a few stock shots for the main title and some background footage for process and blue-screen scenes, the entire picture was filmed at Rank's Denham Studio just outside of London. Fortunately for our enterprise, the Denham artists, artisans, and technicians were the equal of any in the world, and the realization of Brooklyn in London was flawlessly achieved.

During these months, Jean was having a rougher time than I was. She was making a home for us, listening to my problems with the film, trying to obey the doctor's orders to get several hours of bed rest every day, and worrying about which would come first, the baby or our return to the States—a date imposed by the federal courts. Keeping a tight rein on me, the judge had extended my passport for only one year; it was valid until the middle of August.

At 4 A.M. on July 27, 1949, our son Richard was born, and our education on the subject of private medical practice in Britain began. We had allowed a consideration for ethics to overcome our common sense; we had opted for a private nursing home and a private physician because we paid no taxes and felt that accepting something for nothing was not the proper thing to do. And for that silly rationalization, Jean nearly paid with her life. (I might add that our doctor had been a member of the British equivalent of the Lincoln Brigade.)

It was a very difficult, high-forceps delivery, and Jean's doctor called for help; his former mentor arrived with an assistant who carried his kit. Some time in the early morning they judged everything was a-ok, sent me off to the studio, and left the nurses in charge. They were soon complaining about their work load; Jean kept flooding the sheets with her blood, making their jobs too laborious. The realization that she might be hemmorhaging did not enter their minds until she sank into a deep coma. Alarmed at last, the nurses called her doctor, who arrived accompanied by his mentor and the mentor's assistant. Noting that Jean was devoid of blood, they called a transfusion expert, who arrived with *his* assistant; then they called me to hurry down in case the transfusion failed. And it nearly did. By the time I arrived from the studio, they had found the normal transfusion was ineffective, had cut a large hole in her ankle (the scar remains) and were literally pouring blood into her body. They also called in a specialist to inject adrenaline directly into her heart, since it wasn't doing too well. Then they informed me she was within a gasp of dying.

We learned (before the birth of our next baby) that Jean was Rh negative, but of course, she had not been tested for that, nor had they checked the blood used in the transfusions. How she defeated the concerted efforts of that battalion of experts I'll never know. But she did. And though she was very weak for many days to come, we got her out of the nursing home as soon as possible and into the safety of our own home.

Now to rewind a bit. While still in production, I had received permission from the steward's committee to spend one evening a week with my editor, cutting the film. (That's how it was done in England in 1949.

Odd Man Out

The unions and the stewards were very powerful.) At the completion of shooting, only a few weeks remained in which to finish all the elements of postproduction, so I sought the committee's approval for a second evening's work each week. They turned me down on the ground that it was impossible for me to finish the job in the time available. Fortunately, there was an appeals board, composed largely of those villains, the executives; they approved my request. With the nearly superhuman cooperation of composer Ben Frankl and the postproduction crew, the "answer print" was in my hands a day or two before our departure deadline.

Britain's very strict religious censorship would not allow the word *Christ* to appear on the title, and our film had been retitled, *Give Us This Day*.[6] I ran it for all the VIPs involved in its making. Rank, Davis, and the other financial contributors as well as Geiger and Bronston were seated in front of me in the projection room, and when the end title faded out, no one spoke or turned in my direction for what seemed an interminable length of time. When finally they did, it was apparent that all, even the stone-faced John Davis, had been crying. Then there were congratulations all around, and I went home to my wife and family quite pleased with myself. Two days later, Jean, fully capable, though not yet fully recovered, our baby, and I were on the long, long flight to L.A. and limbo.

---

6. Later, in an effort to break the Legion's boycott in the United States, the film's name was changed again. It became *Salt to the Devil*, a phrase taken from a line of dialogue in the film. The boycott took the change in stride.

14

On **Sunset Boulevard,** the Sunset Tower, the tallest and the toniest apartment building in Hollywood, seemed to lord it over that part of town. George Raft was a permanent resident at the height of his career, as were a number of slightly less glittering film lights. I remembered an earlier time, walking by the landmark with a communist friend. He stopped and looked up in the general direction of the penthouse. "Some day," he growled, "*I'm* going to be up there and *he's* going to be down here." I also remembered thinking that wasn't communism as I saw it, but I was naive then. The place never appealed to me, but there was a time when I could have afforded to live up there. Now, however, just back from England, Jean, the baby, and I were living in the tower's shadow in a two-bedroom apartment on DeLongpre Avenue. Here, the disillusionment, or more properly, the awareness, which had started nearly two years earlier in a District of Columbia hotel, was to continue expanding for the next ten months. But first came the all-important problem of living.

Soon after settling, there was a wonderful surprise. One of Adrian Scott's very wealthy and moderately liberal friends offered to lend us each $10,000. The unwelcome surprise followed swiftly; he withdrew his beneficent offer before I had the time to stretch my hand out for it. I had been away from Hollywood for over a year, and England's political tolerance had had its effect. I had never experienced one instance of prejudice or ostracism at the hands of class or party, and although I had been ever conscious of American government persecution, my reaction to individuals was, on the whole, benign. So the surprising demonstration of the power of social and political pressure in California, which was the only explanation for our would-be benefactor's change of heart, was shocking. Willy-nilly, it bound me more securely to the group I wanted to leave behind. Associates, it seemed, would have to stand in for friends.

Once more, I was facing a decision that gave me no choice. Although by now I had some practice in the art, I still hated borrowing. When one's word is not an assignable collateral, borrowing is just another form of begging. But necessity's pinch can overcome repugnance, and I borrowed $2,000 from one of the few men I could still call friend, Harry Gerstad. I hasten to add he was far to the right of communism. That was a seeming contradiction that puzzles me even now; without a single exception, help came from moderate Republicans, in one instance, from a right-winger with whom arguing politics was an occasion for mayhem. (As I write these words, I am reminded of Mary Shelley's plaint—"If I have ever found kindness it has not been from the liberals"—and I wonder why I call myself a socialist, although with reservations.)

In a diatribe written to Herbert Biberman on May 3, 1951, Albert Maltz referred to me as "that scientist"; his use of the term implied no compliment. I only wish I could accept that label because there is great art in much of science. But, pursuant to Albert's point of view, in those rare moments when I have nothing better to ponder, I contemplate an imaginary graph that plots my lifeline (not its length but its quality). The high points I take for granted, but the low points call for reflection and expecially for reexamination of the sources of succor that have forced the line to move upward once more.

This particular plunge bottomed out unexpectedly with aid from my agent, Charles Feldman. He was one of Hollywood's top talent managers, a man of ambition and broad enterprise. One of his enterprises involved the purchase of story properties, usually scripts, from some of his writer clients. When these were reworked to his satisfaction, Feldman would sell them to the studios as his properties, and his top-level roster of stars, directors, and writers gave him great leverage in such deals. He was, of course, doing no more than many independent producers did, but his status as an agent who made a secondary profit off some of his clients rendered the activity questionable. (Val Lewton told me that when he was head of Selznick's story department, he was expected to show an anual profit on the resale of stories and scripts.) Not too much later, the Writers Guild outlawed the practice as unethical.

However, at this time, Feldman's moonlighting worked to my advantage. I had never claimed an original writing talent, which effectively barred me from functioning under an alias, as some of the Hollywood Ten were able to do. But I could function, as most better-than-competent directors can, as a script doctor. During the following months, I recruited two nonblacklisted friends, Charles O'Neal and Tom Reed, both members of Hollywood's considerable pool of ignored talent. We worked on three scripts for Feldman. One of these was later made into a film with John Wayne, another with Clifton Webb; the third, suffering a fate not unusual with the best of the lot, still molders on some dusty shelf. Feldman was no more generous than any other producer who bought blacklisted goods, but he made it possible for us to keep our heads above water, and Jean and I were grateful; we were sustaining life, not looking for bonuses.

Phil Yordan also ran a "script factory," though the times had little to do with it. Still, he probably used the services of as many blacklisted writers as were available, but he slipped them in through the front entrance and out of the back door with such well-timed precision that I never ran into another writer in his apartment. Leo Townsend, another blacklisted excommunist, and I worked on a Yordan idea, but Leo was no better at original creation than I, and the script never got off the ground. It did, however, earn each of us a few dollars, which helped to keep us off the streets.

(I am sickened now to think that we were grateful for the scraps thrown our way, and I still feel anger when remembering that, to the best of my knowledge, with one exception, no producer who took advantage of that sick period in our history ever paid an honest price for the scripts he bought under the table. It would be charitable to say that honest producers, of whom there must have been a few, were dutifully obeying the injunctions of the Waldorf-Astoria Declaration, but I think they feared it more than they respected it. The one exception: Geiger paid Barzman what would probably have been his going salary in an unfrightened Hollywood.)

The Ten were together again. Those who had fled to Mexico, England, or wherever were back, and joined by at least two of our attorneys, Katz and Margolis, were meeting weekly to discuss legal strategy, fund promotion, and occasional incidental business. Dalton Trumbo avoided most sessions, and he left strict orders that his name or signature was never to be used without his specific permission. As a party member of experience, he emphasized the *never*.

In the careless pre-HUAC days, with such characters involved, our meetings would have been frequently interrupted by laughter; now they were extremely dull. But there were exceptions. And those exceptions had a profound influence on me and on the rest of my life. The first exception was on a point of legal strategy. (These meetings, designed to discuss strategy and sustain morale, are pooled in my memory with those few that had taken place before I went to England, and the first of the specific incidents may have taken place then.)

During a discussion of possible prosecution ploys, one of our lawyers posed a hypothetical question: "Suppose the prosecutor asks if you believe in free speech for the Communists. What is your answer?" There was a chorus of "Yes!"

"Now," continued the lawyer, "if he asks you if you believe in freedom of speech for fascists, what do you say?" The "Yes!" chorus once more. To my surprise, but not to the lawyer's, John Howard Lawson rasied a warning hand.

"It's not that simple," he said. And as he had no doubt planned, the discussion continued into the second week, when a six-to-three majority voted to allow fascists the freedom of speech. Unfortunately, our leader was one of the minority, and he now proceeded to shepherd our minds toward the correct answer.

"The answer," he said with finality, "is that you do *not* believe in freedom of speech for fascists." I was a little slow.

"Why not?" I asked. Lawson regarded me as he would an innocent neophyte.

"You believe in freedom of speech for communists," he said, patiently, "because what they say is true. You do *not* believe in freedom of speech for fascists because what they say is a lie."

QED. Who could argue the logic of that? It was so simple, so plausible, so jesuitical, and so contradictory. All of us had invoked the First Amendment as the basis for our refusal to cooperate with HUAC, and now we were expected to deny its protection to those who might disagree with us. But of course! Later, careful examination of Lawson's statements and testimony showed that although he claimed the absolute right of free speech for himself and for selected others, he did not ever mention it as a basically guaranteed right of *all* others. And for the first time, I clearly realized that Lawson's positions were not contradictory— not to him. He had *never* specifically backed everybody's right to freedom of speech. The seeming contradiction, which led to puzzlement and reluctant acquiescence, had always been in my mind, not his. That was one of my longest steps on my walk to freedom of conscience.

The most important exception to the Ten's dull routines came much later, not too long before I went to jail. It could only be considered incidental business since it had nothing to do with the Ten or with our legal problems. It had to do with Robert Rossen.

Rossen was a man of great talent; in some ways, he was an ideal filmmaker. He was a casual friend for years, but I never came to know him well. To me, he always seemed quite insecure, as if he were trying to take his bearings in an alien community in which he inexplicably found himself, and I was always surprised that none of this showed in his work. He had just written, produced, and directed *All the King's Men*, the acclaimed Oscar winner of 1950. And he was being called on the carpet by John Howard Lawson.

Censure is too flabby a word. Rossen's *excoriation* took place during a meeting of the Ten held at Maltz's home. Thoroughly bewildered, he was, for the better part of the evening pilloried by Lawson and those two acid-tongued specialists in the Party's disciplinary procedures, Biberman and Bessie, three men who, lumped together, had not one-tenth of Bob's talent. I was dumbfounded. It was *Cornered* all over again, equally unreasonable but much more cruel, and involving a more worthwhile film. The theme of *All the King's Men* was "Power corrupts," a phrase we often used to denigrate conservatives in general and HUAC in particular. Yet Bob's comrades were now giving him hell for dramatizing it. The reason behind the attack was never verbally expressed, and it took me some time to recognize it: Rossen was really getting hell for exposing the evils of dictatorship, the rock on which the Communist Party was founded. Once more, I found it impossible to reconcile Lawson, the man who had accused the Committee of "conspiring against the American way of life," with the Lawson who now led the attack against Rossen's exposure of the evils of one-man rule.

Bob did his best to fight back, but he was outnumbered, and there was no meeting ground. Eventually, he had more than enough. "Stick the whole Party up your ass!" he said and walked out of the house. And out of the Party. Although that made more sense than anything else that evening, I knew it wouldn't be that easy for me. The fact that a kangaroo court considering a purely party matter had been held in my presence indicated they now considered me one of them again, or at least a party hostage. The same thought had hit me at the end of the hearings, but my long stay in Europe had obliterated that perception. Now I knew for certain that getting out of the Party would require much more than a verbal or written resignation.

"Heaven has no rage . . . nor hell a fury like a woman scorned," wrote William Congreve. That was certainly not an original thought in 1697, nor for millenia before, but that neatly turned phrase survives because it says it all.

All right! Call me a sexist, but in one of those about-faces women probably understand better than men, my ex-wife had chosen this troublesome time to supplement our woes. Long before the hearings, when my career was beginning to bloom, and long before I met and fell in love with Jean, she had left me (and Michael) permanently, was living with someone else in New York, and had suggested a quick divorce in the Bahamas. After I started going with Jean, everything changed. She abandoned the concept of quick freedom in favor of a California divorce, which at that time meant an interlocutory decree and a full year's wait for the final decision. She upped her alimony and childcare demands astronomically, which I more or less cheerfully agreed to, then she neglected to pick up the final papers. Somewhere in the middle of all this came the HUAC hearings, which blighted our hopes for quick riches.

However, during my stay in London, Rank had been kind enough to allow me a payment of $10,000 besides my expenses, and to use his influence with the Ministry of the Exchequer to send it all to my ex-wife. In spite of that, and the public knowledge that I was officially deprived of an opportunity to work in the United States, she had gone to court in an attempt to claim the Agoura property, which was really Jean's. She had also succeeded in obtaining an order to hold my plane (which was now rotting away on a field at the Glendale Airport) in receivership. The order also held me subject to a prison sentence for, believe it or not, contempt of court if I failed to pay up all back alimony and child support. For the hour he spent at the bar to achieve his victory, her attorney demanded $9,000. Even the judge was shocked, but he recognized that lawyers had to live and he allowed him $5,000. I knew the income from the apartments under my ex-wife's control guaranteed both her and my son comfortably more than the necessities, and I felt no guilt in avoiding payments of money I did not have. Feldman's largesse kept us functioning but allowed no frills. However, unknown to me, another attack was in the works.

On April 10, 1950, the new Supreme Court refused, by a vote of six to two, to hear our appeal. The customary petition for a rehearing held off the inevitable for another two months but finally our sentencing was set for June 29.

A week before I was to leave for Washington, I received a shocking call from an attorney, Ed Mosk, a friend of long standing. That morning he had been at the courthouse filing some papers and noticed a subpoena lying on the counter. Even upside down the spelling made an impression, and a covert peek informed him that the summons was, indeed, meant for me. Just one week before going into a federal prison, I

A Memoir of the Hollywood Ten

was being summoned to answer contempt of court charges for failure to meet my alimony and child support payments.

I hung up in a daze. Of all the black dawns Jean and I had survived in the last two years, this was the darkest. We spent the rest of of the evening trying to plan our time until my departure, but nothing made sense. We only knew that we had an edge; the process server would not be aware that we were.

We were up and dressed very early the next morning, and sure enough, at about 7:00 A.M., an unfamiliar car pulled up at the curb outside our apartment and a man knocked on our door. Jean answered, and during the short conversation learned that the man's business was only with me. She told him I was out for my morning stroll. He walked back to his car and settled down to wait. I kissed Jean good-bye and took advantage of our apartment's architectural setup; I sneaked out the back door and down the back stairs to the garage, which opened on the alley below the apartment. Fortunately, the alley joined the street outside the process server's field of vision.

I was in flight, with no roost in mind, but the coast was always more inviting than the city, so I headed out Sunset Boulevard. When I reached Brentwood, I realized I was near the home of an old friend and colleague, Bill Castle. It was still early, and he was having breakfast. I accepted a cup of coffee, explained my predicament, and in keeping with his character, Bill invited me to spend my last few days of freedom with him and his wife. I called Jean, who told me the process server was still at his post. She arranged to have a friend bring her out to Bill's house, where she picked up the car.

The bitterness that might have ruined the next few days was at least partially alleviated by the Castles' hospitality and the excitement of Jean's daily duel with the law. Each morning she left the apartment tailed by the now wised-up server, maneuvered to lose him in the heavy traffic (Jean drove a car the way she flew our plane—by the seat of her pants) and came out to spend the day in Brentwood. On June 28, she took me out to the airport for my tearful departure for Washington, D.C. Neither Jean nor I will ever forget or forgive those responsible for that one week of our lives.

15

On **June 9, 1950,** Dalton Trumbo and John Howard Larson, the defendants in our pilot cases, were each tried and sentenced to the maximum penalty allowable, one year in prison and a $1,000 fine. They were already building time. Sam Ornitz was a frail, sickly man, but our attorneys' request to have him excused on those grounds was denied; he started serving his one-year sentence on June 30 and succeeded in surviving the ordeal, although in due time he was the first of the Ten to die. Adrian Scott had suffered severely from asthma as long as I had known him. On his doctor's testimony, he evaded imprisonment for several weeks, then followed the rest of us with the full sentence. And on June 29, the six with no special pleas or problems went through the established legal moves and motions before three different judges in three separate courtrooms. Except for the day I had been sworn in as an American citizen, it was the first time I had seen judges in action; it was an eye-opening experience—but not to the first judge.

This one listened to his assigned two defendants with closed eyes and mind; then he listened perfunctorily to the lawyers' matter-of-fact motions and handed down sentences of one year in jail and $1,000 fine to each of his victims. The second judge made no pretense of hiding his dislike for the next two offenders, nor did he apologize for his ignorance of the law. He sat sideways at his bench, looked our way only when necessary, argued with our lawyers, and had to be instructed on the law by the prosecutor. So much for political appointments. But he knew what was expected of him, and he gave each of his defendants sentences of one year and $1,000. That left Biberman and me.

We entered a third courtroom and faced a Judge Keech. Older than the others, he looked and acted as one would expect a federal judge to look and act. Like the others, he probably had his mind already made up, but he paid attention to the brief procedure and fined each of us $1,000. However, his sentence called for only six months per culprit. If I had still been lighting candles in church as I did when I was eight, I would have kept one perpetually burning in his memory. To quote the golden oldie, "What a difference a day makes, twenty-four little hours." Unless you've lived it, you can't possibly know or properly imagine what a difference 182 days can really make in a prisoner's life.

Federal bureaucracies may move slowly; the Justice Department is an occasional exception. We were handcuffed on the spot, escorted out of the building and into a police van, and driven to the District of Columbia penitentiary, a maximum-security prison. (Jean later told me she had been expecting that "one phone call" from Washington. "That's for people just arrested," I told her, "not for convicts.") There our handcuffs were removed, and we were ushered into the "tank." (Incidentally, at no time while I was in jail, either maximum security or prison camp, did any guard give me that shove on the back or the shoulder that all filmmakers treat as an obligatory feature of the prison scene. In fact, prison officials, from guards to wardens, were much more decent and polite than the congressional members of the House UnAmerican Activities Committee.)

The tank was a large, barred room, furnished with wooden benches on which twenty-five to thirty nondescript men were sitting. They paid little attention to us or to each other; their own problems were probably of more concern than the sight of six clean-shaven spiffs in suits and ties. My own conception of prison and its inmates had been based on films I had seen, and I had always assumed there was at least one menacing jailbird in every group of prisoners—another stereotype shot to hell. I was to learn that menaces existed in plenty, but they largely took shape in your own mind and your own guts. To balance the picture, however, there were indignities.

My name was called, and I was asked to surrender my personal possessions and to take off my clothes. A trusty bundled them up and carried then away. I assumed I would be getting prison garb, but I stood there in the buff until I was led into a cavernous reception space that adjoined the tank. There I was steered from one desk to another; I was fingerprinted, I answered questions, and filled out forms. The wooden chairs were startingly cold to my bare bottom, but more keenly felt was the indignity of the bare-ass promenade. How can this differ, I wondered in a hazy sort of way, from the treatment received by a Russian who questions the wisdom of Stalin or a local Red commissar? And there was more to come.

The routine was interrupted by an interesting interlude when a tall, youngish man in gray prison clothes approached the desk and identified himself. I dimly remembered him as a stand-in for the Duke in *Back to Bataan*. He was serving time for some sort of car sales scam and had been there long enough to become a trusty. He assured me that my

Odd Man Out

slightest wish was a command; anything I wanted, short of freedom, he could arrange to get. With a friendly shake of the hand and a pat on the back, he left me to carry on with his routine. I wondered how he had learned of my presence so quickly, and decided that, as rumored, the prison grapevine was truly the only thing faster than light. Through the haziness of mind that was my protective companion that afternoon, I was sorry that the only thing I could possibly want he couldn't give me.

The final rite of passage took place in a huge, sunken, wide-open shower room, where I bathed, dried off, then peppered my private parts with powdered antiseptic. When I climbed back up to the reception area, I found my own clothes waiting for me. They, too, had undergone disinfection, and they were to be my prison uniform. I had been warned of this possibility before I left Hollywood, and except for a decently tailored brown suit, I had worn only nylon because of its quick, drip-drying qualities. For the rest of my stay at the Washington penitentiary, I washed my shirt, shorts, and socks every evening in my cell. By the time I arrived at the prison camp, they were almost completely in shreds.

We had been processed separately. I remember vaguely that Maltz was in the shower room with me, but outside of that each of us was alone. My own private escort (for the moment) now led me through narrow, iron-barred passages, locked steel doors, and up metal stairways. We ended up at a short four-foot passage locked at both ends; it looked something like a porous air lock on a sci-fi spaceship. It was obviously designed to limit the rate of flow of inmates passing through. After unlocking the doors, we came out on the third tier of cellblock one—a huge, extremely high room with five tiers of cells hugging the wall on our side. The opposite wall of this room was broken by a five-story-high window of frosted glass, topped by a rose window near the ceiling. The room's open area occupied a good 80 percent of the cellblock, and part of its floor space was filled with wooden benches and tables at which the inmates ate three meals each day. The first four tiers on our side each held twelve to fourteen cells (I never got around to counting them), but the fifth tier was a bare, fenced-in area with a concrete floor, which served as a small exercise yard when the outside weather was inhospitable, or when the guards chose to keep us in our cellblock. At the far end, all five tiers were connected by a metal stairway that debouched on the ground floor.

The guard had stopped me in the air lock and had manipulated a switch or two; all the cell doors on the third tier slid open with an ungodly metallic crash. After warning the tier's occupants to stay inside, he marched me past five or six cells, stopped beside one of the open doors, and waved me inside. Cautioning the inmates once more, the guard stalked back to the entry port and pulled the door-closing switch. The gates of hell could not have been more thunderous than the sound of all the tier's steel doors crashing shut simultaneously, creating a volume of noise no tape could possibly record. Stupefied, unfocusing, I stared through the bars, convinced that I would never see Jean again. This sensation of complete and utter loneliness stayed with me until Bartley Crum came to see me two days later. But it lasted long enough to teach me the meaning of that florid phrase, "the depth of *despair*."

It was some time before I pulled myself together and turned to inspect my living quarters. Slowly, my eyes took in the six-by-eight-foot cell; a metal double-deck bunk with a pallet and a blanket apiece, a man sitting on a stool, a compact sink with one tap (cold), a small open toilet, first cousin to a boat's head—my eyes swiveled back to the man on the stool. He was a skinny, seedy character of uncertain age, wearing worn-out slacks, shirt, and shoes—no socks. Another surprise: I hadn't anticipated a "pen" pal. I was wary at first, a natural animal reaction in a foreign environment (animal reactions come easily in jail), but I soon found him to be a harmless, decent, and rather pitiable man. He had been canned two months previously for selling a bottle of "corn," and was awaiting trial. Unfortunately, this was the start of the vacation season for justice, and he would have to wait at least another three months before appearing in court. And though that was probably as long as the penalty he would get if he were found guilty, it was dead time, which, in those days, was not subtracted from the sentence. On the other hand, he might be found innocent.

I felt for the man, but I was in no position to do anything about it, except get angry. Most of the people in our great (quantitatively) middle class like to believe the purely American myth that a person is innocent until proven guilty, but that is hogwash in the halls of justice as well as in the minds of aware citizens. If you are too poor to furnish bail, you're in trouble the moment the heavy hand of the law is laid on your shoulder, innocent or not. It is a complex problem, with probably no satisfactory solution, but one should at least be honest about it. One of the average American's greatest faults as a citizen is self-deception; the belief that, ideologically, America is perfect, which is not quite true, as most of us learn the hard way from time to time.

Odd Man Out

My cellmate was a rum-dum in rather questionable physical condition. He walked with a pronounced limp. Naturally, he was nicknamed "Gimpy" or simply "the Gimp." He had a deck of cards, and for the next three weeks, we played a lot of gin. It was no different from playing with my agent or the head of a studio, but the language was cleaner.

Besides playing cards, there was little to do. I was in no mood to read books, and I avoided the daily press, which I could have gotten through my Hollywood contact, the trusty. It seemed better not to know about the world; the contrast with my present life-style could only make matters worse, and unlike Albert Maltz, I was in little doubt about who started the Korean War. When I was a very young child I had learned, out of necessity, how to adjust to almost any environment; the secret was to "go with the flow." Two days after I entered my cell, when Bartley Crum dropped in to see me and I realized there was still contact with the world and, by extension, with Jean, I started to settle in.

Seeing my lawyer was a special event. I was able to leave my cell and, led by a guard, weave my way downstairs to the legal conference area. On the way, we passed a long corridor-like room where inmates were talking with visitors. And here another stereotype I'd had of prison life bit the dust: visitors and inmates weren't sitting at counters and talking through a wire mesh, as I had so often seen on the screen, but standing on either side of a solid wall, looking at each other through small, diamond-shaped windows and talking on telephones. It seemed a little more inhumane than one would expect, but a few years later, when I shot a prison visit between Monty Clift and Hope Lange in *The Young Lions*, I used such a phone arrangement although, for dramatic reasons, I used much more glass. I believe it was the first time that sort of communication set-up was used in films, though I've seen it often since then.

Then, there was the count. It was taken six times a day, and every inmate had to be accounted for. The counts were usually taken before breakfast, at midmorning, before lunch, in midafternoon, before supper, and just before bedtime. The count was taken to make sure no one had escaped, or secreted himself for an eventual escape attempt. After the guard on duty had checked all the locked-in inmates, we waited breathlessly until the loudspeaker announced, "The count is clear!" Then things got back to the normal routine. On a few occasions, the final announcement was unaccountably delayed, and the suspense, the hope that somebody had "made it" built rapidly. But in my time, nothing that exciting happened; the count was always clear.

At another time, during a game of gin, I was startled by a loud, rhythmic, unearthly rat-a-tat-tat, a titanic paradiddle echoing eerily through our cellblock. I glanced questioningly at "the Gimp"; he waved a casual hand. In a moment, a guard walked by, bending over as he held a billy club against the lowest set of vertical bars, much like a boy would drag a stick along a picket fence (at least, where I grew up). But this sound was much more explosive and startling. My cellmate explained that was their way of checking the bars to make sure that none had been partially sawed through by some desperate convict. It seems that once in a great while they did have such a problem. Sawing through a steel bar takes a good deal of time, and between sessions the kerf would be filled with soap and colored black. That would make it invisible to a casual inspector, but the bar would not resound with a true metallic ring when struck by a bouncing nightstick. No, I've never had the occasion to use the scene in a film, but what a sound effect it would make!

The block's inmates were permitted to leave their cells four times a day—three times for meals and once for exercise or washup. Before my first meal, which was supper, my cellmate advised me to accept no more food than I was sure I could eat. I could refuse a helping, even ask a server to take back part of an over-generous dollop, but once away from the steamtable I had to "lick my platter clean." The food, served on metal plates, was passable. Spoons were dealt out to each inmate, but no knives or forks, for obvious reasons. And every spoon had to be picked up and accounted for before a single inmate could leave his table at the end of a meal. A missing spoon once kept us on our benches for an extra fifteen minutes; it was eventually found under a table. No one assumed it had been dropped by accident, because everyone knew, and I later found out, that an experienced con can turn a spoon into a lethal weapon within a matter of minutes—and you'd better believe it.

As for the first regulation: One day I was urged to notice a slight, pasty-faced prisoner, who looked like a teenager. In whispers (talking was not allowed at meals), I was told he had just finished spending twenty-four days "in the hole" for some infraction of prison rules. This was his first day up in the relative sunlight. Toward the end of the meal, there was a commotion at his table; a guard was leaning over him, exhorting him to finish the gristly stuff on his plate. Silent, but adamant, he refused. The guard called for help, but help couldn't budge the kid. In the end, he was picked up and taken back to solitary confinement. It seemed a very costly and futile exercise in rebellion, but he had beaten the minions of society, which was his enemy, and he had done it in the presence of those who envied his will. It was probably the only kind of victory he knew he could win, but he had established his place in his world.

Twice a week, we showered and shaved, and once or twice each week, depending on the weather, we were herded out into a large yard for about an hour, where we would walk, meet acquaintances, smoke, and talk. The yard couldn't accommodate all the prison's population at any one session, but Maltz, the only one of the Ten in my cellblock, and I did run into our colleagues on one or two occasions. During inclement weather our cellblock was given the freedom of the fifth tier. Many of the inmates smoked, some gambled for cigarettes, and others, including Maltz and me, would pace the length of the concrete floor, striding back and forth until we were recalled to our cells.

During one of our indoor exercise periods, Maltz confessed to being troubled. The Korean War had erupted on June 25, four days before we were imprisoned. Here it was, at least a week later, and he still didn't know who had started the war. The war was the farthest thing from my mind, and I was surprised by his concern. I pointed out what everybody had been able to read in the press on June 26 and every day since; the North Koreans had invaded South Korea, taking the South Koreans and the Americans by surprise. Maltz pooh-poohed the information; he had, of course, read those accounts but who, he asked, could trust the capitalist press? The only information he would believe must come from Moscow. And it soon did. Maltz had a visit from one of our New York lawyers, a party member, and he was finally able to pass on the party line: The Americans and the South Koreans had invaded the North, and that "democratic" country was only striking back—somewhere deep in South Korea. Maltz could now sleep better, and so could I. I was more certain than ever of the divergent path I had chosen. Maltz's reliance on Moscow's word was becoming downright ludicrous.

On another day, as we paced the fifth-tier floor, we noticed a tall, pleasant-looking young man clinging to the chain-link fencing that caged the tier. He seemed to be looking out through a broken pane in the rose window on the far wall. We made several turns on the floor, and he was still at his position. I was curious.

"What are you looking for?" I asked.

"My family." He couldn't have been in long enough to be prison-simple, so I decided to watch with him. The view through the broken window disclosed a small segment of a street that bordered the penitentiary grounds; it was at least a hundred yards away. But sure enough, in a little while a car pulled up at the curb, a young woman got out, helped a girl of three or four down to the sidewalk, then reached in and brought out a baby. Carrying the infant in one arm and pulling the little girl by the hand, she walked back and forth a few paces past each end of the car. They didn't look in our direction; they probably didn't know just where the husband/father was. Instead, they just walked up and down the street. And on tier five, their husband/father was crying, and so was I. I didn't know why the man was in jail, and my only words of comfort were, "Why did you do it, you son-of-a-bitch! Why did you do it?"

Why and for what? For those who might care, the "why" was that he was out of work. The "what" was that he tried to hold up a liquor store. Halfway in, he lost his nerve, turned, and ran right into the arms of a policeman. He was charged with attempted armed robbery, and unless, come autumn, he was lucky enough to face a judge like Keech, he was in for a hefty stretch—in a block where he couldn't see his family through a broken window.

One other aspect of those dreary days impacted my film-trained mind. Bedtime was nine o'clock sharp, and lights were turned off at that hour, except for one or two that beamed down from the ceiling. They gave the cavernous room a soft, highly contrasting texture that would have delighted the eye of any good film noir cameraman. It was spooky—a mood that was helped by the dead silence of the cells. That was a hard and fast rule: no talking after lights out. However, there are always a few who can't sleep. And as for rules, if there is anything a man learns in prison, it is, "What can they do to me that they aren't already doing?"—which bit of jail wisdom led to an experience imprinted so thoroughly on my mind that I can picture it in full Technicolor to this day.

His accent was southern black, and his clear tones echoed eerily through space, as a man on the third tier started talking in a sing-song voice.

"Hey, Joe, I got the all-American band." Another tier, and another voice.

"I hear you, man." A pause.

Odd Man Out

"Ol' Satchmo on the trumpet."

"Yeah, man."

"How 'bout Jess Stacy on the piano?" No ethnic bias here.

"I hear you, man."

"Barney Bigard on the stick."

"I hear you, brother."

"An' Big Sid Catlett on the drums."

"Yeah, yeah, yeah!"

And so it went, pure lyricism in a primeval world. But there is always a serpent in paradise.

I saw the fingers of his hand crawl like a squid's tentacles on the outside edge of my cell. In a moment, the guard slithered quietly past my door and stopped at the other side of my the cell, preparing for his next move. Then he disappeared. A few held breaths later, I heard his triumphant semihysterical cry, "Gotcha! I gotcha!" Several seconds went by; the doors crashed open, and with a black man in tow, the guard walked grinning past my cell on the way to the hole. The doors crashed shut.

I am a jazz buff. I hated to see him go.

Contempt of Congress is only a misdemeanor and calls for incarceration in a minimum-security facility. We were in the Washington penitentiary only to be processed, which is why we had to wear our own clothes, but this time the Justice Department had disappointed me. It took them eighteen days to do the job, and those days were material. A prison camp awards more "good time" than a maximum-security jail, and each week in Washington cost us another day or two. But what's a few extra days in prison to the attorney general of the United States?

The federal authorities must have feared the Ten together might start a revolution, because they split us up into pairs. Maltz and I were being transferred to the prison camp at Mill Point, West Virginia; we were fitted with leg irons, handcuffs, and chained to each other. We clanked as we crawled into the back seat of an unmarked police sedan. The front seat held the driver and a guard.

About two hours out of Washington, we had to take a leak. The driver pulled the car to the side of the road, climbed out, and drew his revolver while the guard unlocked our leg irons. Still chained together, we lumbered over to some roadside bushes and unzipped our pants. I pictured myself driving by and seeing this tableau; a couple of hardened criminals, I would have thought.

I had to laugh.

16

West Virginia is an attractive state. Its mountains are especially beautiful, their thick, green forests encompassing, yet friendly. On this day, in mid-July, they were also cool, and looked deceptively free. We had been traveling through backcountry for some time, and as we rounded a curve, we could see a collective that included a sawmill, complete with a flume, piles of logs, stacks of rough-sawed lumber, and a number of one-story buildings surrounding several barracks. The settlement reminded me of the CCC camps I had seen during the depression era.

"Mill Point," announced the guard. I was confused.

"The town?" I asked.

"The prison camp."

It required some adjustment. I could see a few men working in the sawmill yard, but no uniformed guards. And where were the watchtowers and the walls? I decided the guard was kidding me.

"Where are the fences?" I asked.

"Don't need none," said the guard. "You can get out, but there ain't no place to go."

I worried the thought as the car turned into a gravel drive and pulled up before a sprawling, one-story, wooden building. Stretching toward the hills on the other side of the driveway was a row of brown, bungalow-type cottages, which, I later learned, were the homes of the warden, the guards, and their families. The houses faced an expanse of lawn badly in need of cutting.

We were helped out of the car, and our fetters were removed as if, indeed, our physical freedom was no longer a threat. We were conducted into the building that contained what appeared to be the prison's headquarters and turned over to the officer in charge. The several offices seemed to be staffed largely by trusties. After a short wait, we were launched into the now-familiar processing procedure. At the routine's finale, our pictures were taken by a tall, friendly, black trusty, and the placard he pinned to my chest for the sitting identified me as number 3568. Somewhere along the line, we were given the obligatory short lecture on the proper institutional behavior and told if we followed the rules, there was nothing to fear. I hadn't seen anything that might be scary if we *didn't* follow the rules, but in any event, I didn't feel rebellious that day.

Odd Man Out

Outside of the office workers, we had seen few signs of life; like the Washington court system, the camp seemed on vacation. We were led out of the barracks side of the office building, marched thirty or forty yards along a wide, empty parkway, and dropped off at quarantine. This small building contained eight double-deck bunk beds packed tightly together, and an open shower and toilet. Later, as I became a more experienced "con," I realized that the naked openness of the showers and toilets was designed to discourage lingering and misbehavior and to protect inmates from unwelcome molestation more than to destroy any sense of dignity. It did a good job at both.

At quarantine, we were turned over to another guard, a medic. (We found out in time he was an ex–army sergeant and an alcoholic who knew nothing about medicine.) Once more, we stripped, showered, and dried off. Then, because the camp mistrusted us and the hygienic procedure at the capital, the medic sprayed our private parts with an antiseptic powder.

So far, the procedure had been a shorter, cozier version of the experience in the Washington jail, with one element added—we had an onstage audience. A few days before our arrival, the camp had received five or six hillbillies; they were still in quarantine. A dead-accurate takeoff on the mountain folk in the *New Yorker* cartoons, though more menacing, they slouched in a tight group against a double bunk about eight feet from the shower, and watched the medic do his thing. In time, these men turned out to be human beings. But on this day, their slack-mouthed, unblinking, dead-eyed stares showed no spark of friendship. I almost wished for the security of a prison cell.

The Mill Point Federal Prison was a working minimum-security facility; there were no fences, and the guards weren't armed. The inmates felled oak and walnut trees in the surrounding woods. The native hardwood was sawed into large planks at the camp sawmill and sold on the open market. The officials boasted that it was the only federal penal institution to turn a profit, and that was probably true. The camp population fluctuated between three hundred and four hundred inmates, two-thirds of whom were black. Aside from a few figures of national notoriety, like Howard Fast, Maltz, and me, most of the inmates were locals, serving short sentences of from three months to two years. Although it was not its main purpose, the camp also served as a halfway house for a few hardened criminals preparing to enter society. One man, who became a friend, was completing a ten-year sentence for homicide.

The camp's white inmates were mostly hillbillies who were doing time for distilling or selling booze, or both. At least half of the total population was completely illiterate, men barely able to make their marks when they signed for cigarettes, tobacco, candy, or other allowables they bought on semiweekly visits to the canteen. (I never learned how one could legally distinguish one X from another.) The camp was only partially segregated; the blacks occupied two dormitories, as did the whites, and the races were also kept to their sections of the mess hall. But there, discrimination stopped. On work detail and in recreational activities, there was total integration. (Remember, we're talking 1950.) Although there were occasional fights in the camp, those, too, were segregated. I never saw the slightest sign of trouble between whites and blacks.

The most noticeable segregation was that of class, not race; it was the sharp division between the hillbillies and the slightly more sophisticated urban types, and I don't remember seeing the former participate in the baseball games we played on long summer nights and on the weekends. Fast-pitch softball was the camp's favorite sport; we even played against visiting teams from some of the nearby towns, and usually did well. One of our stars had been given a tryout in the majors, and two or three could have made any semi-pro club. For those who couldn't rough it on the gravelly diamond, or when the evenings grew short on visibility, chess and checkers were the games of choice. At that time, TV was beyond the facility's budget.

Once in a great while, there was a film, but that was a budgetary sacrifice. The warden told me the prison received about 70 cents per inmate per day, for food, clothing, and recreation, and even in 1950, that was chicken feed. To eke out the budget, the camp grew many of its own vegetables, canning some for winter use. It raised chickens for eggs and occasional dinners and pigs for pork that was served only on high holidays such as the Fourth of July and Thanksgiving. It also worked its own strip mine for coal in the fall and winter.

The seasonal labor requirements were filled serendipitously. It seems that in spring and summer, local crimes were committed largely by men with green thumbs, while lawbreaking in fall and winter was monopolized by men with heavily calloused hands. The prison's luck spilled over into other areas. I remember a conversation with the man who operated the mill's buzz saw, which ripped raw logs into rough lumber. It is a job that requires skill and caution, and there were just two men with the necessary experience; one was black, the other white. Fortunately, they never served their sentences simultaneously. The white inmate who was currently on the job had done time at Mill Point on a number of occasions.

"You know," he said dryly, "I've been here a lot and I usually know what I'm in for, but this time I ain't got clue what I did wrong."

Be that as it may, the two men had been alternating for several years, and the mill had yet to chalk up any dead time.

Some of my fellow inmates were winos, often taking self-imposed cures. From these, I learned of an economic strategem that helped support another segment of our society. When I mention Mill Point's local population, I am referring to men from areas in Kentucky, Tennessee, Virginia, West Virginia, Ohio, and Pennsylvania; hillbilly country covers a lot of ground. Most of these states employed magistrates to hear and sentence petty offenders. (I believe the practice still persists in many localities.) Some of these low-ranking judicial officers were paid on a piecework basis; each joker sent to jail earned the magistrate about $15. For a dead-broke rum-dum badly in need of a drink, the last resort was a justice of the peace who could lend him two bucks, the price of a jug of cheap wine. The only condition of the loan was that the wino report to the magistrate when he was able to walk again. He would then be sentenced to jail for drunkenness, usually for a term of ninety days, and the magistrate would collect $15. Fifteen minus two equals thirteen, a very good return on such a short-term loan.

And if that makes you feel that some of the citizens of this great nation of ours aren't getting a fair deal, let me remind you that we have it on the highest authority that every man and woman in the country can get a job that pays well enough to enable him or her to live a life of decency and quality, that is, if he or she really wants to—which brings me to the subject of prison myths.

It is common knowledge that most, if not all prisoners claim to be in on a bum rap. Yet I have never talked to a man in my short stay in the Washington jail or my longer time at Mill Point who didn't admit his crime. Many took a quiet pride in it. Of course, they all rationalized their sins, justifying them on the ground that lots of people have done things equally wrong, but they had been lucky enough to escape getting caught. And they were not far off the mark. Our warden, K. E. Thieman, remarked that criminologists concede that almost every person in the country would probably serve some time in jail if our hundreds of thousands of laws were strictly enforced. Even the hermit who shuns society and the freeways is probably trespassing on private property as he wends his way to the cave he calls home.

Under present conditions and attitudes, rehabilitation is another pipe dream, equivalent to our delusion that we can get the drug dealer off the streets without giving him the opportunity to make a living legitimately. The percentage of prisoners who will volunteer to learn a trade and agree to practice it on their release is exceedingly small. Of all the prisoners I talked futures with, only the murderer vowed he would never return to crime after he hit the streets. A friendly con man (and aren't they all?) who worked beside me during my first weeks in prison spent all his time perfecting an improved sting. Although he had been arrested and sentenced numerous times in the past, we all knew his talent for sweet talk would assure his release at the prison's next parole session. And it did. We also knew, because he had told us, that he would immediately start work with his new version of the old scam. To him, a prison sentence was a sabbatical.

The man who slept in the bunk below mine, with whom I spent many evenings in conversation, assured me he would return to selling drugs. But the next time, he would go into business for himself; he would never again take the rap for his boss. I asked him if he wasn't ashamed to sell heroin to junkies?

"Ashamed!" He was astounded. "Why should I be ashamed? I am a benefactor. Have you ever seen a guy who is dying for a fix? Have you any idea how he suffers? For just a few bucks I give him relief from pain. Ashamed? I deserve a medal—not this purgatory!"

And he sincerely meant it.

Some of the hillbillies were not that unselfish. A tall, spare man bearing the good old mountain name of Jeeter was one of the few pleasant-faced hillbillies in the institution. He was spending a fifth hitch at Mill Point, this time accompanied by his son. He was always welcome here—he was our best chain saw operator.

"Hell!" he said. "After I'm out I want just enough time to cook a couple hundred gallons. I'll sell a hundred and drink the rest. Then they can come and get me."

He too sincerely meant it. But with a chuckle.

After talking to him and listening to others like him talk about each other, I came away from that alien land with the impression that at least some of them were periodically turned in by their wives to get them off their backs. The wives also received the greater share of their husbands' prison earnings, which, though small, was more certain and the source of fewer personal demands than what they received when their husbands were home.

One hears a great deal about prison homosexuality. In Washington, I had not known any hard-core, long-term convicts, so I can say nothing about their sexual habits or behavior. At Mill Point, there were three or four youthful types who kept their own company, which included the visiting chaplain, a divinity student from Duke, and a gay man. He rewarded his disciples with an occasional trip into town; nobody censured them, nor as far as I knew, did anyone envy them. As for the others, the only example I can offer is my own. When I left home for prison, my mind automatically rejected any thoughts of sex, and it continued to do so until shortly before I got out—but that is another story. At the Washington maximum-security prison and at Mill Point, I felt absolutely no sexual urge; it was never on my mind and it never entered into my conversation. Nor can I recall any such talk from any of the others—except from one of the officers who was always guardedly on the make and, as far as I knew, getting nowhere. As for the inmates, their most vulgar jokes were scatalogical, not sexual. I believe celibacy is a practice (or nonpractice) many inmates can assume, at least those who know they have a short, finite time to wait.

Maltz and I remained in quarantine for two weeks. During that time, we were assigned a variety of jobs; we mowed the extensive lawn near the guards' cottages, peeled potatoes, plucked chickens, and skinned boiled beets for several hundred inmates. For three or four days, we shoveled sand at the homemade filtration plant that purified the camp water system. Howard Fast, who had arrived at the camp two weeks before us to serve a three-month sentence for contempt of Congress in a case involving the Joint Anti-Fascist Refugee Committee, stopped by after completing his garbage-collecting duties for a quick hello; longer contact during quarantine was discouraged.

The camp's offices were staffed largely by trusties, and our personal statistics were soon camp property. The inmates regarded us with casual interest, but the guards eyed us with a mixture of awe and suspicion. They knew I had earned more in two weeks than they earned in a year; on top of that, they were afraid we might be intellectuals. Some of them had had trouble during the war with interned conscientious objectors who were in the habit of belying their philosophy of nonbelligerence by breaking up everything available. When the guards discovered we were relatively unpretentious, willing to attack any chore without complaint, and not inclined to disruption or destruction, their attitudes, with one or two exceptions, changed. A few became friends. On the whole, quarantine was far more valuable as a means of insinuating us into the prison population than in protecting us from exotic diseases.

Discharge from quarantine meant assignment to long-term duties, and we were asked our preferences in the matter. The camp's attempt at education was half-hearted, not because the administration wasn't willing to try, but because the inmates weren't. However, Maltz and I both indicated a preference for teaching. In answer, we got a peek into the Federal Prison Administration's mode of reasoning. Howard Fast was one of America's good writers. A colleague who came to prison with him on the same charge was a professor of Germanic languages at NYU. Maltz was a writer of some note, and I was a good speller. No one else at camp could claim equal credentials. Yet none of us was assigned to teach the pitifully few illiterates who opted for self-improvement. It seemed the Washington administration's fear of possible indoctrination was stronger than their desire for rehabilitation.

Maltz drew duty as an orderly at the tiny four-bed camp hospital, a position for which he was well qualified; he was a godsend to the ailing. The medic was happy to limit his own contributions to signing requisitions while leaving the medical chores to Albert. I was asked to replace the soon-to-be-released garage clerk, an elderly corporation finance executive who was completing a two-year term for fraud. Since the camp's industry relied heavily on transportation, the garage served as a sort of camp action center. My duties consisted of opening up the "carbarn" at six o'clock every morning except Sunday, handing out the keys to the drivers of the forty or fifty cars and trucks used in the camp's lumbering operations, ordering replacement parts for all the vehicles, including tractors and bulldozers, when needed, servicing and fueling the work fleet and the passenger cars used by the prison staff, then refueling and parking all the vehicles as they were brought in after the day's work was finished. I also kept the garage records and helped with the servicing and repairs when an extra hand was called for. With the exception of Maltz, who was on call twenty-four hours a day, my workday was longer than that of any other prisoner, a circumstance that allowed me certain privileges. I ate my meals when it was convenient, and I was excused from the daily counts. Along with the night guards and Albert, I could visit the mess hall after hours for a doughnut, a cup of coffee, and some conversation about events of the day both in prison and in the outside world. The guards, at least, did read the daily press.

Maltz slept in the hospital, and I was assigned a bunk in the white barracks. Prison life was now becoming an established routine. In the normal street sense, the only cruel and unjust punishment I suffered was being jarred awake at 5:30 each morning by the cheery voice of a sadistic guard. But there is a variety of punishments.

17

"It's a *beautiful* **morning** on Cranberry Mountain!"[7] Whether it was raining torrents, bitter cold, or dark as the hidden regions of hell, that phrase, delivered by our resident psychologist (?) over the camp loudspeakers in ridiculously cheerful tones, awakened us each morning to the reality of a deadly routine. Question: "What makes this day different from the other day?" Answer: "Not one damned thing!"

Still, life at Mill Point was not necessarily as immutable as that inane wake-up call. In the absence of any kind of creative endeavor, and in the effort to avoid idle time spent in self-pity, I was able to fill in the slack hours learning how to operate tractors, bulldozers, and the great variety of small and large trucks I parked every evening. I also learned how to weld; how to build a working still, complete with "thumper keg," an art that I have had no opportunity to cash in on; how to deice a frozen lock at six o'clock on a snowy morning; and how to transform a wood rasp into a first-class knife. Knives, and stills, were plentiful in jail; it was impossible to eliminate them. The guards could shake down the entire prison and confiscate dozens of knives, but within a few weeks, these would be back in full supply. I also learned that the safest place to stash a shiv was inside the double layer of cloth that constitutes the trouser's fly. Guards never touched that part of the anatomy for fear of being accused of homosexual advances, a cause for dismissal—or so the inmates wanted to believe. Although I doubted the guards would behave with such delicate concern, I never had the occasion to test the hypothesis.

As for the stills, at one time there were five in operation on or near the premises, all apparently unknown to the staff. Just before my release, one was found under the kitchen floor. It distilled alcohol out of the fruit juices that were surreptitiously skimmed whenever we had canned fruit for dessert, which was quite often.

In the evenings, a few of us usually assembled for chess—Maltz, Fast, the prison photographer, the convicted murderer, and I. I often wondered about Fast's colleague, the professor from NYU. He remained aloof from us and from the rest of the inmates. (Fast maintains they were very close, but I never saw the two together, day or night). Obviously, it

7. Cranberry Mountain was a small hill behind the prison camp.

could have been called a partial withdrawal, either psychological or political—perhaps a little of each. But since he performed his daily duties without complaint, I assumed that it was chiefly political and that he was probably in the same position in which I found myself; both Fast and Maltz were confirmed communists and hardly the men to discuss doubts with (although Fast renounced communism in 1956 after Khrushchev confirmed the slaughter of millions of dissidents under Stalin). You could get confirmation from these two creed-bound men but not impartial examination. During our brief discussion in Washington concerning the start of the Korean War, Maltz had nearly turned apopletic when I questioned the Comintern line. I had made up my mind then to keep my own counsel. As for Fast, his desire to win new recruits for the Party led him to tempt our black photographer friend with strange bait; he assured him that blacks were better than whites. The backfire lost Fast a convert.

"He must think I'm stupid to think I'd accept that crap as something he really believes!" the photographer told me.

The naïveté of ploys such as Fast's no longer surprised me. Blind belief can do strange things to the most intelligent men and women. And ideological reassessment is a trying procedure. The NYU professor avoided our company because he had probably not yet reached my stage of rethinking, or perhaps he was far beyond it. At any rate, he was not up to assuming those necessary pretenses that Maltz, in a later assessment of my attitude, called "devious."

Because of my long working days, I had persuaded the warden to allow me a free hour at the primitive gym during the slack period of early afternoon. I had worked out with barbells since I was fourteen, and I used the time for weight-lifting exercises. I also organized and taught an evening weight-lifting class, attended by three other inmates. One of my black students, who had a muscular body to begin with, quickly developed into a first-class lifter. I have often wondered if he carried on after I left.

A second member of the class was Fast's friend, a thirtyish man who was completing his sentence for murder. He had been a seaman in the merchant marine during the war. In a North African port, a fellow sailor had attacked him with a knife. He had wrenched the weapon from his assailant's hand and had killed him in self-defense. Although the truth of his testimony was confirmed by a number of witnesses, a military court ruled he had defended himself with too much vigor and had decreed a ten-year sentence, probably for manslaughter. As is customary in military decisions, there was no possibility for parole. With accrued "good time," he was finally released in the fall of 1950. He was luckier than most. On Fast's recommendation, he was reporting for a job at a publishing house in Boston.

Legally, an inmate can leave prison immediately after midnight on the day of release; in practice, he is usually let out after the camp awakens in the morning to minimize disruption of the day's routine. In this instance, the warden had agreed to discharge our friend at midnight, and he allowed Fast, Maltz, and me to stay with him until his departure. As usual with the warden, it was a wise decision. Long before "the witching hour," and in spite of our attempts to get his mind off his immediate future, this man with enough guts to face an armed sailor was a sweating and shivering mess. It was hard to guess what he might have done if left alone, but by the time he walked out a free man, he was ready to commit another murder to avoid going out "into the streets."

"Into the streets." That apt convict's phrase is not exactly a happy reference to freedom. Its specific significance depends upon the convict's prison history. According to most old hands, about two years is all a person can take before going stir-crazy or becoming prison-simple. I was familiar with the first expression, but the second was new to me. When the difference between the two conditions was explained, I could see examples of each on all sides.

The stir-crazy prisoner becomes psychotically irritable and rebellious; the prison-simple inmate retreats into a state of quasi-idiocy. It is this second type who is most commonly a recidivist. In prison, he feels protected; in the streets, he is terrified. An elderly kitchen worker had the most benign temperament I had seen at Mill Point. He was released while I was still in residence. Mr. Balzer, a fatherly guard with whom I frequently talked at snack time, assured me that the discharged con would be back within a week. He overestimated by three days. The kindly man, terrified by the outside world, had used a knife to attack a stranger in the streets. He hadn't cut his apparent victim, but he got his wish: a quick return to the kitchen detail at Mill Point.

To some extent, I also experienced the feeling of security. I had long suffered from the film directors' occupational disease—an irritable stomach. It had never become ulcerous, but dyspepsia can be extremely painful, and I had always kept a roll of Tums n my pocket. When I learned they were banned in jail, I dreaded the prospect of doing without them. To my physical and mental relief, I experienced not one moment of heartburn throughout my months in prison. I almost felt guilty. I had often said my incarceration would be harder on Jean than on me, and at least in one way, I was proving it. But it was quite logical. In prison, I had not one decision of substance to make, hence nothing to worry about. It would appear that freedom is more conducive to gas on the stomach than is captivity.

I realize that much of what I have written sounds like a vacation at a working dude ranch where reformed dilettantes pay for the privilege of stacking hay and feeding the stock, but the inescapable punitive features of life in prison are nearly impossible to describe. They are essentially psychological and self-inflictive and made manifest largely through action or reaction. I first became conscious of one of them while playing chess with Fast. His game, to put it gently, was adventurous; he took far too many chances. Early in the game, Howard made a move that would have delighted a sane opponent—but not me. To my own surprise, I reacted violently, overturned the chessboard, and uttered a few choice expletives. Because *he* had made a silly move that guaranteed an easy win for me, *I* was on the point of commiting mayhem, and I stalked angrily out of the room. I paced in the cool night air and tried to analyze my emotions. I soon realized that however benign the prison's staff, however lenient the conditions of imprisonment, it was impossible to anticipate or to understand the feelings of despair, of lost hopes, of irreplaceable days and nights with loved ones, and nearly as impossible to repress the maniacal irritability that confinement, especially open confinement, where fenceless boundaries are a constant temptation, inevitably brings.

The warden, Thieman, an experienced and compassionate man, understood the last condition. Because, in a way, he was as imprisoned as I was, he probably felt its spurs, and he tried to protect his charges against additional irritation from the outside. One day, to my surprise, he called me into his office, chatted casually for a few minutes, then handed me a newspaper clipping. I could feel his eyes on me as I read it. It was a Winchell column, and that asinine, self-proclaimed tsar of American public opinion had reported that Jean Porter Dmytryk was filing for a divorce. (Later, I realized that in Winchell's untidy mind, one member of the Hollywood Ten was equivalent to another. I believe it was about the time that Ann Shirley Scott was divorcing Adrian.) Obviously, the warden knew less about the mistakes and excesses of journalists than I did, and he certainly didn't know Jean. He was concerned that if I first heard this startling news from some other source, I might try something rash, like escaping from prison. In this instance, I felt more secure than he did. I assured him I had the utmost faith in my wife, and he decided to believe me. He allowed me a few more minutes to persuade him to share my jaundiced view of the press, then sent me back to work.

Alone at the garage, I didn't feel nearly as secure as I had in Thieman's office. The waits between Jean's letters were, at best, periods of impatient expectancy. For the first time, my impatience was laced with a growing sense of doubt. Could I be sure? However, Jean's next letter, and the next, recounted only her daily activities along with glowing reports of our son. I was back to seeing it through.

Sometime later Thieman was neither concerned nor careful when he called me in to tell me I had won the First Masterpiece Award at Venice for *Give Us This Day*. K. E. Thieman and Arthur Rank, two men professionaly and financially poles apart, yet so similar in their understanding, tolerance, and compassion. If such qualities were more accessible in more people, this tattered world might be made whole.

Outside of the uncommon psychological distress and aggravation that confinement brings, life at Mill Point was not always a battle with monotony. On rereading some letters I had written to Jean while in jail, I was reminded that I commented on a meal I had enjoyed, and I wasn't trying to flatter the chef. But besides a decent regard for the inmates' stomachs, there were moments of action, of drama, and of suspense; if one could find the will to test the razor's edge, jail was a huge stewpot of experience. First, the action.

Fighting at the camp was uncommon, since it could easily become a killing. Most fights were quickly broken up by the nearest neutrals before they got the guards' attention, lest the participants suffer a return to maximum security or the loss of good time. In one bizarre instance, a rather frail, harmless, middle-aged black, the master of the chicken coops and the pigsty, whose irritability quotient must have climbed into the red, senselessly attacked Clean-head, the prison's most formidable inmate. Clean-head was the camp's Mr. T, but taller, stronger, and minus the Iroquoian hairdo—he was totally real. The little man carried a long steel pry-bar, which must have given him a false sense of invincibility. He swung at Clean-head's bald pate, and the big man caught the bar as if it were a pussywillow wand, tossed it aside, and set about strangling his hapless opponent.

It took a full squad of black inmates to pry him loose. (Since prison teaches the value of common sense, no whites got involved in the scrimmage.) But the scuffle had lasted long enough to attract the attention of several guards who could hardly take it lightly. The camp had no barred facility, and Clean-head was taken to jail in the nearby town of Mill Point. I never saw him again, though he may have returned after my release. The baseball team missed him; he was our leading home-run hitter.

Now for the suspense: Late one Saturday night I almost had to fight a battle of my own. Mill Point is situated in the middle of a number of states that share a love of things classical, like the Grand Ol' Opry. In hillbilly country, the show was aired for its full four hours! To accommodate the local aficionados, the loudspeakers, one of which was just a foot above my pillow, ran full blast until 11:00 P.M., the show's sign-off time. I had had a very full day and was trying to get some sleep but "If you got the money, honey, I've got the time . . ." was splitting my skull. I reached up and turned off the speaker. In less than ten seconds, a young hillbilly who occupied a bed across the room climbed up on my bunk and turned it back on. As he walked away, I switched the speaker off a second time. He stopped, turned, and took a step in my direction, glaring ominously. I glared right back. He decided not to choose me, which was a relief because most inmates carried knives. But the Opry continued to blare its arias from the other speakers in the room. I am aware the music probably made the young man's stay at the camp a trifle more sufferable, but I've never been able to tolerate country music since my stay in West Virginia.

There were, of course, more unsavory incidents from time to time, but the more dramatic, even tragic, the prisoner's situation, the greater the need for comedy. Most especially in prison, humor is an antidote for depression; the more nearly one cancels out the other, the greater the chances of winnowing some good out of the bad and making the "building" of time a constructive operation. And so we were lucky one day to have a fire drill that Buster Keaton could have made into a masterpiece.

When the whistle tootled its short, sharp blasts, I paid little attention. Then Mr. Farmer, an ace mechanic who doubled as the garage guard, informed me that the garage clerk was also the camp's fire chief, and that the small building next door, the one with the rusted lock and the unyielding hinges, housed the fire engine. I adjusted to the call of command more quickly than General Haig, and assumed I had to get into the station to retrieve the fire equipment. But where was the key? My two assistants and I scrambled wildly through the garage and my office—I could picture the camp going up in flames—and we finally found a stray key whose patina of rust matched that of the lock on the firehouse door. A few generous squirts of oil on lock and key, some careful pressure on the tumblers, a final yank, and it worked. The doors screeched open, and I discovered why they had been so securely locked. Inside was a treasure, an exhibit for the Smithsonian, at least. Under layers of dust, on solid rubber tires that couldn't go flat, sat a pre-1920 fire engine, a relic from the days of the Toonerville Trolley. (If it's still at Mill Point, it's worth more than the camp and all its timber.)

The urgent whistle brought us back to earth. We jumped onto the engine and jumped right off again. The battery was dead. With the garage next door, that was no problem, but it did take time, and somewhere a fire was raging. Once more back on board, we cruised the grounds like a troop of Mack Sennet's cops—with the camp's few spectators urging us on in all directions. Finally, near the sawmill, we found the small bonfire that Balzer had set. It was nearly out, but we leaped off the truck, grabbed fire extinguishers, and started spraying. Nothing. The extinguishers were bone-dry, as was the engine's water tank. Undaunted, we stamped out the fire with our boots. The camp was safe.

For the next few days we scraped, scrubbed, washed, cleaned, and polished. The fire engine and the newly filled extinguishers blinded us with their brilliance. And everything was functional, including the battery. Then I backed the fire engine into its garage, locked the door, and tossed the key into the back of the most heavily stuffed drawer in my desk. When I left the prison I didn't tell my successor about the fire engine, his duties as the fire chief, or the key's hiding place. I hoped that he, too, could appreciate a little fun.

Since then, I have hypothesized that the keepers of the keys may have set the whole thing up as a psychological safety valve, but—the Federal Prison Administration? Naah!

In real life, such an unusual occurrence would serve to mark the passage of time, but not in prison. In prison, it is not the happening, but the hours, the days, the years, that count. Here, even more than in the physicist's or philosopher's classrooms, those are the elements of another real dimension. Inmates, with an accuracy based on experience, call it "building time," and the daily greetings are not "Hi," "Hello," or "How are you?" which bespeak the present time, but a query indicative of continuty: "How're you buildin' it?" And the question implicitly concerns the health of your morale, and of the state of your mind in its permutations. The question is much more to the point than is the free person's casual greeting.

A con may not know his friends' ages, birthplaces, or religions, but he will know as much about his friends' time as he does about his own. It was not uncommon for the driver of a lumber truck, coming in for gas, to shout, "Hey, Dmytryk—two months and nine days, right?"

"Right! And yours is one year, three months, and seventeen days. How're you makin' it?'

"No sweat."

The answer had a literal meaning. We never discussed time philo-sophically, but we all developed similar techniques for greasing its pas-sage. Example: We got clean laundry twice a week; when I picked up mine, my reaction was automatic. "Thirty more laundry days," I said to myself. "Thirty more!" Sunday was special—it carried a bundle of seven days: "Fifteen more Sundays—fifteen more!" Ah, but the full moon was a huge bale of twenty-eight days, and you could watch it grow: "Just three more full moons—only three more!" It worked to make time pass a little more quickly. It worked too well. Forty-four years in the streets and I still find myself counting full moons. To what . . .?

18

The one certain thing in life is death; for most cons, the second is release from prison. Unless the reaper chooses to assert his prerogative, once in, you must come out. With some exceptions, that is a prisoner's most eagerly anticipated day—the day when his only meaningful project is complete; time has been built. I was lucky. Because of an accident (?) of assignment, I had two days of happy anticipation; the day of my release and, before that, the day Jean came to visit.

I would like to correct myself; there *was* a real, a glaring, instance of cruel and unusual punishment on the part of the Federal Prison Administration, a punishment that extended, in all its calculated cruelty, to our innocent wives and families. With only two exceptions, all of the Hollywood Ten were sequestered east of the Mississippi. The two exceptions sweated out their time in Texas, which was hardly an improvement. There were, of course, federal prison camps in the West, including one, at Lompoc, California, which is within 150 miles of Hollywood, and visits from wives and relatives would have been no problem. But for those in our financial straits, a cross-country trip was extremely difficult and prohibitively expensive. I could never see any real purpose for the FPA's choice of prisons except as a small, mean act of some sort of patriotic vengeance, far beyond the bounds of humane penalization. It is ironic, but the smaller and meaner the unkindness, the longer it is remembered and the more difficult it is to forgive. My gorge still rises in anger when a chance word or sign brings that particular aspect of my imprisonment to mind.

Through our letters, Jean and I decided that only one visit was affordable, and it should take place about midterm. Jean first considered coming by bus, but when Margaret Maltz agreed to visit Albert at the same time, Jean found the means to come by air. Toward the end of August, they flew to Charleston, West Virginia, shared a room in a motel that night, and drove to Mill Point the next morning in a rental car. They arrived at the prison about noon. Thieman provided an unused office as a meeting place and allowed us the whole afternoon for the visit. However, it was hot that day, and we spent most of our hours in a little outdoor patio.

What does one do at such a rare time and under such unusual conditions? We cried a little, smiled a lot, kissed a good deal, and occasionally bubbled with laughter at the happiness of being together. Jean told me of our son's rapid development, and we made plans for the future, plans that could be realized, plans that were very different from those that Margaret and Albert, murmuring together across the patio, might have suspected.

Jean and I had tentatively discussed our possibilities before I left Hollywood, but two months of undisturbed thinking showed me the light, and a positive decision could not now be postponed. My "comrades'" proclamations of carrying the torch for freedom of speech and thought were proven frauds, and it became obvious the Ten had been sacrificed to the Party's purpose as a pipeline for the Comintern's propaganda. If it so pleased them, the other nine could wear hair shirts, but if I were going to be a martyr, I wanted the privilege of choosing my martyrdom, and making my family suffer to protect the American representatives of a foreign agency would certainly not be it.

I wanted out!—certainly not out of jail, since my sentence had only two months to run, but out of my *real* imprisonment, my association with the Hollywood Ten and, by extension, my publicly perceived ties with the Communist Party. In 1945, I had tried the quiet way, and it hadn't worked; to be effective, my separation from the Party had to be as noisy as my association with it had been. And a voice from inside the prison would be more widely trumpeted than one from the outside. The time was definitely now, and who better to set the wheels in motion than my wife?

Jean was ecstatic! For the first time in four years, we could see a future! Suppressing our enthusiasm, we pretended we were saying sweet nothings to each other rather than plotting rebellion, but Jean was practically rehearsing the call she would make to Bartley Crum the minute she got back to Hollywood. And even then, the whole procedure had to be carried out in secrecy. Jean was open to attack, and if one word of our plans got out before it hit the press, she would be deluged by the communists and their left-wing friends pressuring her to make me change my mind.

It was a most productive afternoon, even for Albert and Margaret. In her bag, she carried away a very special package of Pall Mall cigarettes, which had been emptied of its original contents. These had been replaced with a number of small pieces of paper, tightly coiled to resemble cigarettes. They were covered with writing that Maltz couldn't get past the censor. And who would ever suspect Albert or Margaret Maltz of such deception? We all said tearful but, at least in my case, not unhappy goodbyes, and Jean and Margaret headed back to Charleston and the next plane to LAX. At their highest altitude, they couldn't have been higher that I was as I floated back to the garage for my evening chores.

When Jean goes into action there is no stop, look, or listen, and now she had the help she needed. Under such unprecedented circumstances, Bartley Crum was the best intermediary we could have had. He had been a friend for three years. We had even been with him in New York on May 14, 1948, two days after our marriage, when President Truman had phoned to tell him he was recognizing Israel as a sovereign state on the following morning. But what is more to the point here is that, in representing us, Crum suffered greatly from the righteous wrath of the conservative extremists, even though his political interests in no way matched those of the group he had represented out of principle.

One evening stands out in my memory. Some time after our return from the hearings, Scott and I flew up to see Crum on a matter of business. He invited us out to dinner, but first we had to have drinks at the famous Bohemian Club of San Francisco, of which he was a proud member. As we passed small groups of men on our way to the bar, few of his fellow members met his look. There was no friendly "Good evening," no smiling "Hello, Bart." Quite isolated, we stood at the bar while he quickly swallowed his drink. "My God," I thought, "is it a sin to come to the aid of someone in trouble? Is this democracy at work?" I believe it was such narrow-minded ostracism that, a short time later, forced Crum to leave his beloved San Francisco for New York, which is where Jean contacted him.

Bartley went to work immediately after he talked with Jean. There were two or three phone calls to Mill Point, then, on September 9, but allow me to reproduce a letter I sent to Jean the next day:

From: Edward Dmytryk   Sept.–10,–1950
        #3568   8338 De Longpre Ave.
To: Mrs. Jean Dmytryk   Hollywood, 46, Calif.

Darling—It's done! I don't know whether it will turn out good or bad—but we'll just have to sit back and see what happens. The reason I'm writing this airmail is that things have happened so fast the last few days, I haven't had time to warn you of some possibilities . . . you will be on the receiving end of a lot of stuff. Most of it will be good, I think, but some of it may be pretty unpleasant. Probably the wives will be brutal . . .

Bart came in style. Brought the lawyer Diamond (the one who almost succeeded in negotiating the settlement with the studios) with him, and a secretary. He dictated the statement, which is just what I would have wanted to say—no more, no less—then several papers having to do with substituting Crum for the other attorneys in my civil cases, and kept the office in a general uproar with calls to the White House, Attorney General McGrath, places for plane reservations to Washington, etc. I'm sure the local telephone central has never had such a day. I told them I'd have to get back to work to pay their expenses, but they have high hopes for a decent settlement with the studios on my civil cases . . .

Darling, the next few weeks may be a bit rough—hang on— we'll make it—then it'll probably be smooth sailing again. I love you more than anything, and hope you're happy about everything. Love to Ricky.

Edward Dmytryk #3568

[The formal sign-off was a prison regulation.]

The warden witnessed my statement on September 9, 1950. It said simply that I was not a communist or a communist sympathizer and that I had not been a communist at the time of the congressional hearings. It did not mention my earlier party membership. It was short and straightforward, and I hoped it would take me off the blacklist. And it might have, if it hadn't been for Herbert Biberman.

The statement received worldwide distribution, and in general, it had the hoped-for effect. But at Mill Point, Maltz was shocked and deeply disappointed. I believe he thought he had betrayed the Party by not keeping my toes on the line. Naturally, he insisted it was a great mistake, but I thought it was the most sensible thing I had done in three years. Since we had never been close, there was little change in our relationship. As for Howard Fast, he had been released three weeks before. Our friends in Hollywood, with only a few exceptions, were not communists; they were very pleased with the statement and called Jean to tell her so. Our communist-oriented friends never spoke to Jean or me again, at least not until later, when some of them also appeared as friendly witnesses before a reconstructed HUAC. A few held off until after the aborted attempts at freedom in Hungary and, several years later, in Czechoslovakia; some, like the man to whom I had given employment and friendship, Bill Watts, and his wife, Flo, were never seen or heard from again, except once.

In October, Hollywood experienced an exciting turn of events. The Screen Directors Guild of America was set on self-destruct. But at Mill Point, there was little on my mind save the building of nearly completed time, and word of the affair did not seep through the prison's invisible walls. I learned the details from friends on my return to Hollywood and, some thirty-eight years after the fact, from Elia Kazan's recapitulation of Joe Mankiewicz's version of the incident; it is probably the most accurate account of the lot.

In the three years since Cecil Blount DeMille had invaded the Directors Guild and declared war on liberalism, he had assiduously constructed an extremely reactionary board of directors, of which he was currently a member. And now that the evil genie McCarthy was out of the bottle, conservatism was on the ascendance, and the guild's president, Joe Mankiewicz, was in Europe, DeMille judged the time propitious for a long-planned coup. His actions created a moral and political crisis within the guild.

C. B. and his adherents on the board convened a special meeting of the guild membership and, using the totalitarian open-ballot technique, steamrollered a resolution mandating a membership loyalty oath. In typical DeMille fashion, C. B. created a blacklist to top all previous blacklists; his plan called for the listing of all who refused to sign a loyalty pledge and the distribution of that information to the studio heads, producers, and distributors. There were further connotations, but that was enough to start with.

Mankiewicz returned from Europe just in time. He learned of the guild action in New York, hurried to Hollywood, and called a meeting of the national board. Supported this time by men like John Ford and George Stephens, he challenged DeMille and called a special membership meeting for the following Sunday. Its purpose was to take another vote on the loyalty oath, but this time by secret ballot.

The next few days saw the DeMille forces engaged in hectic activity. Dozens of motorcyclists scoured Hollywood and Beverly Hills searching for enough votes to impeach Joe and to cancel the meeting. As a back-up, they called Joe into a meeting with DeMille and his cohorts and, in their arrogance, suggested he make an act of contrition. After an appropriate response, Mankiewicz and his allies took effective counteraction. They hired one of L.A.'s leading lawyers, Martin Gang, to obtain a quick court injunction against Cecil's interference.

Sunday arrived, and so did more than six hundred guild members. The hall was packed. Joe delivered a well-received speech, and after some give and take, DeMille rose in rebuttal. Apparently, he had decided to try a technique that had been used earlier by Congressman Rankin during the congressional debates on the Hollywood Ten. (It would be used again by McCarthy.) He read a list of names he identified as "Mr. Mankiewicz's 'champions,' " and he pronounced them with a Yiddish accent: "Mr. Villy Vyler, Mr. Fred S-s-s-ini-mon" (Kazan, *A Life*, 391), and so on. But there were more decent people on hand than C. B. ever dreamt of in his worst nightmares. He didn't get too far before the booing began—and it continued in a crescendo until Cecil was forced to shut up and sit down.

After the directors had vented their displeasure, Admiral Jack Ford, a revered member of the guild, stood to speak.

"My name is John Ford," he said. "I make westerns. [Laughter.] I don't agree with DeMille. I admire him, but I don't like him." (Those words have become immortalized in the history of Hollywood.)

Then, Fritz Lang, the famous German director, had his turn.

"Mr. DeMille, I want you to know that for the first time since I am in America, I am frightened—because I have an accent. You've made me frightened, Mr. DeMille" (Kazan, *A Life*, 392).

And so it went with Willie Wyler, Delmer Daves, and others, until the vote was taken that wiped DeMille's alternatives off the books. To cap a perfect evening, the membership let it be known that they wanted the resignation of the national board, and the election of a new one. And C. B. learned to leave sleeping lions alone.

In *A Life*, Elia Kazan makes an especially relevant statement on the affair: "I saw that what my guild brothers were defending was the middle road. The men who beat DeMille, an extremist of the right, were not from the left. Many were 'reactionaries' like John Farrow or Jack Ford. But all were for the way of fairness and decency . . . [for] classic Americanism, our basic way of living with each other in this country. And they'd succeeded" (393).

I am not a strong advocate of revenge as a rule of life, but I would have tremendously enjoyed witnessing the comeuppance of Cecil B. DeMille, a man difficult to like but oh so easy to detest. However, at the time, Hollywood's problems were light years away from Mill Point, where things went on just as they had before. The weather got colder, the waiting got harder, but each day did finally end, and soon it was time to leave. I turned over my garage duties to another inmate and settled down to wait out the longest week of my life.

Balzer had told me that the last few days of a man's sentence was the period during which he was most likely to attempt an escape. Now I found out why. All those thoughts of sex that I had so successfully put out of my mind came flooding back. There is no aphrodisiac like the thought of a beautiful, desirable woman, especially if she is the wife you love. Each day got worse. Jean was driving back to pick me up, and each day I pictured her getting closer and closer to West Virginia. The morning of November 14 finally arrived, and at 6:00 A.M., Jean pulled up in her car and brought in a suitcase full of fresh clothing. I changed and signed out. I don't remember saying good-bye to anyone. Thank God, it was still pitch-dark. We must have gotten a mile away from camp before I pulled the car over to the side of the road and turned off the lights. I had missed a hell of a lot, but I hadn't forgotten a thing.

19

After a long, slow trip across the country, Jean and I arrived home a few days before Thanksgiving (my fourth since I had been fired). But now we had something to be thankful for; I was free, the uncertainties of trial and punishment were behind me, I was with my beloved wife, and I was getting reacquainted with my son, but like a fogged-in long shot in a suspense film, the environment was opaque and ominous. I was aware of things around me, but this wasn't my world. I almost wished I could remake *Till the End of Time*; I now understood, if only a little, how a returning veteran must have felt after a couple of years at the front. But nature's greatest gift to mankind is a crumbling memory, and I soon came back to solid earth—the hard way.

Charles Feldman and Jack Gordean, my agents, had opened contract discussions with Columbia soon after my statement had been released. This was the golden age, before the studios were run by conglomerates, and Harry Cohn, head of Columbia Studios, had always been a fierce individualist. He had fought the Waldorf Committee to the bitter end and had always been uncomfortable with the Producers Association position. He was the one executive in Hollywood who was interested in putting me back to work, and he and Feldman were negotiating a deal starting at $60,000 a picture. But I forgot to knock on wood.

Herbert Biberman, whose sentence and release date coincided with mine, had arrived in town a few days before I did. He was already at work preparing ointment for unwary flies, and he found it in the likeness of the parole board. Some time after Thanksgiving, I was surprised to see him at my front door. I dearly wished, and has assumed, that my prison statement had permanently removed me from the good graces of the communists in general and the Ten in particular. But here he was, all smiles and sunshine, and he needed help.

The eight still in prison were applying for parole hearings, and Herbert was rounding up outside support for their pleas. Both he and I had applied for similar hearings at the earliest allowable time, but our requests had been denied. (By the way, official notice of the denial reached me two weeks after I got home.) At that time, we had both been told, and had no reason to doubt, that paroles were rarely granted for political misdemeanors; nevertheless, Biberman had been directed to make a show of strength and solidarity. Since my wounds were still fresh, I could certainly empathize; I finally agreed. But my agreement was conditional. I strongly stressed that in view of my desire to distance myself from the Party and of the delicate state of my contract negotiations, my support could be made known only to the parole board; it was not to be released to the press or in any way linked to the Hollywood Ten. Biberman solemnly promised to respect my wishes. But two days later, my name was splashed all over the front pages of both trade papers.

That afternoon Feldman delivered the feared message—the deal was off!

My first reaction was one of extreme anger, followed by self-righteous blame and unrestrained self-pity. But the mood wore itself out, and I decided to take a long, hard look at what had happened, and why. First, I said to myself, You're not stupid, but you have behaved stupidly indeed, and you have only yourself to blame. You know these men, and something of those behind them. To quote an old Hungarian proverb, they "talk water but drink wine," and you're known that for the last five years. You know they preach freedom of speech but censor unorthodox opinion; you know they talk democracy but prepare the way for the most inhuman autocracy in modern history. So why do you expect them to keep their word, and why are you still protecting them and the brutal principles they stand for? Could it be that you want to believe those first false promises you heard? Could you still be searching for utopia? Or could you still subconsciously believe there is a possibility of a decent world through Stalinism?

Now that the remnants of a bankrupt idealism had been brought out into the open and considered, I knew the answers to those questions would forever be, "No!" But though my mind was cleared, the situation in which I found myself had deteriorated; my chances to make a living in Hollywood had been reduced to zero. And what were the alternatives? I had received offers of work from Arthur Rank and other producers in Europe, but as I had discovered, it was one thing to be an honored guest artist in a friendly country and quite a different kettle of fish to be a foreigner accepting a high-class form of charity, and as the only director of the Ten, I could not take cover under a pseudonym.

Besides, the United States was my country as much as it was DeMille's—mine and Jean's—and this is where we had a constitutional right to live, work, and raise a family. I could not allow Biberman's selfish—no, I suddenly realized, more than selfish—downright mali-

cious and probably planned action to take those rights away from us,
even though all hope had disappeared. I added up the amount of money
I owed in back taxes, child support, alimony, and assorted IOUs; it was
impressive. I was close to a half-million dollars in debt—not bad for a
kid who had run away from home with 30 cents in his pocket. But the
very size of my indebtedness limited my alternatives; so-called common
work could hardly handle that amount in one lifetime. My ex-wife and
her attorney were still trying to bleed the turnip (they had attached
Jean's car), but the IRS had priority, and they were adamant. Trying to
find an easier way out, I broached the possibility of a settlement, noting
that a well-known sports figure had recently arranged to pay a small
percentage per dollar. The tax examiner smiled a predacious smile.

"Your situation is entirely different from his," he said cheerfully. "He
no longer has an earning potential, so we'll take what we can get. You,
on the other hand, are only forty-two and a long way from finished."

Those were the first encouraging words I had heard in four years
from a disinterested party—or was he? Yet his expression of faith would
have little influence on Hollywood's frightened producers.

In *Murder, My Sweet*, Philip Marlowe is pistol-whipped, carried away
to a phony sanitarium, and drugged to the gills. After two days of DTs,
he awakens to find himself literally befogged. As he struggles to dispel
his hallucinations, his progress is monitored, metaphorically, by the
gradual attenuation of the web of smoke that overlays the scene. When
it has disappeared entirely, we know that his mind is finally clear. And
so does he. "I was ready to talk to somebody!" he narrates.

After a measurable amount of self-examination, situational analysis,
and discussion with Jean, the sensible member of the family, the fog had
lifted. I was no longer angry. Instead, I, too, "was ready to talk to somebody!"

Jean and Bartley Crum were both happy with my decision. Bart, the
hardest-working unpaid lawyer in the country, had searched for any
possible means of breaking the blacklist; he, too, had found only one—I
had to purge myself. HUAC and the Hollywood right each had to have
its pound of flesh, and neither would accept a compromise. They had an
eye-for-an-eye attitude, and they weren't letting anyone off the hook.
Now that I was looking at things from a less-doctrinaire point of view, I
couldn't blame them. After all, their collective self-esteem had taken a
bad beating during the hearings, a beating headlined in the press of the
literate world. A few pretty bright men, who cleverly avoided being

pinned down, had convinced a lot of pretty bright people that they were the true defenders of liberty. (This was especially true in Hollywood.) In the early days of the struggle, when laughter came more easily, we often chuckled at some sharp put-down of the Committee or the producers. Time had staled the arrogant humor, but those who were ridiculed had long memories. Now, *they* were riding high, victory in hand, but they still needed confirmation from the camp of the defeated, and they insisted on getting it. For three years, they had been waiting for someone to say, "Okay, I'm sorry. You were right all along." Well, I was not in the least ashamed to admit that, at least in part, they may have been justified.

Bart took the first step. He approached the Motion Picture Industry Council, the committee responsible for the anticipated rehabilitation of blacklisted workers. At our meeting, I found some of the committee were old friends, and all were thoroughly decent men. They were intent on putting this business behind them as soon as possible, and some would have preferred to put it aside altogether. ("This business" lasted a good ten years before suffering a slow death—a death not yet fully realized. Some remnants of the studios' fear of political pressure still remain.) To expedite the clearance process, only one of their requirements was an absolute. The rest were open to compromise. Each was some form of public relations activity designed to pave the way for a favorable response from that portion of the general citizenry that makes up the movie audience.

The period of the blacklist is often regarded as a heavily one-sided tug-of-war between HUAC and a few film industry Reds, and it is assumed the Producers Association was coerced by the Committee to follow its lead. Comfortable, but simplistic. "The troubles," to borrow an old Irish expression, had their origin in some failing artists' jealousies and in some congressmen's grabs for the brass ring of publicity. But artistic jealousies are almost a tradition in show business, and certainly no movie mogul had ever feared the fire of a few bigoted congressmen as individuals. No, there was more to it than that; an endemic fear does exist in Hollywood—the fear of an audience turned off. And the producers were not so much intimidated by the Committee as they were scared to death by the cumulative effect of its influence on their collective constituency.

Art lives on appreciation, either eventual or immediate; the cinema, which is more a business than an art, lives on immediate acceptance. As most people know, to be successful, American films must reach a considerable cross section of the world public. If they lose a large bloc of viewers, for whatever reason, they will surely fail. A nationwide boycott would be a disaster. The cold war was exceptionally hot in the years after World War II, and the American Legion had grown enormously in size and influence. When I met with the Motion Picture Industry Council, a show of the Legion's power had already been demonstrated against one of my films. *Give Us This Day* had opened to exceptional reviews, but on the following day, the theaters were visited by Legionaires who informed the managers that continuation of the run would bring a boycott not only of my film but of all others for the foreseeable future.[8] Exhibitors are no smarter than the next man, but they are no dumber, either. With a few exceptions, they closed shop, and in effect, my film never saw the light of day in the United States.

Though these were the exhibitors' problems, they were implicitly also mine. I could clear the record only by returning to where it all began. I would have to appear a second time before the House Committee on Un-American Activities. And *that* was the absolute.

The optional requirements were easier. Essentially, they entailed interviews and appearances to exhibit my changed attitude to the people. That was no problem, since I knew the media would be on my tail once the word got out. (In fact, they've never completely let go.) But one interview was quite important at the time. Richard English, a well-known Hollywood writer who often appeared in national magazines, volunteered to do my story for the *Saturday Evening Post*, a very influential publication in 1951. We spent a full two weeks together, one of them sequestered in a San Diego hotel, during which he interrogated me like a prosecutor; then he wrote a lengthy and fairly comprehensive article explaining my involvement with the Party and the Hollywood Ten. No communists were identified in the story, yet it evoked a violent reaction. English's article appeared in the May 19, 1951 edition of the *Post*, but nearly a month before, I had been the chief actor in a much-publicized drama.

The most important element in the reinstatement procedure was an appearance before the HUAC. I had no doubts, no second thoughts;

8. According to a widespread view, the failure of *Citizen Kane* when it opened is an example of a tacit nationwide boycott promulgated by an influential portion of the press.

those were all behind me. It is quite likely that I was the only one of those who purged themselves to approach my second ordeal without fear.

Naturally, the Committee was pleased that I was going to cooperate, and they put me in touch with their investigators. They were all tired of being accused of bypassing the Bill of Rights by people who would have made its abolishment their first order of business if positions had been reversed. The investigators laid down only one stricture; there could be no mention of anyone whose party membership was not verifiable. None of those I named was unknown to the investigators, although two or three surprised the public.

At one of these preparatory meetings, I learned that Larry Parks was also making a committee appearance and that it was scheduled before mine. I suggested to Larry that I testify first. I must have sensed that he was in deadly fear of an inquisition and totally unprepared for what, to him, was certain to be an ordeal. But for some reason that now escapes me, he insisted on sticking to the schedule. This he did, and his tortured testimony was so copiously, so unsympathetically reported that it haunted him throughout the rest of his life.

My appearance before the Committee on April 25, 1951, took everyone by surprise. No one (except committee members and staff) even knew I was in Washington. As I approached the hearing room door, I ran into one of our former party lawyers, Marty Popper, who was there to represent a new batch of unfriendly witnesses. He looked at me in astonishment,

"What are you doing here?" he asked.

"I'm making an appearance," I said.

He blanched. I went into the hearing room.

20

Mr. Tavenner.	**What is your name, please?**
Mr. Dmytryk.	Edward Dmytryk.
Mr. Tavenner.	And the spelling is D-m-y-t-r-y-k?
Mr. Dmytryk.	That is right.
Mr. Tavenner.	When and where were you born, Mr. Dmytryk?
Mr. Dmytryk.	I was born in Canada, Grand Forks, British Columbia, September 4, 1908.
Mr. Tavenner.	Are you a naturalized American citizen?
Mr. Dmytryk.	I am.
Mr. Tavenner.	When were you naturalized?
Mr. Dmytryk.	I was naturalized in 1939.
Mr. Tavenner.	What is your profession?
Mr. Dmytryk.	I am a screen director.

It was anything but a game of questions and answers. Still, there was a similarity to the release of tension that follows the opening action in any sport; the cold feet and the sweating palms were returning to normal. And so was my awareness. "Here we go again," I thought. But I knew that wasn't true—this was not a rerun. Today I was on my own, alone. To quote a cartoon character of my childhood, "I wore no man's collar." I had no lawyer at my side, and I was no longer held captive by false group loyalty. Whatever I said, whatever stand I took (and I realized how controversial both would be), these would come from a free man following his own conscience, guided by his own ideals.

It was April 25, 1951, and I was making my second appearance before HUAC. The Committee's purpose was the same: it was still trying to measure the extent of the Communist Party's inroads into American society. But its personnel were different in more ways than one. J. Parnell Thomas was long gone, and his gavel had gone with him. The present members were Representatives John S. Wood (chairman), Frances E. Walter, James B. Frazier, Bernard W. Kearney, Donald L. Jackson, and Charles E. Potter. Frank S. Tavenner was the Committee's chief counsel.

This group of men was doing its best to maintain a professional demeanor and to adopt a dignified role in the hearings that had only recently been resumed to continue its long-term investigation into the entertainment industries. In short, its members were trying hard to make people forget their predecessors and to convince those who would be watching their performances that they were gentlemen. This may have thrown Larry Parks somewhat off guard.

In spite of my effort to head him off, on March 21, Larry was the first friendly Hollywood witness to appear before the reconstituted committee. He testified willingly, and yet unwillingly. He had still to learn the lesson that had been driven home to me after the release of my prison statement; in this political environment, there was no such thing as a half-measure. You couldn't just get your feet wet. You either dove in over your head or you did not go in at all. But, to show the cosmetic difference in the present Committee's attitude, here is an exchange between Congressman Walter and Counsel Tavenner.

Mr. Walter.   Mr. Chairman, may I ask the counsel a question? How can it be material to the purpose of this enquiry to have the names of people when we already know them?

Mr. Tavenner.   . . . the Committee ought to be entitled to receive proof of information which it has in the files. There would be no way to really investigate Communist infiltration into labor without asking who are (the) Communists in labor. And the same thing is true of Hollywood,

Walter found no fault with Tavenner's position, although the most important question of all was not included in the brief exchange. However, subsequent dialogue between the counsel and Parks approached the heart of the matter.

Mr. Tavenner.   Do you believe . . . that the persons who are in those responsible positions [of turning out films] should be people who are antagonistic to the principles of democracy . . . and are members of a conspiracy to overthrow our government?

Mr. Parks.   Most assuredly, I don't.

Mr. Tavenner.   Then what is your opinion as to whether or not members of the Communist Party should be in positions of power and influence in the various

	unions which control the writing of scripts, the actors, and various other things which we have mentioned during the course of this hearing relating to the great industry of moving pictures?
Mr. Parks.	I certainly do not believe that those people should be in any position of power to be able to direct this.
Mr. Tavenner.	Then I will ask your cooperation, before this hearing is over, in helping us ascertain those who are or have been members of the Communist Party.

And there Tavenner had him. For *people* are the lifeblood, the *all*, of an industry or an association, and it is futile to admit abhorrence of the evils of an organization but refuse to identify any of the individuals who help to make that organization evil. And how does one deal with those members who, as Larry maintained, do not believe in overthrowing the government, but belong to a party that does? Obviously, here is a matter involving an extremely deep contradiction that has nothing to do with decency or reality but with some vague superstition about conscience. Larry's failure to reconcile the contradiction led him to take a very weak position.

Mr. Parks.	Don't present me with the choice of either being in contempt of the Committee and going to jail or forcing me to crawl through the mud to be an informer.

At last it was out—out in the open, though nobody seemed to recognize it, especially Larry. What he was saying, and what thousands of confused liberals have believed since then was that one must allow a seditious Party to destroy one's country rather than expose the men or women who *are* the Party. In other words, naming names is a greater crime than subversion. That's what I call the "Mafia Syndrome," and I find no shame or indignity in rejecting it.

In time, Parks, too, was able to see the fallacy inherent in that point of view and to understand that there were many factors involved in whether or not informing was morally defensible. The presumption that there is an immutable, unwritten law against informing is sheer nonsense. It is simply a rule of self-preservation, and its validity depends solely on whether society is benefited or harmed by its imposition. The

Communist Party was unquestionably an agent of an autocratic foreign power, and exposure of its purposes or its personnel was no threat to a clear conscience. And those sympathizers who argue that the Party was too small to merit concern should be reminded that Hitler started his death-dealing career in a Munich beer hall with only a few hundred drunken adherents.

Just over two years after this appearance before HUAC, Larry Parks wrote a letter to the new chairman of the Committee, the Honorable Harold Velde. Though chronologically out of sequence, it belongs here thematically, and I will quote a few passages from Parks's letter of July 15, 1953.

> In light of the events which have transpired since I appeared as a witness before the Committee, it is crystal clear that no one who really believes in a progressive program for humanity can support any part of the Communist program . . . Soviet Communism constitutes as grave a threat to the rights of man today as once did Hitler Fascism . . . the enemy is the same though the labels have changed.
>
> . . . if I were to testify today I would not testify as I did in 1951 . . . but on the contrary I would recognize that [my] cooperation would help to further the cause in which many of us were sincerely interested when we were duped into joining and taking part in the Communist Party. (*Congressional Record*, July 23, 1953)

The last sentence is an interesting example of what many excommunists had to learn before their break with the Party was complete: we were not obligated to sacrifice our beliefs in those liberal ideals that led us into the Party; they were still ours to contemplate and to live by. That consideration became more persuasive as the pressures of the blacklists and of ostracism continued to grow.

In her book *Lost Illusion*, Freda Utley wrote: "You believe what you wish to believe until experience bangs your head against the wall and awakens you from dreams founded on hope, a misreading of history, and ignorance both of human psychology and science (25). During the early fifties, a number of men and women awakened to the realization that they had been banging their heads against the wall for the wrong reasons and for far too long. As their distaste for snitching diminished in the face of their need to fulfill their lives and their careers, scores of such people, many of whom had been party members while others had merely been sympathizers, made their way into the Committee's offices to rid themselves of the stain of Stalinism.

For its part, the Committee had sensibly diminished the pain of the sort of public grilling suffered by Larry Parks and held most of the hearings behind closed doors. Among those who took advantage of the Committee's more accommodating behavior were Robert Rossen, Elia Kazan, Budd Schulberg, Lloyd Bridges, Isobel Lennert, Jose Ferrer, Lee Cobb, Michael Blankfort, David Raksin, and Clifford Odets. There were close to a hundred others. Although the testimony of these witnesses was placed in the record and circulated in the studios to facilitate open employment, it was rarely published in the daily press.

But in 1951, the experiences of the past four years had already taught me lessons that Larry and the others had yet to learn, and my hearing was a very different story.

Mr. Tavenner.	Mr. Dmytryk . . . you are one of those commonly referred to as the "Hollywood Ten"?
Mr. Dmytryk.	I was.
Mr. Tavenner.	I notice you say "was" rather than "are."
Mr. Dmytryk.	I don't think I will be considered so much longer.
Mr. Tavenner.	Your testimony today will throw considerable light on the subject?
Mr. Dmytryk.	I imagine so, yes.
Mr. Tavenner.	I believe you are one of the group who were prosecuted for contempt of Congress, and that you received a sentence, and that you have served that sentence?
Mr. Dmytryk.	I have, yes.
Mr. Tavenner.	Were you a member of the Communist Party at the time you were subpoenaed before this Committee in 1947?
Mr. Dmytryk.	No, I was not.
Mr. Tavenner.	Had you ever been a member of the Communist Party?
Mr. Dmytryk.	Yes, I had been a member from sometime around the spring or early summer of 1944 until about the fall of 1945. Most of this was during the period the Communist Party as such dissolved and the

	Communist Political Association had taken its place.
Mr. Tavenner.	While you were a member of the so-called Hollywood Ten, did you have an opportunity to further observe the workings of the Communist Party.
Mr. Dmytryk.	I think I can truthfully say that I had much more opportunity to observe the workings of the Communist Party while I was a member of the Hollywood Ten than I did while I was a member of the Communist Party.

That established, Frank Tavenner confirmed my willingness to testify and my reasons for finally agreeing to cooperate. Then he asked my opinion concerning the Party's true objectives in Hollywood.

Mr. Tavenner.	I would like to have you state to this Committee what the real object of the Communist Party is in its efforts to organize and infiltrate the moving-picture industry in Hollywood.
Mr. Dmytryk.	Well, I have no access to inner-Party circles, so I can't tell you officially, but my opinion is they had probably three chief purposes. The first one was to get money . . . the next one was to get prestige. And the third and most important was, through the infiltration and eventual take-over of Hollywood's guilds and unions, to control the content of pictures. The only way they could control the content of pictures was to control the studios, and the only way to do that was to completely take over the guilds and the unions.

There followed a routine exchange about money, dues, and other minor issues; then Tavenner went on to the second point. This concerned the Party's creation or infiltration of popular fronts, usually headed by men and women of national prestige who were rarely, if ever, party members. The communists' ability to control such fronts, even though they were a tiny minority, has already been mentioned in chapter 2. The counsel then asked about the third point.

Mr. Tavenner.   You spoke of the third and most important aim and object of the Communist Party as being the purpose of eventually obtaining control of the guilds and unions, as I understood you to say?

Mr. Dmytryk.   Yes.

Mr. Tavenner.   What guilds were they you referred to?

Mr. Dmytryk.   In the first two points I mentioned I think the Communists had considerable success in Hollywood. In the last point they had only limited success. Hollywood is split up into probably two sections. First, the talent guilds—Screen Writers Guild, unaffiliated; Screen Directors Guild, unaffiliated; and Screen Actors Guild, which is affiliated with the American Federation of Labor, but is largely autonomous. Then there are the craft unions, mostly IATSE—International Association of Theatrical and Stage Employees. I know the Communists were successful for a time in . . . largely controlling . . . the Screen Writers Guild . . . They were not successful at all in the Screen Directors Guild. There were only a few Communists in the Directors Guild at any time.

Mr. Tavenner.   Were you in the Screen Directors Guild?

Mr. Dmytryk.   Yes, from 1939 on.

Mr. Tavenner.   How many were there in the Screen Directors Guild?

Mr. Dmytryk.   The total membership, full directors, was 225 or 230.

Mr. Tavenner.   And of that number there were a few known to you to be members of the Communist Party?

Mr. Dmytryk.   As far as I know there were seven.

Mr. Tavenner.   Will you give us the names of the seven?

Mr. Dmytryk.   Yes. Frank Tuttle.

Mr. Tavenner.   He was a director?

Mr. Dmytryk.   Yes. Herbert Biberman. Jack Berry.

Mr. Tavenner.   Can you identify him further?

Mr. Dmytryk.   I heard the Chairman this morning give the address. He is the Berry who lives on King's Road. The meeting was at his house. That is why I knew. Bernard Vorhaus.

Mr. Tavenner.   I believe you have named four.

Mr. Dmytryk.	Then Jules Dassin. And myself.
Mr. Tavenner.	Do you have any definite knowledge of any of the others having left the Party?
Mr. Dmytryk.	No, I don't. I think it is quite possible that some of them have.

For some reason, I only named six directors, including myself. If I had named a seventh, it would have been Joe Losey. Tavenner then went on to establish infiltration.

Mr. Tavenner.	I understood you to say the meeting you described was held at the home of Jack Berry?
Mr. Dmytryk.	That is right.
Mr. Tavenner.	What was the purpose of the meeting?
Mr. Dmytryk.	. . . I think it had to do with trying to elect one of us to the board of directors of the Directors Guild.
Mr. Tavenner.	Why was the Communist Party interested at that particular time in placing one of its members on the board of directors of the Guild.
Mr. Dmytryk.	. . . that was a part of a long-term plan. They wanted to get as many people as they could on the board of directors of all the guilds, particularly in relation to an eventual coalition for the backing of the various unions.
Mr. Tavenner.	In other words, this is one instance in which the Communist Party was endeavoring to obtain control of the guilds?
Mr. Dmytryk.	Yes.
Mr. Tavenner.	. . . what other efforts do you know of that the Communist Party resorted to (in order to) control either pictures, or the guilds, or the executives of the industry?
Mr. Dmytryk.	The chief effect was in the craft unions. In my opinion, the Communist Party never had any control over any major executive in any major studio, nor did they at any time have effective control over the content of pictures. It is true that somebody might have slipped in a line, or something, that made him happy, but that is not

> the kind of thing that would be effective in the
> least degree ... But in craft unions they were
> successful in organizing a group called the
> Conference of Studio Unions that had a great deal
> to do with the policies. They eventually got so
> strong they risked a strike against IATSE. However,
> they lost the strike after a very, very long and
> serious battle, and that attempt came to nothing.

The next series of questions and answers concerned the strike of the
Painters' Union, which belonged to the Conference of Studio Unions,
and to the activity of the Communist Party within the Writers Guild,
particularly as it related to its efforts to control the content of story material. This led to the first public disclosure of the *Cornered* episode, of
Albert's losing tussle with the Party on the question of free expression,
and of my exit from the Party (as discussed in chapter 3).

Mr. Tavenner.   Have you anything further to say regarding point
three that you mentioned, as the most important
aims of the Communist Party in Hollywood?

Mr. Dmytryk.   I feel sure that the Communist Party is now a
completely ineffective element in Hollywood.

Mr. Tavenner.   I have been rather struck with some of the testimony
here as to the station in life and the measure of
success that various people have when they
become members of the Communist Party. What
appeal was there in the Communist Party which
aided them in recruiting members—for instance,
such as Jarrico, as to whom there has been
testimony that he was a member of the Communist
Party—how was it they would become members?

Mr. Dmytryk.   Writers are ... traditionally concerned with people.
These are the bones of their work. To understand
people properly they had to understand the society
in which they live and the economic conditions
under which they live. So any writer worthy of the
name studies those problems. Probably he became
a writer because he is a humanitarian. There is at
least a streak of altruistic idealism in him ... They

have become troubled about poverty, especially
when there is such discrepancy; where a man
making twenty-five hundred dollars a week is
working next to a man making twenty-five dollars
a week. They consider this unfair. It is . . .
characteristic . . . of Hollywood. You hear in
Hollywood more than anywhere else the word
"break" used. If you ask a successful person in
Hollywood how he got there, he will never say, "I
got there by hard work and personality." He will
say, "I got the breaks." Of course, hard work and
personality count a great deal, but "breaks" count,
too. We think, there but for the grace of God, go I,
when we see somebody not so successful. As a
result, a person in Hollywood is really interested in
bringing up the general level of the people around
him. He knows he can't do it individually. He
knows it wouldn't do any good to give five bucks
here or there. He looks around for an organization
in which he can work that does these things. He
finds Marxism because it is waiting for him . . . The
Communist Party has laid clever fly-traps for him.
Those organizations are all around him . . . their
overt purpose is certainly good . . . They not only
attract those who become Communists, they attract
many who never become Communists, but give
Communists the advantage of their time, their
work, and their money. [But] the average person
who goes in [eventually] finds there is no freedom
of thought; that the discipline is a very harsh one.
If it had not been for my experience with *Cornered*,
I might have gone on [being a Communist] for
some time. The Party has a very good explanation
for everything that troubles a man. If he says he
doesn't have freedom, the Great Explainer,
whoever he is in that locality, will point out that he
has freedom to tell the truth: that the Communist
Party has discovered the ultimate truth, and within
that limit he can speak. Anything outside of the

Party Line is a lie. Of course, anything capitalistic is basically a lie because it came from a system they consider dishonest to begin with. So when a man accepts this thinking, he believes he is following the truth ... I would say the majority of members are not used in subversive activities. They are concerned with the organization and running the Communist fronts, and many go to their deaths believing they were working in a decent organization. It is the "end" policy of the Communist Party which explains everything. Whatever is done, they say, "This had to be done to achieve a good end" ... For instance; many people questioned the Communist purges. The answer was, "Those people are revolutionaries. We must hold them back." My wife had an interesting experience while I was in jail. My wife is not political at all, but she wanted to get me home very badly and was doing what she could, together with the other wives of the Ten, to get me home. She was asked to go with one of the wives ... to Sacramento, where all three parties—Democratic, Republican, and Progressive—were holding conventions. My wife noticed that the woman she was with, and others she had contacted up there, were doing things she didn't think quite proper. In one particular instance they asked a small clerk, getting a small salary, to give them a secret list. My wife said, "You are asking him to risk his livelihood. He might lose his job and his reputation." The answer was, "It doesn't matter if one person gets hurt if thousands will eventually benefit."

Mr. Walter. How do the Communists explain the eighteen million slave laborers in Russia?

Mr. Dmytryk. In this country they deny it. They say the capitalist press does not print the truth. .... They will admit some people are liquidated, but they say it is for the good of humanity.

There were more questions about how and why I had joined the Party, about meetings I had attended, and what members were present at those meetings. Tavenner also inquired about my activities with the Ten after my return from England.

Mr. Dmytryk.   When I came back to this country, we had a great many meetings of the Hollywood Ten . . . I noticed a change had taken place . . . and that the group was, without question, following the Party line. That is, they put stuff out in the defense of the New York Seven (the Communists in New York), the Harry Bridges case, and every case of this sort that came up. Sometimes others would agree with me . . . but . . . when the argument got hot, somebody would call on John Howard Lawson, and . . . Ben Margolis, and the dialectical reasoning would come . . . In the long run it would wind up as always, of course, in favor of the broad Communist Party line of action.

Mr. Tavenner.   The time you were subpoenaed to come before the Committee, was there any indication to you that the Communist Party was endeavoring in any way to influence the course of action that you as a group should take?

Mr. Dmytryk.   Well, I certainly had no idea of it at the time. In looking back, of course, and remembering how the Nineteen were organized, I would say the answer to that would probably be yes.

Tavenner posed the question of the suppression of works of art that appeared to stray from the strict party line. He cited an example in the USSR of party discipline censoring an orchestra.

Mr. Tavenner.   Now, is that the type of discipline you refer to as being objectionable and as being accepted in the Communist Party?

Mr. Dmytryk.   It certainly is. For instance, in the famous case of the Communist musicians who were reprimanded by the Party, I remember asking, "How can any commissar or committee say what is people's music? ... a note doesn't propagandize as far as I'm concerned." But they said, "No ... There is a certain kind of music people understand. If they understand it, it is people's music, and it should be done. On the other hand, if the music isn't understood by the people, then it is counter-revolutionary and as such should be forbidden."

Mr. Tavenner. And was that argument equally valid with regard to the Duclos letter, which has been mentioned here in the testimony a number of times?

Mr. Dmytryk. The Duclos letter was a little bit different. I'd say this is what happened. Browder [the head of the U.S. Communist Party during my time as a member] and his associates decided they could cooperate with the capitalistic government, that revolution and war [were] not necessary ... Now, after the war was over and there was no longer need on the part of Russia to cooperate with the United States, Duclos ... a French Communist, went to Russia. When he came back to Paris he wrote the famous letter in which he criticized severely the American Party line as it had been followed under the Communist Political Association. This even had some percussions in Hollywood, because John Howard Lawson, who had been a strong preacher for the cooperative policy, had to do a lot of very fast tightrope walking to save himself.

Mr. Tavenner. Well, do you recall any instance in which a leader in the Party may have argued in behalf of one thing at one time and then very shortly afterward been compelled to change entirely?

Mr. Dmytryk. There was a well known incident that everybody got a laugh out of in Hollywood, even the Communists ... Herbert Biberman had made a very powerful, impassioned speech in favor of a personality or the Party line one day. The official Party line changed the next afternoon. The following day he made an equally impassioned speech in direct contrast to the speech he had made two days before.

One more bit of testimony about my prison affidavit, although out of sequence here, is relevant to the hearing as a whole.

Mr. Dmytryk.   I have heard rumors; two different kinds: One that I made the affidavit because I had been offered a job at MGM at five thousand dollars a week . . . This obviously has been proven untrue. [Not only was there no offer of work or money from MGM, but the clearance involved my agreement to abandon my contractual civil action against RKO.] The other is [that] Bartley Crum said somebody, not a Communist, had approached him in New York and said, "I understand that they really put the works to Dmytryk in jail, they put the pressure on him, and that is why he made his affidavit." That is not true. There was no pressure, nor has there been, of any kind, nor have I ever been offered a bribe or job of any kind—I wish I had—to make either the affidavit or to come here.

As I thought about it later, I realized that from the end of the hearings in 1947 until those of 1951, no representative of the Committee or the government ever tried to pressure me, Jean, or Crum to change position. In truth, the investigators who, at that time, were my enemies, never came in sight—until my enemies became my supporters.

21

The FBI finally paid me a visit. The agency had been the communists' number one bogeyman as long as I had known the Party, but FBI officials had been completely absent at both my committee appearances and during the years in between—unless, of course, the tapping of our phones in Washington and at home had been their handiwork. I never knew for certain whether the eavesdroppers were from the FBI or some agency of the Committee. I had never liked J. Edgar Hoover on general principles, and the stories I heard from members of the Washington media in the know did nothing to brighten his image, but I am somewhat sorry to say, on the basis of personal experience, I cannot confirm any of the horrendous tales I often listened to during coffee-break chatter at leftist affairs. They had never knocked on my door at 3:00 A.M. when I was drugged with sleep, they had never threatened me with the loss of my job (when I had one), and they had never, in any way, behaved like American clones of the KGB.

Now, however, I was a possible source of information. On several occasions, the agents either called on me or asked me to drop in at their downtown office when they were seeking verification of charges. As might be expected, direct and anonymous accusations flooded the agency during those unhappy years. I was not under oath before a legal body, and therefore under no compulsion to answer questions or to tell the truth, but I was in a quandry; I reckoned that, decent as they seemed to be, G-men could make dangerous enemies, and I didn't want to appear uncooperative. Fortunately, I was never faced with a difficult decision; I was unable to identify any of their suspects as communists. I really knew so few. Perhaps the following bit of transcript will clarify the apparent inconsistency, which appears in the testimony of nearly all who cooperated with the Committee.

Mr. Tavenner.	Did you sit in on a Communist Party meeting at any time with Richard Collins?
Mr. Dmytryk.	Only in this particular affair [the meetings on *Cornered*]. A person can be in the Communist Party for a long time and still not know which people are Communists, because these groups are kept

	fairly separate. There is no secret handshake or password, and I have never had anybody come up to me and say, "I am a Communist." It just doesn't happen. You can suspect fifty or a hundred people, but you cannot be sure unless you have worked with them in a meeting.
Mr. Tavenner.	Now, for instance, Richard Collins, to give an example, testifies that he had been a member of the Party in Hollywood for around nine years, that he attended meetings about twice a week during all that period, and yet you never sat in a meeting with him?
Mr. Dmytryk.	Never sat in a meeting with him outside of the incident I mentioned.
Mr. Tavenner.	Sterling Hayden was one who testified that he had attended a number of meetings. Did you ever sit in a meeting with him?
Mr. Dmytryk.	I was very surprised when he admitted being a member of the Communist Party. I had no idea he was even close.
Mr. Tavenner.	Larry Parks has testified he was a member of the Communist Party and attended meetings. Did you ever attend a meeting at which he was present?
Mr. Dmytryk.	No. At the time of the original hearings I was convinced Larry Parks was one of those—and there were several in the Nineteen—who were not Communists.

All that was true, and whether the agents believed me or just tired of my negative responses, they soon terminated our rendezvous. But before that happened one interesting name popped up. Frank Sinatra had applied for a passport. In that dim, distant past, he had a reputation as a liberal, and the State Department decided to check him out. I had never met Sinatra, but I gave him the highest marks in Americanism, which I thought he deserved. I'm sure I was not the only one who did; I mention the incident only to illustrate the ridiculous extent to which the un-American hysteria had spread; to establish a police state in the defense of freedom is a very profound and unhappy contradiction. But it was kind of funny—Frankie a communist? I could imagine the action when a cultural commissar, say John Howard Lawson, would order, "Just go back and rephrase the last eight bars, Blue Eyes." A little imagination and a slight touch of humor could have saved our State Department a lot of time, trouble, and money.

But I'm vaulting too far into the future, and the weeks and months immediately after my HUAC appearance deserve some scrutiny. After my return from the nation's capital—freer of mind but no richer in pocket—nothing happened. No calls from my agents, no studio offers, no movement of any kind. Then, after four weeks of wondering whether I had been buried and forgotten, the *Saturday Evening Post* issue of May 19, 1951 hit the stands.

The publishers had done an excellent job of advertising the issue, and it was a sellout. My noncommunist friends were pleased and relieved, believing that four years of misery could now be set aside. My former comrades and their many leftist supporters were extremely distressed. When wounded, communist apologists resort to vituperation so immoderate, it can scarcely be believed—ask any excommunist. Although they had branded me a liar from the time of my second HUAC appearance, the *Post* article drove them into a fury, which, in its vehemence, could only be equaled by the piranha's feeding frenzy. Clearly, the article had scored a bullseye. Nothing but the truth could elicit such a violent reaction. Their shrill cries of "Liar!" alerted the *Post* publishers to a possible suit. English suggested they conduct their own investigation. This they did, and their fears were exorcised. The absence of any libel action further corroborated my account.

The effort to whitewash the Ten, the Party, and its supporters had been severely damaged. In a last-gasp attempt at a resuscitation, the Party commissioned my erstwhile best man to write an open letter, which occupied the center spread of both trade papers. (Maltz had never been my best man in reality. He simply shared a ride with Jean and me to Philadelphia, and was present to witness our simple ceremony. He was no more a best man in the accepted sense of the words than the secretary we had borrowed as a witness from the Ellicott City Town Hall was a maid of honor.) In his diatribe, Maltz employed his creative talent to concoct a series of questions to which he supplied his own lopsided answers. But only one statement needs mentioning here. Near the end of his lengthy invective, he quoted me as saying, "I'm still the same man I always was—but it is necessary for progressives to go underground for a while." In his obstinate adherence to the Ten's tactic for avoiding any use of the word *communist*, Maltz shot himself in the foot. Progressives were not communists, and communists certainly were not progressive. *Progressive* was a nonparty term that could be borrowed by any group, and nobody who had any knowledge of the politics of the time would suggest that the Progressives should go underground any more than the Democrats, the Elks, or members of the clergy. The whole thing was so palpably ridiculous that on June 6, 1951, the Motion Picture Industry Council took out a somewhat more modest one-page ad in the trades entitled, "You Can Be A Free Man Again!" Among other items brought out in my defense was the following statement: "The one thing we could not know in advance . . . was the one BIG LIE in the attack on Dmytryk, namely the unsupported claim that Dmytryk said progressives must go underground. We are certain Dmytryk never said anything like that. The BIG LIE was fashioned as a supposed 'clincher' for a collection of half-truths and distortions in time and fact. The BIG LIE is an official technique of the Communist Party."

The statement was signed by the following: Roy Brewer, I. E. Chadwick, Art Arthur, Jack Dales, Alexander Kempner, and Ronald Reagan.

However, none of these names was magic—at least not yet, and the major studios showed no eagerness to test the blacklist or the boycott. Since my *big* agents talked or played gin only with the *big* producers, most of my possible opportunities were eliminated. Then an old policy of mine paid off; in my salad days, my door was always open to actors and agents, and the great majority of those who took advantage of the practice were the so-called small fry. Now one of these minor agents, Bert Marx, who had always been a sympathetic friend, told me the King Brothers, B producers extraordinaire, had expressed interest, and would I like to talk to them? That was one of the easiest decisions of my life: I went over to the Monogram Studio, which was situated a short block away from the home I had escaped nearly thirty years before, and talked to them.

The King Brothers were an odd lot; there were three of them, none married. Maury, the oldest, had been a newsboy, a bootblack, a pugilist, a bootlegger, and according to the scuttlebutt, a small-time gangster. I saw no evidence of the last during the years I knew him, although he did insist on sitting in the outside seat facing the front door in any restaurant booth he occupied at mealtime. Maury had lived the American

Dream, and with the capable help of "Mama," he had kept the family together through the depression and the "thin" times. When I first met him, he was continuing to do so through the "thick."

Brother number two, Frank, was, in my opinion, the brightest of the lot and had the advantage of a high school education. He was an extremely knowledgeable film man and could have become a top producer at any major studio if he had been willing to break up the family. Frank and Maury shared a large office and took turns sitting in the one chair behind the one desk.

Hymie was the youngest—the one with the easy, pleasant, and relatively polished manner whom one talked with while waiting to see the two one dealt with.

Between them, Frank and Maury had all the attributes of a top producer, except one—they refused to risk much money on any film, no matter what its potential. As a result, they made only the cheapest of B films, although occasionally they made a good one. After 1947, they took full advantage of the blacklist. To my knowledge, at least two of their scripts were written by Dalton Trumbo for a fraction of his former salary.

Now that I was certified as "clear," though not yet "checked out," the King Brothers took a chance on me. The story was *Mutiny* (a strange coincidence), the cast included Angela Lansbury, Patrick Knowles, and Mark Stevens, the schedule was eighteen days, and the salary was $5,000. Instead of Louie B. Mayer and $5,000 per week, as the communists had insinuated, I got the King Brothers and $5,000 for what, counting preparation, shooting, and editing, amounted to about five months' work. And that amounted to about $250 per week, my starting salary at Paramount in 1939. But it was more than I had been making in the last four years, and since Jean was pregnant again, I was grateful. I liked Maury and Frank a lot—and Mama.

Mutiny was probably a little better than the average King Brothers film, but it created no heat at the box office, which couldn't have made me happier. The picture was a routine potboiler, and any excitement caused by its release could only have been managed by the patriotic watchdog organizations; it was significant that the film failed to arouse a single protest.

My comeback had advanced another giant step, then came to a jolting halt. The ensuing hiatus, which, as always in such situations, appeared endless, was one of the most disturbing constituents of "the troubles." Since I believed the last obstacle to my rehabilitation had been removed,

I found it hard to understand the studios' indifference in the matter or to know where to place the blame. It was then I began to realize that my decision—about which I have never had any doubts—had made my road back even rockier than it had been. That was a scary perception, and only three hours a day at the weights and, most especially, Jean's never-failing understanding and support enabled me to challenge it. Then, as has happened so often in my life, help came my way from one of Hollywood's most fearless risk-takers.

"On any list of independents expected to challenge the powers that be, the producer Stanley Kramer would have been at the top," wrote Victor Navasky in his book, *Naming Names* (156). For me, he was at the top in more ways than one: He hired me when no other producer of substance was knocking at my door; he gave me full freedom with my films; and he subsequently assigned me to direct the best and most popular film he ever produced. For me, he finally broke down the resistance to blacklisted filmmakers, and he opened the way to a career that no one else of the marked group could match and only a couple could distantly approach. And for all that, I have been ever grateful.

Stanley had just concluded a pact with Harry Cohn and Columbia to make more than twenty films, none of which (with one or two exceptions) was to cost more than $1 million. This differed from other low-budget programs in that the pictures would not be "cheap" but "inexpensive films of quality." And on that point, Kramer and I saw eye to eye. When I signed a four-feature deal, starting at $60,000 a picture (a far cry from the King Brothers' $5,000, and an immediate boost to my pride and my sense of worth), Kramer already had under way, or in preparation, the film versions of three popular plays: *Death of a Salesman* (director, Lazlo Benedick); *The Four Poster* (Irving Reis); *Member of the Wedding* (Fred Zinnemann); and a film version of the book, *My Six Convicts* (Hugo Fregonese). The casts included stars like Fredric March, Rex Harrison, Julie Harris, and Akim Tamiroff. I was happy to be associated with that quality of product and talent, and for the second time in my life, I felt I was on my way. And that was true as far as films were concerned, but when it came to understanding human nature, I still had a lot to learn.

My first film for Kramer was *The Sniper*, cowritten and coproduced by Edward and Edna Anhalt. The story of a psychopathic killer, it was aimed at an understanding of the victim of a twisted mind and its uncontrollable impulses. It featured a newcomer to films, Arthur Franz, as the killer; Richard Kiley as the psychiatrist; and Adolphe Menjou, whose casting was a twenty-four-hour sensation in Hollywood. Probably for perverse, but subconscious, reasons, I suggested Menjou for the role of the police inspector who hunts down the murderer. My more rational reasons for the choice were, first, to see if an actor of such far-right stance would work with me; second, to take the screen's leading sophisticate, trade his waxed moustache for a stubble beard, and dress him in a wrinkled, off-the-rack suit; and third, I had always considered him a fine actor. (This is called "casting against type," and is often a disaster.) Menjou accepted the part and the suit, shaved off his mustache, and gave one of his best performances. Now, let me present the incident from another point of view.

David Platt, in the *New York Daily Worker* of November 15, 1951, treated the story this way:

> Movie director Edward Dmytryk, ex-member of the Hollywood Ten who turned informer for the FBI, is now palsy-walsy with his erstwhile foe—the rabid witch-hunter and the haberdasher's gentleman—Adolphe Menjou.
>
> Four years ago Menjou gave frame-up evidence about "Communist activities in Hollywood" to the Un-American Committee, the committee which hounded Dmytryk and nine other screen artists to jail for a year.
>
> Now Dmytryk and Menjou are together again—this time as friends. Menjou has the leading role in "The Sniper," which Dmytryk, gone over to warmongering and restored to the favor of Big Money, is now directing for Stanley Kramer Productions.

The buzzwords were all there—"informer for the FBI," "rabid witch-hunter," "frame-up evidence," "warmongering," and "Big Money." There was more along that line, but communist writers favored redundancy—it allowed space for more misinformation. Let me point out some of the flawed statements in the article: (1) I never informed on anyone to the FBI; (2) although we worked well together, I was by no means "palsy-walsy" with Menjou; (3) I was the opposite of a "warmonger," as some of my later films showed, and there was certainly no warmongering in this picture (an old ploy of the communist press is to throw in anything that can be harmful because most people believe what they see in print); and (4) although I had no quarrel with the terms of my contract, I was not yet in the "Big Money."

Menjou, in his turn, was attacked by *his* colleagues. He adopted an interesting defense. One of his disturbed friends, feeling betrayed, asked how he could possibly work with that ex-"commie," Dmytryk.

"I'm a whore!" snapped Menjou, and that cut short the conversation. As for me, I have always preferred wit to vilification, regardless of the politics.

22

The Menjou anecdote is more than an amusing story; it is an example of a nationwide aberration that had developed immediately after the war, ballooned through the fifties and sixties, and which, to an ever greater degree since Reagan's substitution of the "L word" for the "C word" (in the 1980s), is still with us—political polarization. This warp in our political system asserts that political partisanship is of greater significance than political programs.

Menjou was a wealthy man and in no need of a job for the job's sake. He was undoubtedly intrigued by the role offered him in *The Sniper*, which was something new for him, but a greater motivation was probably a curiosity about a timely question, as it was with me (and, I suspect, with Kramer): Was it possible for two men who were poles apart politically to work together productively?

In our case, fruitful collaboration was more than just possible. Menjou was an extremely intelligent man, and we had common interests in filmmaking and Chinese food. Our exterior locations were all in San Francisco, and we often ate our evening meals together. Political debate was tacitly tabooed, but we were pleased to find a grab bag full of discussable subjects besides politics, war, and haberdashery, and we managed lively and un-self-conscious conversations.

Menjou's disturbed friend, however, was more in tune with the discordant times. He assumed that political bias was the principle element in a working and social relationship. He would probably have been surprised to learn the Party was years ahead of him. Complete polarization was *the* basic rule in the Soviet Union, and only those who followed the party line, or pretended to, could have any hope of success in their lives or careers. In the United States, the Party was too weak to admit its ties to totalitarianism, and it based its appeal on altruistic idealism. Sooner or later, most American communists saw through the Party's false front, but even a misty sighting of pie in the sky was preferable to the arrogant "let them eat cake" attitude of the opposition. It was not love for communism that kept me aligned with the Ten so long after disillusionment had set in, but hatred for its alternative. For political and social polarization was openly flaunted by the extremists of the right.

This point of view had been promoted nationally by HUAC and locally by organizations such as the Motion Picture Alliance for the Preservation of American Ideals. It had been nourished by men like J. Parnell Thomas in Washington and by C. B. DeMille in Hollywood. Then, in the early fifties, Joe McCarthy added a great deal of insult to injury by his one-man campaign to brand those of whom he disapproved as enemies of his country. Eventually, he overreached himself and committed political suicide. Unfortunately, the human species being what it is, his bigotry will live forever.

Hollywood has always feared audience polarization. (For instance, we had to overcome a great deal of inside opposition in the making of *Crossfire*, a film that attacked racism.) In an effort to eliminate such a possibility, the studios unwisely created a polarization of their own through the imposition of blacklists and graylists on an industry-wide basis. Political ostracism by individuals and groups inevitably followed.

A few Hollywood spokesmen, including former actors and senator George Murphy and actor and ex-president Ronald Reagan, have denied the existence of such protective measures, but that is like neo-Nazis denying Hitler's concentration camps. In truth, there were a number of blacklists, and no one in full possession of his senses would dream of denying the fact that many men and women in the entertainment media were barred from working for reasons that had nothing to do with their qualifications or the quality of their work. The Waldorf-Astoria Declaration, later amended to include many besides the original Hollywood Ten, was a publicly released full-fledged blacklist that "names those in disfavor." A number of periodicals, including *Red Channels, Counterattack*, and the *American Legion Magazine*, published lists of suspected un-American individuals and organizations (often without confirmation), and several syndicated columnists were on the alert to report their own suspicions; George Sokolsky, especially, was a self-appointed naming and clearing committee of one. And finally, every major studio had an employee who checked the political backgrounds and records of all those seeking a place on the company payroll.

The term *graylist* sounds less sinister than *blacklist*, but the opposite is true. For instance, I was blacklisted, I knew why I was blacklisted, and when I so desired, I knew how to get off the blacklist. Both the responsibility and the remedy were under my control. The graylisted, on the other hand, although generally left-wingers, were almost never communists and usually had no knowledge of their transgressions or even that they had transgressed. They knew they weren't working, but they didn't know why, and by the time they found the last pieces of the puzzle, they had lost a lot of ground. Even their agents, if they had them, often didn't know the truth, and if they did, they kept it to themselves. It was unquestionably a conspiracy, and many who might have ultimately found success in Hollywood disappeared from the scene. To be on the studio graylist was to be anonymous.

I was thoroughly aware of the blacklists, but I knew nothing of the graylists until I was putting together a crew for *The Sniper*. I had asked for a certain man as a dialogue director and learned I had to await studio approval. A few days later, my request was denied. There was nothing specifically damning in the man's record, but I was told, it "would just be safer not to hire him." When I persisted, I found that "safer not to" meant "absolutely not!" The clearance man was actually the equivalent of a communist commissar with veto power, and the studio backed him to the limit. The spineless Eric Johnson no longer made brave statements about the un-American nature of the blacklist, and the studio was taking no chances, which made hiring writers and actors more difficult than selecting a crew.

The many sacrifices of the war years had conditioned a number of decent people to feelings of sympathy and charity. Scores of actors and writers had signed activist petitions and donated to what appeared to be worthy causes—and most of them were. But how was one to know which was the brainchild of a communist front? Not one writer in twenty, and even fewer actors, were aware that such fronts existed, and so they remained ignorant of their "blunders." But now, as work opportunities mysteriously slipped away and idle time accumulated, they began to wonder why they were unemployable. Sooner or later, some sympathetic producer or director would inform them that they were on the list. The first step was to absorb the shock; the second was to find out what crime they had committed. That was no easy task, since many of them didn't know the Motion Picture Industry Council existed. However, once in touch, they were informed that their approval or their money had been given to some group working with or for the Communist Party. That was the second shock; the realization that they were now crimeless victims as well as the realization that they must expiate an act they had considered humanitarian propelled the accused into the real world at last.

The bleeding hearts wept for those who fled to Europe or Mexico rather than face the music; my sympathies went out to those unselfish actors and writers who had never made a procommunist move but were forced to flail at shadows in defending themselves against the amorphous allegations of the arbitrary graylist. Contempt of Congress was a much more honest charge!

During this period, and for many years thereafter, ostracism was rampant in Hollywood. The extreme right, whose motto was "Once a commie, always a commie," recoiled at the slightest tinge of red. In a strange and unholy alliance, they were joined by the extreme left, which turned its back on those who had cooperated with the Committee and those who were *rumored* to have cooperated with the Committee. But perhaps the most disturbing and least-understandable group to join in the ostracism consisted of wandering liberals who, though not party members, were sympathetic to its cause. Such liberals were called "Pinkos."

Those who still embraced communism because they believed in it, or those who held what Victor Navasky in *Naming Names* calls a "moral presumption" against denouncing it or its members, were only an occasional problem, actors in minor bits of drama that might be called "Awkward Moments." Their reactions were basic and understandable. But they suffered from their confrontational attitudes more than did those they ostracized, for those reactions were invariably manifestations of bitterness and hate, which is a sign of inner rot.

My first brush with a person of this category occurred a few months after my second appearance before HUAC. Jean and I, while spending a weekend in Palm Springs, were dinner guests of a hotel owner and his wife. The day had been perfect, and we were enjoying a lively conversation. A couple seated nearby had been eyeing us somewhat grimly, but since they were strangers to me, I assumed only that we might have been too boisterous for their taste. We were having our dessert and coffee when the couple got up to leave. On their way out, the man walked behind me and uttered a string of vituperation and profanity. The sudden verbal blast caught me by surprise, and I missed most of the words but heard enough to know it had to do with my cooperation with HUAC. And I could smell the hate. By the time I had collected my scattered thoughts, the couple was out of the room and I saw no point in rushing after them for a confrontation. Our hosts were embarrassed, and Jean, whose hearing is better than mine, was angry. I was emotionally confused.

A bit later, as our hosts politely steered the conversation away from the incident, my confusion had subsided, and I found I could only feel a cold pity for the stranger who harbored so much hate for a man he recognized but didn't know. I had done him no personal harm, so in his boorish way, he must have been avenging the damage I had done to his organization. After a few more similar, though not as vulgar, incidents, I came to realize that his reactions may have been aggravated as he watched me enjoying myself. I learned that those on the other side of the line expected me to carry a full load of guilt. When my behavior disappointed them, some got angry, but most rationalized that I must be grievously suffering inside.

An anecdote included in Navasky's *Naming Names*, is a perfect example of such a sublimation. I had never known Adrian Scott's widow, Joan. When Adrian and I worked together or attended party meetings, he had been married to Ann Shirley, who divorced him not long after the 1947 hearings, apparently because of his refusal to divorce himself from his comrades. After his release from prison, he had been keeping company with my ex-wife and living at her apartment. My ex-wife died in 1952 from the effects of mixing whiskey with sleeping pills, just as medical research was recognizing that combination as possibly lethal. The communists wanted the world to believe that nobody on their side died a natural death, and they claimed her as a victim of my problems with HUAC.[9] That was nonsense. She had never been a communist, and any problems she shared were Adrian's, not mine. She was certainly not a suicide; she died of drug abuse, a death not uncommon in our society. I am not in possession of the dates, but I assume Scott married Joan some time after my ex-wife's death.

Adrian died in 1973, and Joan Scott chose to carry on his martyrdom, which, unlike the self-sacrificing attitudes of the saints, was rooted in hate and a seemingly unquenchable desire to see the renegades suffer as they themselves were suffering. Such wishful thinking distracts the senses and makes accurate observation impossible. At least so it would appear in the incident that follows. In *Naming Names*, Victor Navasky quotes Joan Scott as saying:

"We bumped into Dmytryk one night in a restaurant sometime in 1956 or 1957. We were seated in a booth adjoining Dmytryk, his wife,

---

9. When Edward Bromberg died of heart failure in 1952, the communists blamed the Committee for hounding him to death. But Bromberg was an ailing man before 1947; he had apparently suffered a rheumatic heart condition for years.

and a guest. Dmytryk pretended not to see Adrian. Adrian said in an aside to me, 'Dmytryk is sitting there with his wife.' So I said, 'Do you want to move?' Adrian said, 'Hell no. I want to look.' And he sat and stared and Dmytryk refused to look back. He just drank. He was miserable" (375).

If Navasky had checked with me, I could have told him that Joan Scott was a questionable witness and less than a middling mind reader. I made no pretense of avoiding Adrian's gaze; our eyes met from time to time, but they weren't eyes I wanted to drink to, and I saw no profit in a schoolboy's staring contest. What's more, I don't drink, and I was by no means miserable. But I *was* sad, sad at the thought of how needlessly futile Adrian's past few years had been; sad that a man whom I had respected as a writer and a producer had become professionally sterile; sad that, if the reports were true, he had once more found refuge in the Party. I could not understand how anyone, given Scott's experiences and knowledge of communist aims and activities, could possibly be so regressive, so self-destructive. Maintaining silence about one's associates was one thing, but making common cause with those largely responsible for his present situation was not the way of wisdom.

Another incident, more typical of the three or four I survived without damage during those years, occurred in San Francisco. Jean and I had dropped in to see Mort Sahl perform at The Hungry Eye and were seated on a cross aisle in the small auditorium. The show was about to start when I noticed a man in work clothes hurrying down the aisle, checking the overhead spotlights. As he neared us he looked down, saw two familiar faces, and broke into a smile. Simultaneously, he held out his hand. But in less than two heartbeats his face froze into the dour expression I had always known, and Alvah Bessie jerked his hand back just as I was reaching for it. He scurried on down the aisle, and for the remainder of the evening, we saw him only from a distance as he worked at his duties—lighting and propping the show. Although the locales were different, my other encounters were carbon copies of my meeting with Bessie.

Then there were two other encounters with close friends that might be of some interest to students of behavioral sciences. Both were rejections of a special sort. Ed Mosk was a lawyer, a nice guy, and a family friend. It was Ed who had put me in touch with Rod Geiger, which had led to my two British films in exile, and it was Ed who had spotted and surreptitiously scanned the carelessly positioned subpoena on the law clerk's counter, which made my last few days before leaving for prison an unusual adventure. He was, after a fashion, my Hollywood attorney. So I was not surprised when, shortly after my return from Washington in 1951, he invited me to lunch on the terrace of the Knickerbocker Hotel.

I expected a pleasant get-together. But I was wrong. Politely, and with some apparent regret, he informed me that, considering the circumstances, he could no longer represent me. Momentarily, I wondered where legal ethics began and where they stopped; he could plead for a child rapist or a pederast, but not for me. Well, a portside lawyer was a mouthpiece I didn't need. He was doing me a favor.

The other incident in which party loyalty ruled above all involved a couple who, at the time, were our best friends. Bill Watts had spent most of his adult life in the theater, with no conspicuous success; nor had he conquered Hollywood. I was responsible for all his gainful employment from 1945 through 1947. In 1946, I took him to England and to the Alps. Between films, Bill and his wife, Flo, toured the West, which included a location hunting trip to the Canadian Rockies, as our guests. When I went to prison, Bill's wife consoled Jean for what, she dolefully assured her, would be my permanent martyrdom. Then my prison statement hit the streets, and so did Bill and Flo—they disappeared from our lives. But there was a P.S.

A few years later I cast Lee Cobb, a mutual friend, in *The Left Hand of God*, a film I made with Bogart. Cobb told me he had run into Bill in New York, and Bill had asked him to give me his regards, but with the stipulation that Flo should never know. "If she hears of this," Bill said, "she will divorce me." You may believe it or not, but it was only then I felt certain that Bill and Flo were communists. But it was not the first time I recognized a wife as the driving force in party loyalty.

One need not sympathize with the hard-core members of the Party to understand their need to retaliate in any way they could. Their organization had been materially damaged by my defection. But the frontline troops, I knew, were hurt by my attack against the purity of their ideals, since that was all that sustained them. Those ideals were their most precious property and had to be defended against all sources of disillusionment.

The ostracizers of the far right, who were just as doctrinaire, also defended their property, but the property they defended was exactly that, property. And in their minds, anyone who had once threatened that property was capable of doing so again. Even my insurance company got into the act; the Southern California Auto Club refused us coverage. I didn't know whether it was a leftist clerk who turned us down because of my second appearance or, what seemed more likely for the auto club, a rightest who had just learned about my first. Whichever, I was branded an "unacceptably high risk." I shuddered to think they possibly knew more about party vengeance than I did. (A long-time party member who defected later told us that if we had gone to Europe soon after my second Committee appearance, I would probably have been "taken care of.") Other companies to whom we appealed followed the auto club's lead. Eventually, Occidental Life agreed to cover us; all it took was a letter from Roy Brewer, another from the president of a film company, and a third from Republican Congressman Donald Jackson. It pays to know the right people.

As for the members of the Motion Picture Alliance for the Preservation of American Ideals, some, like Ward Bond, George Marshall, and Hedda Hopper, were content to husband their hostilities; they leaped into the fray only when I had a possible award-winning film. (More on that later.) But my erstwhile casual friend, who some years before had felt we were taking different paths toward the same end, had apparently changed his mind. When given the opportunity to ventilate his political opinions, the Duke always named me as the quintessential Hollywood commie. However, I never felt that Wayne was, in any way, an obstacle to the reestablishment of my career. There were other heavyweights who were of greater consequence in that area. They are important enough to have a chapter of their own.

23

Once again, I was lucky. I was working for the most progressive film-maker in Hollywood. Stanley Kramer was a man of good mind and strong purpose and unquestionably one of the outstanding producers in motion picture history. I had a few disagreements with his way of working, but they were minor and unspoken. I was sorry when he decided to become a film director. I could gladly have spent the rest of my film career working with him alone. Yes, I was lucky, and happy in my work, but I made a crucial mistake; I assumed my troubles were behind me. I didn't realize that a burgeoning hate had become the losers' only reason for living or that the particular aspect of the cold war in which I had been involved was a virus that could be checked but never wiped out. However, for the next twenty-odd years, the fates were relatively kind; the center was broad and friendly, the sniping from the left never ceased completely, but the sniping from the right was a more frustrating problem.

I made four films for Kramer, with the last, *The Caine Mutiny*, standing out as an Oscar nominee and the box-office champion of its time. My first three films were typical of Stanley's Columbia program; they were made on short schedules, tight budgets, and generally with no-name casts. Each had a strong theme, an involving story, and all were well regarded by the critics; in short, each had everything except the necessary pheromone to attract the required swarms of viewers. But on the fourth, Kramer experimented with a different formula, and my bait bucket was filled to overflowing.

The Kramer program had totaled about twenty films that showed a cumulative loss, but his fade-out production, *The Caine Mutiny*, put Kramer, his entire program, and his financing company, Columbia Pictures, well into the solid black. It was his first film to feature a script based on an international best-seller, it had a tight but decent budget, and an all-star cast that included Humphrey Bogart, in possibly the most memorable role of his great career; Van Johnson, then a top leading man; Fred McMurray; and Jose Ferrer. In short, it had the necessary appeal to attract record-breaking audiences and to catch the special attention of the two political extremes, which justifies a couple of paragraphs of analysis.

There had been some rather noisy resistance to the filming of *The Caine Mutiny* from the far right, on the grounds that it was unflattering to the United States Navy. Kramer must have felt some inner anxiety, but it was not reflected in his demeanor; he seemed unconcerned about the complaints. When we made our preproduction trip to Hawaii to meet the commander in chief of the Pacific and the slew of admirals who were in command of the various facilities our film required, we got a great lift; nowhere did we encounter anything but unequivocal encouragement. The commander of the Navy Yard who, we were told, was our toughest nut to crack, took us off the hook shortly after we shook hands. "*The Caine Mutiny*," he said, "should be required reading for every officer and man in the United States Navy!" That sentiment, which was echoed by every sailor we worked with, was later transferred to the film.

There was one small problem—we would be filming in the Navy Yard at Pearl Harbor, and I had no clearance from security. With typical efficiency, Commander James Shaw, the most helpful technical adviser I had ever worked with, went into action. It seems the Naval Intelligence had placed no data in my dossier after 1947, and that was not an auspicious time to close the book. No bad entries was good, but no good entries was bad. Getting into high gear, the commander slashed through the usual red tape and pressured intelligence units to update their information. Clearance in hand, he returned from Washington within a week. Throughout the production, I found the navy system allowed for quick individual command decisions, which made it possible to shoot a great deal of usable material in an unbelievably short time. Incidentally, of special interest and benefit to me, it also allowed some courageous and independent political action.

The front-page headlines of *The Film Daily* on March 28, 1955, proclaimed, "*Caine Mutiny* heads *Ten Best*." But there was some disagreement from the left, which was ameliorated by a peculiar aspect of the criticism; after 1951, the communist press, both in the States and in Europe did not so much critique my films as they did my status as an enemy of their movement. It was party dogma that the excruciating pangs of a guilty conscience suffered by every renegade also stifled his every effort at creativity. Joan Scott's assumption that "he was miserable" and Phil Brown's expressed pity for any turncoat who found "facing himself in the mirror to shave an almost unbearable experience" (Navasky, *Naming Names*, 345) are based on axioms taken from the communist "Handbook on Wishful Thinking." Since such an assumed conscience and its deadly effects were matters of doctrine, the film itself could be quickly dismissed as worthless, while the remainder of the column could be filled with all the billingsgate at the critic's command.

This hostile attitude on the left never quite disappeared, and it reached its climax with the 1958 release of *The Young Lions*. While I was preparing *A Walk on the Wild Side* at Columbia in 1961, a French journalist dropped into my office. During our conversation, he pulled two tattered clippings out of his wallet. They were reviews of *The Young Lions*, he told me, scissored out of the two leading communist papers in Paris. He had been carrying them for at least three years—I didn't ask why. One review, true to formula, said virtually nothing about the film; it just tore me to shreds, an onslaught to which I was by then completely immune. But the second critic made my day. He did his duty to the Party by also belittling my character, but apparently bewildered, he ended by saying, in effect, "Nevertheless, 'The Young Lions' is an outstanding film, which contains a great deal worth seeing."

If one follows the communist dialectic, the rule that an artist loses his ability to create when he leaves the Party leads to the conclusion that his post-exit output in no way compares to that achieved when he was still a believer. That is an irrational conclusion that has annoyed me no end, and which can easily be refuted by the record. Howard Fast and Budd Schulberg, along with other apostate artists, did some of their best work *after* they renounced the Party, and all of Elia Kazan's outstanding film achievements followed his defection in 1936. The communist point of view could be expected from party critics, but a number of left-leaning scholars, as well as encyclopedists, have uncritically supported the communist position.

Besides *The Caine Mutiny*, my output after 1951 included such films as *The Broken Lance*, named the best western of 1954; *The Left Hand of God; The End of the Affair; Raintree County*, an Oscar nominee; and my personal favorite, *The Young Lions*, which covered a broad field of human relationships, including love, war, and anti-Semitism. Later came *Warlock, A Walk on the Wild Side, The Reluctant Saint*, and *Mirage*. A pertinent fact is that nearly all the films carried messages of social importance, yet were entertaining and absorbing enough to pull in the people.

Almost all the above-mentioned films won international critics' awards of one sort or another, and both in audience appeal and in substance, they far outweighed those I made before 1947. Of course, stars like Spencer Tracy, Humphrey Bogart, Marlon Brando, Elizabeth Taylor,

Monty Clift, Gregory Peck, Henry Fonda, Max Schell, Richard Widmark, Anthony Quinn, and Deborah Kerr, plus well-conceived and well-written scripts didn't hurt. The only films I made during my hitch in the Party were *Till the End of Time*, which had nothing to do with political philosophies, and *Cornered*, which did. The latter was by no means one of my best, though it did serve to get me out of the Party. (This summation is unavoidably self-serving, but its real purpose is to make it possible for reasonable conclusions to be drawn concerning the Party's biased point of view about the moral and ethical results of the renunciation of communism.)

The right wing's reaction was of a different sort; blinded by their continuing antagonism to anyone who might have experimented with the Party, they cheerfully worked the communists' side of the street. DeMille's motorcycle brigade and the telephone squad of the Motion Picture Alliance went into action when they sensed I had a winner. The Academy nominated two of my post-1951 films, *The Caine Mutiny*, and *Raintree County*, for best picture; Elizabeth Taylor got her first nomination for best actress in the latter film. There were other candidates in other categories, and a few eventual winners. I received no mention for either picture. I confess I was a touch peeved, but I am not paranoid. I knew nothing of the telephone campaigns until they were reported to me by friendly directors who had been importuned and by one of my agents who represented some of the callers. I had thought it odd that the films were good enough to grab an assortment of nominations, yet their director wasn't. After once suffering a similar "oversight," Mervyn Leroy had said to me, "How can it be a best picture without the best direction?" Now it's nice to have Spielberg and Streisand for company.

At this stage of my comeback, it was like starting all over again, and *The Caine Mutiny* was more than just a motion picture; it was an anxious but hopeful step leading to the high ground. The first three steps had been short ones; no matter how we tried to deceive ourselves about Kramer's "inexpensive films of taste and quality," we knew they could be rated no higher than B-plus or, to be charitable, A-minus. But *The Caine Mutiny*, a top A in every respect, did more than earn money and prestige for Kramer and Columbia; it returned me to the "acceptable" list. The industry's top stars were thorough professionals then and very picky about their directors; in that epoch of Hollywood's history, only a handful of filmmakers were consistently in demand. So, when the stars of *The*

Caine Mutiny, who represented a mixed bag of political persuasions, agreed to work under my direction, it meant more to me than just the opportunity to make an exceptional film—it proved no star would turn me down.

But my sense of self-satisfaction was tempered by a nagging doubt: Did Kramer have to twist an arm or two in my behalf? Then Twentieth Century producer, Sol Siegel, who had dropped my contract as a B director when he had taken over that department at Paramount in 1940, asked me to make Spencer Tracy's first film away from MGM, and I knew at last that I had finally made a list not labeled "Black" or "Gray," but "Approved."

My luck was holding. Darryl Zanuck, the production chief at Twentieth Century–Fox, was another independent soul. Like Cohn, he had not appeared before HUAC to testify in defense of the industry, and he was one of the few who had fought hard against the Waldorf-Astoria Declaration. On the minus side, he had an industry-wide reputation as a dictatorial and meddling executive, which immediately raises a film director's hackles, and I was apprehensive about working for him. But a big "adult" western with Spencer Tracy, Richard Widmark, Jean Peters, Katy Jurado, Robert Wagner, and E. G. Marshall was too tempting to turn down. Moreover, the IRS was still taking its pound of flesh, and the Fox deal doubled my salary. However, the chief attraction was Richard Murphy's almost-finished script.

The story was sketchily based on *The House of Strangers*, which had been made at Twentieth Century some three years earlier by Joe Mankiewicz. It was a good film but a failure at the box office. Our western borrowed only the basic situation of an iron-willed father in conflict with his sons, then developed a drama of prejudice inherent in the presence of an Indian wife and a half-breed son. Our hope was that *The Broken Lance* would succeed where its progenitor had failed, a hope fulfilled beyond Zanuck's highest expectations. Six years after getting my pink subpoena, I was once again established as a director in demand, and for the next ten years, Jean and I lived the American Dream.

Victoria was born in November of 1951, and Michael was back with us after his mother died. But too many years in the enemy camp had taken their toll, and he found it difficult to adjust. The problem was understandable but impossible to deal with. After some fifteen months, he returned to a nearby private school where he had been boarding before coming to live with us. While these complex changes were taking place,

Jean had found, and leased, a beautiful three-acre estate in old Bel Air. The postwar real estate boom had not yet taken off, and we were able to buy the place at a ridiculously low price; it was to be our home for the next nineteen years.

Accompanied by Jean and the two kids, I flew to England, after filming *The Broken Lance*, to make Graham Greene's *The End of the Affair* for David Rose, (the producer, not the composer). By the time the film was finished and we returned to California, *The Broken Lance* had been released and a nonexclusive, five-picture deal was waiting for me at Twentieth Century. I had passed the test, and so had Zanuck. Ignoring the rumors, I had discovered a rational and supportive executive who showed a quality deeply appreciated in a field as uncertain as our; Zanuck was constructively encouraging but never interfering. I signed my new contract without any reservations.

(I find I have been complimentary about two executive producers in a row, which could get me thrown out of the Directors Guild. Perhaps that was due to a change in *my* attitude. If so, it was an example of something good coming out of something bad. During the first stage of my career, I had been susceptible to one of Hollywood's chronic anxieties: What or who waits around the next bend in the road? But my stint in prison had effectively erased the "who" from the bogeyman list, and now my reaction to tough authority was, "If I could take four-and-a-half months in jail, how can anyone fill me with fear?" Of course, life as a whole is not quite that simplistic, but at that stage of my comeback it was a decided help.)

Over the next few years, I made several films at Twentieth Century, and two, including *Raintree County*, outside of what was now my home studio. After *Raintree*, I was approached about filming *The Young Lions*. I had just finished an extremely long and difficult stint with Monty Clift in *Raintree*, and I was looking forward to a few months rest. But just as I was beginning to feel human again, Twentieth Century approached me with an uncompleted script adapted from Irwin Shaw's novel, *The Young Lions*. I knew the book, and I was high on its possibilities. Clift lived in New York, and my first move was to send him Edward Anhalt's nearly completed script. Monty had a great drinking problem, and after *Raintree* I had sworn that, great actor, good friend, and exceptional person that he was, I would never work with him again—but who else could play Noah? A few days later, I received a brief telegram, "Yes." Well, risks are there to be taken. Then, through a strange combination of circumstances, I hit the jackpot; Marlon Brando, who had hesitated to play in *On the Waterfront* because of Kazan's defection from the Party, agreed to play the part of the German, Christian Diestl. Dean Martin made his dramatic debut as the third member of the trio. Hope Lange, Barbara Rush, and two newcomers, Mai Britt, who could speak English, and Maximillian Schell, who couldn't, were the heart of another great cast. A couple of weeks with the dialogue coach we had brought with us to Paris, and Max was ready to go. The rest is movie history. Schell won the Oscar for best actor with his performance in his second English-language film, Kramer's *Judgement at Nuremberg*, and though he now devotes much of his time to the theater and to directing, in my opinion he is one of the five best actors in the world.

As is customary, we started shooting locations in Paris, outside of Strasbourg, and in Germany. We had good luck and bad luck. The good luck was that Monty didn't cost us one lost hour; the bad luck was that our French crew cost us many weeks. Twentieth Century's man in Paris had no experience with production, and he had rounded up a hodge-podge gang of workers, half of whom were members of the communist film union. We were (or rather, I was) sabotaged at every turn. That we made any progress at all was due to the nonparty members of the crew, who did their best in spite of repeated threats of future job boycotts. "Dmytryk is going back to Hollywood when he is finished, but you have to stay and work here," was the communists' threat. One actress, who was brought to Hollywood for interior scenes, was blacklisted for several years after her return to Paris. But in spite of the Party's campaign, we were getting great work from Brando, Monty, et al., and after some three months away from "home and mother," we left Paris with a huge collective sigh of relief. Strangely, my irritating and time-consuming hassle with the communists of Paris had made me forget the problems building at home.

24

In 1926, I was enrolled at Cal Tech to study mathematical physics; one year later, I changed my mind. I looked at the students and professors around me, and I had a vague feeling that films, which were just beginning to show signs of a potential broader than pantomime with titles, might, in the long run, prove of more value to the world than science. The modern-day spate of gratuitous vulgarity and sickening violence, both physical and sexual, makes it hard to keep the faith, but my hopes are sustained by rare films, like *Dead Poets Society*; there is still a chance that filmmakers like Tom Schulman, Peter Weir, and Robin Williams *can* make a difference. And while science (still my favorite avocation) has probably made life easier, it is doubtful that it has made life better, and it has unquestionably raised the world's index of insecurity.

A long-term (I'm talking generations) improvement in ethics, morals, and quality standards will do more to improve life than teflon frying pans or a search for the rascal who set off the Big Bang. Ethics, morals, and standards are, to a considerable extent, in the hands of the people's representatives, therefore in the hands of the people. That's where the buck really stops. The cliché says, correctly, that selecting the best government is a good citizen's responsibility; so it was with dismay that Jean and I, who hoped to do our part as good citizens, discovered quite suddenly that neither of us was able to engage in any meaningful political activity; shoving our ballots into the ballot box was as dedicated as we could get.

The rude awakening came in 1952, when we volunteered to work in Adlai Stevenson's presidential campaign. With no attempt at diplomacy, it was pointed out that our help would be the kiss of death. My involvement with communism and HUAC was all too recent for clear distinctions to be made, and the local Republicans would certainly take advantage of the opportunities. McCarthy's star was in the ascendant, and branding liberals guilty by association was the sport of the decade. Our concern was appreciated, but our support was not wanted.

We accepted the harsh reality of the situation, but eight years and ten films later, we tried again. Jean was becoming an efficient activist in purely local circles, and carried away by a fading memory and growing optimism, we decided to extend our parochial freedom to a broader field of political activity. We discussed the advantages of a local film campaign for Jack Kennedy, and primed with plans and good intentions, we approached a good friend who was a wheel in southern California Democratic politics. Startled at our suggestions, he looked at us for a moment, then broke into a laugh.

"Boy!" he said, "You *really* want to see Kennedy lose, don't you?"

There was nothing more to be said—the stigma was still there. But that was the way it was. We could donate money—anonymously—but our names could not appear on the fliers or the ads we helped pay for. We were not welcome at political rallies or demonstrations. No Oscar nominations? Hell, regardless of the quality of my films, I couldn't even get elected to my guild's board of directors. Over the years, Jean and I have concluded that this was by far the most baneful result of my association with the Hollywood Ten. Like a feebly felt, deeply buried ache of old age, it has remained with us ever since. But as time passed, a few attitudes were slowly changing, and there were different and sharper irritations to scratch.

The fifties were drawing to a close, and faced with competition from "the box," disappearing profits, and terminal attrition in the executive ranks of men who knew and loved motion pictures even better than money, the studios were floundering. As a good studio man, I didn't realize that I was floundering with them.

Still, my record and my Paramount contract saw me through the sixties and into the seventies. I made *A Walk on the Wild Side* for Charles Feldman and Columbia; produced and directed *The Reluctant Saint*, with Max Schell, one of my favorite films and my biggest flop, also for Columbia; and *Mirage*, with Gregory Peck and Walter Matthau, for Universal. Nothing to be ashamed of there. For Paramount I made two films: *The Carpetbaggers* was hit and miss with the critics but a tremendous success with the public, whereas *Where Love Has Gone* was a dismal failure, both from the critics' point of view and from mine. Then my past caught up with me—again.

After a long and relatively quiet period politically, I was hit fore and aft or, to put it more properly, from both port and starboard. Milton Sperling, whom I had known for forty years, sent me a script of *The Battle of the Bulge*. After I read it, we spent several hours in enthusiastic discussion of the project. I liked the story, and I liked the prospective cast; by the end of the evening, we had reached a verbal agreement. But the film was being backed by Warners, where Jack Warner was still the boss, and as I said "Good night," I voiced a fleeting thought.

"You'd better check with Jack," I said. "He has been quoted as saying, 'Dmytryk will work in my studio only over my dead body.' "

Milton, a quick thinker, barely flinched. "Don't worry," he said. "I'll take care of it."

I didn't worry, but neither did I carry a full load of confidence out of Sperling's apartment that night. The Royal Air Force motto, "Crash on regardless!" was not to his taste. I never heard from him again, but I was becoming adept at reading silence; I assumed the deal was off. So much for the hard right.

On the other side were the communists' greatest asset, the "parlor pinks," to whom ignorance of the facts hardly mattered. They knew I was a backslider and a renegade, and that was enough; in their judgment, blind loyalty to a questionable cause was more important than common sense or talent. In company with Richard Widmark and a friendly agent, I had set up *The Buffalo Soldiers* at United Artists, and once more the systems were "go" until the deal reached the top for final approval and the reigning liberal executive squashed it.

I was a leaking balloon, but I wasn't the only one in Hollywood crying "Foul!" Inexorably, the pendulum's swing had reached the other side. The Actors and Writers Guilds had once more veered toward the left which, in itself, was not unhealthy, but so had the executive branch of the industry, and a growing number of conservative and right-wing artists, who felt that they, too, had a constitutional right to work, complained out loud of the pinko blacklists. A shoe on the other foot always pinches.

My own problems, however, were in a category apart, and the third incident in that area had a familiar ring, but a most unusual reaction. Sergio Leone signed a three-picture deal with Paramount (where my profit sheet showed a healthy balance). He planned to shoot two of them himself and asked me to make the third. The story sounded possible, the deal was good, and my bank balance was low; besides, I liked what little I knew and everything I had heard about the man (I didn't know the half of it). I agreed to make the film.

A few days later, I got a call from New York. It took me a moment to make out the caller's identity—Sergio, the maker of those tough spaghetti westerns, was crying!

He had tried every form of persuasion at his command, but the studio had the right of approval and the adamant answer had been, "Over my dead body!" No, it wasn't Jack Warner; it was someone who had borrowed Warner's hackneyed line, the executive who had turned me down earlier at United Artists. Playing Hollywood's version of musical chairs for executives, one of his rounds had dropped him on the throne of Paramount for a short stay. It was easy to put two and two together; the difficult part to accept was that I, who was losing a much-needed job, was consoling a man who had three. I hung up the phone lamenting that I could not do the film, but for only one reason: a man who could cry over the misfortune of a fellow director was a man eminently worth knowing.

The above anecdote nicely illustrates that my bouts with the opposition often had interesting, beneficial, even humanizing counterreactions to offset their more unpleasant aspects. But once more, the decent people, at least from my point of view, were in the middle. Old left-wingers, like John Houseman, whose influence was in the ascendance, now felt it safe to be open enemies. My life had accustomed me to downhill rides on the roller-coaster, and I could swallow my disappointments, but my kids were now growing up (Rebecca had been born in 1961), and readers with a realistic awareness of human nature have probably guessed that no such emotional escape was available to our children. They were occasionally the targets of "slings and arrows" aimed at them by other children, who must have gotten their ammunition from their parents, and even by the adults themselves. There was, for instance, the incident at the prestigious Westlake School for Girls. Our daughter, Victoria, had already been accepted as a day student when she was blackballed at the last hour by two school mothers who could not allow their children to attend classes with the Dmytryk's daughter. Victoria never got over the humiliation.

However, such incidents are more properly material for Jean's book, which will concern the trials, tribulations, and joys of a wife who chose to share the trials, tribulations, and joys of her husband. Her anger burns more hotly than mine, and I shall leave it to her to do them justice. As for those who find it difficult to believe that such a deep desire for vengeance and so much hate can vigorously survive the passage of forty years, the next chapter will bring things up to date.

25

The **July 20, 1988 issue** of the *Hollywood Daily Variety* features Tom Pryor's column, "From the Sidelines," carrying this headline:

> Enlightenment Opportunity
> Lost at Barcelona Festival

The film festival was the year's highlight in a most hospitable Catalonia. For two weeks early in July, Barcelona's hotels and theaters were hosts to dozens of Hollywood personalities and film aficionados from Europe and the Americas, while the members of the press and air media haunted them for interviews during all hours of the day and night. But, as Pryor mentioned insightfully, the activity that will be longest remembered by the festival's guests was the "homage" paid to a few of Hollywood's blacklisted artists.

A panel of five men and one woman had been invited to discuss the trials and tribulations of Hollywood's darkest days, now some forty years in the past. The discussion was being held in a long, narrow room that was apparently a civic council chamber, with desks at each seat equipped with a microphone connected to a speaking system. Jean and I sat in the front row, and I had activated my "mike" to be able to join the discussion if an opportunity presented itself. And it did, often, but it was not the kind I had hoped for.

A panel discussion is usually guided and controlled by its moderator, and I hoped we would have one who was neutral, though I doubted that the three chief panelists would have accepted an unbiased chairman. To do their best—or their worst—appeal to emotionalism was crucial, and they needed a moderator who was an ally. They got one. He was Spanish film scholar Ruben Gubern, and his introduction of the panelists indicated his political stance. He wanted his hearers to believe they were listening to crusaders just back from reclaiming Jerusalem for our side.

The invited panelists, originally, were writer Wilbur Bernstein; directors John Berry, Jules Dassin, Edward Dmytryk; Spanish actress Rosaura Revueltas; and Daniel Taradash, a Hollywood writer-director, and the only member of the panel who had not been a communist sympathizer, nor had he been blacklisted. He was the moderator's nod to neutrality.

Taradash was not only neutral, he was nearly nonexistent. Apparently bemused, he sat like a man who had wandered into the wrong arena, a strong reminder of the placid protect-yourself-at-all-cost liberals of the late forties and fifties. He was unwilling to contradict or even comment on the most flagrant misstatements, or to object to the vicious scurrility from the American members of the panel, perhaps in fear of becoming an instant target for their vilification. It is a fear that has afflicted many "neutrals" in Hollywood.

As for the three communists (now possibly excommunists), I had named Julie Dassin and John Berry in 1951 as members of the Party, but I had not been aware of writer William Bernstein until I saw his credit on one of Woody Allen's lesser efforts, a film that did no justice to the communists, the producers, or the blacklisted writers.

Dassin and Berry had told the Committee that my presence on the panel would not be tolerated, and I had been asked to excuse myself. I agreed, and accompanied by my wife, I was seated in the audience. Although I had vivid memories of the Party's roughhouse tactics, after a forty-year hiatus I hoped for a civilized discussion. However, after the moderator's reverent introduction of the three excommunists, I knew there would be no attempt at evenhandedness. Still, I was taken off-guard.

Once the discussion was under way, the air was filled with epithets like "Judas," "informer," and "scum," all directed at me, of course. My few quiet responses had no effect on the volume or the burden of my enemies' tirades, and the ranting, revilement, and vilification continued throughout the shortened session. Any honest discussion of the blacklists and other results of HUAC's hearings were completely forgotten.

I was conscious of Jean's anger and pent-up tears as she sat rigidly at my side. Some of their lies about our pre-1951 association included Jean, especially the distortions of Dassin. During a brief moment of relative calm, he had said, "If my memory serves me correctly, I took care of Dmytryk's children while he was in jail." If that was not an out-and-out fabrication, he should have sued his memory. We were living in Europe before I was imprisoned, and neither Jean nor I remember seeing Julie after early 1948, some months before the birth of our first child.

Those misstatements were minor, and Jean could shrug them off as easily as she did the invective of the other panelists, but Dassin's insults and lies nearly crushed her. She and Julie had worked together at MGM in the early forties when they were both under contract to that studio.

They had established a warm friendship that continued after our marriage—we had become part of a small group that met weekly for food and charades. I could understand Dassin's enmity toward me, but Jean found his virulence hard to accept, especially since she had done nothing to deserve his animosity. Of course, she *was* my wife.

As Pryor began and ended his article on the affair, it was "too bad"—an opportunity for enlightenment had been lost. And Jean had finally lost her composure. No longer rigid, her arms on the desk and her head on her arms, she gave vent to her emotions in a burst of tears. I realized that I should not have brought her with me, though I seriously doubted I could have kept her away. She had just witnessed some of the same kind of noisy and lurid demonstrations I had seen when Lawson and Biberman had appeared before the Committee forty-one years ago, except here there had been no chairman to shut them up or sit them down.

Bulbs flashed all around us as the photographers enjoyed a field day. This was much more than they had expected. Jean pulled herself together, for the time being, and we prepared to leave the chamber. We were surrounded by a crowd of sympathizers when a serious-looking man urgently pushed his way toward us. He had scribbled his name and address on a used envelope, and reaching between bodies and over shoulders, he handed it to me. He spoke hurriedly.

"I am your greatest admirer," he said, "for your work and for your stance. Don't give up on either."

His name was Valery Fried, and he was from Moscow, here to represent the Russian filmmakers. Shades of glasnost! A Russian—possibly a communist—and on our side! Even in times of disaster, there may be encouragement and occasional small triumphs.

Over the next two years, I gave the Barcelona incident a great deal of thought, and it was only after the disintregration of the Soviet Union that things came together—a possible explanation for the panel's behavior and the attitude of the Russian writer. In 1988, Valery Fried was already breathing whiffs of *svoboda*, and feeling free enough to express an anticommunist opinion. On the other hand, the American panelists were beginning to sense, at least subliminally, that their world was collapsing, and their near-hysterical behavior was probably caused as much by a feeling of the approaching loss of their reason for being as by their hatred for me.

For these men were essentially political beings, and their nerve center was dissolving into nothingness. Just as Albert Maltz was utterly lost until he got the word from the Comintern about the causes of the Korean War, so these men could have no opinions without dispatches from headquarters to tell them how to think and what attitude to adopt.

In *Witness*, Whittaker Chambers, once a most-dedicated Communist, wrote: "No Communist can be loyal to the Communist International or any of its component parties without being loyal to the Soviet Union. No Communist knows any higher loyalty or he could not be a Communist" (288).

With the collapse of the USSR, the Comintern went out of business, leaving its followers hopelessly lost, with no new icon to worship and no hint of where to go for solace and for solid ground.

However, the past still lingers, and many people are still bothered by the Mafia Syndrome. On the whole, they are more concerned with the naming of names than with the political and social imperatives of my decision. The two questions I have most often heard are "Why did you desert your comrades?" and "Why did you name names?"

The answer to both questions should be obvious; I deserted my comrades *because* they were "comrades"; because as Chambers pointed out, American communists had to be loyal to the Comintern and the Soviet Union, and as another dedicated party member, John Howard Lawson, testified in 1947 "divided loyalty . . . is another word for treason [and] the most despicable crime of which any man or woman can be accused."

These reasons alone make a presumption against informing completely unsupportable, especially when a very real cold war was at its height.

26

It is odd, but amusing, that most people consider a crisis survivor a seer, especially if the survivor's experiences have claimed a good deal of attention from the press. Esoteric questions are asked and profound answers are anticipated; and the third question most frequently asked of me is, "Do you think it can happen again?" That depends. A governmental attack on creative freedoms in Hollywood? Possibly. Senator Jesse Helms is on the prowl again. An organizational attack on constitutional rights in general? Almost certainly.

Experience plays no part in my answers; they are based only on what I have learned from history, that is, what goes around, comes around. The hearings and their aftermath were not unique; in fact, they were classic examples of regression, a cyclical phenomenon in all advanced societies, since many people are not convinced that *progress* is a synonym for *improvement*. That leads them to organize movements of resistance. Usually based on political or religious dogma, most regression is a form of extremism. Our generation has seen examples of religious regression in most of the Islamic countries, among the Hasidim in Israel, and among our own fundamentalists, and religious regression always leads to political regression, as any moderate Iranian will testify. And for more than seven decades, the political regression of communism brought religious and social suppression of the most inhumane kind.

In my own time, I have witnessed major regressive reactions against labor and an assortment of ethnics. At present, we have seen the rise of skinheads, the Aryan Brotherhood, the neo-Nazis, and the resurgence of the KKK, though none of these movements is yet powerful enough to arouse wide public reaction, or thank God, attraction. In a relatively stable system such as ours, regressive movements are usually initiated in reaction to political and social activity deemed dangerous by one extreme or the other, and in the last few decades, most attempts to play fast and loose with our constitutional guarantees have been the result of the cold war.

After having been a source of great damage, rationalization of the cold war with the Soviet Union has lost its validity. But since the end of World War II, we have been conducting bush wars in places like Vietnam, Cuba, Panama, Grenada, Nicaragua, and a bigger war in the Mesopotamian desert. We will probably continue to wage such wars for some time to come. So the answer to the third question, which is asked only by the politically naive, is a very positive "Inevitably!"

The fourth most frequently asked question, "Has your experience made you bitter?" is somewhat more troublesome. For years, my answer to that question was, "No," even when some thirteen or fourteen years ago my life was nearly blighted by a long overdue midlife crisis, whose roots had been nourished by my political, professional, and social experiences after HUAC. However, after surviving that ordeal (thanks to an obstinate wife), I was forced to take a hard and honest look at the state of my mind (without benefit of professional help), and I uncovered a large pool of gall deep in my psyche. Its existence was a complete surprise, as was its reason for being.

All those who knew me, friend or foe, would have assumed that such bitterness would be directed at my former party associates and/or the Committee, but those assumptions would have been far off the track. I understood the sources of the differing points of view, even though I disapproved of their extreme biases. From the very beginning, I had considered the events of 1947 through the 1950s as battles of the cold war, whose rules were similar to those of any conflict, and in which there were no predetermined winners.

My battles as one of the Ten were losses, and though I hated the defeats, I could not complain. I violently disagreed with the Committee's tactics, but I understood that its members were battling for what they considered right at that time in our history. And after I reversed my stand in 1951, I could also understand the bitterness of those excomrades who were clinging desperately to the remnants of a dream I had helped to shatter. I had only to place myself a few years back in time to see how they could mistakenly consider my attack against the organization that they had elevated to a religion as an attack against their ideals, some of which I still shared.

My problem was to identify the real source of my rancor. I did not have far to look. In my saga, the scoundrels were not members of the Committee or the Party, but fellows of the liberal chic, the hypocrites who rated snitching a higher crime than treason and who, from no-risk positions, kept the conflict alive into the present decade, to the detriment of Hollywood and its chief industry. I was indeed bitter toward the Billys, the Johns, the Morts, and the scores of less clever others, who, though not members of the Party, unknowingly aided and abetted the real renegades of our community, while making snide jokes at the expense of those who prized their country more than the party of Stalin and Brezhnev. In his book of atonement, *The Naked God*, Howard Fast, using a derisory style honed during his tenure on the *Daily Worker*, put it neatly and honestly: "All over the nation the mental revolutionaries, the parlor pinks, the living-room warriors, the mink-coated allies of the working class wept that people like myself had betrayed the holy cause of Communism" (66).

After all the political and social analysis, I realized that a very human factor had always been part of the equation: the liberal chic was understandably missing the fetid forest because of a few healthy trees. Specifically, Trumbo, Lardner, and Scott were, apart from their talents, nice guys, and few of their "mink-coated allies" wanted to look deeper than that.

The rest followed quickly. It was no problem for me to separate the good from the bad in the parlor pinks' logic or to recognize the simplistic rationalization disguised as principle. And while conceding the legitimacy of the precepts against informing adopted by those suffering willful persecution, as have the Jews through most of their existence, it was still completely logical to deny the legal and moral validity of such precepts when used by criminals and members of covert, subversive organizations as a shield against justifiable exposure.

It suddenly strikes me that this book is too much about conspirators, scoundrels, misguided idealists, fascist-minded Americans, would-be traitors, and naive patriots. But, largely between the lines, it is also about friends.

I had not seen Dore Schary since 1956, the year he was fired by MGM. Though in the next ten years he wrote and produced a very successful play and film, *Sunrise at Campobello*, his next play was a total flop. From the early 1920s to 1956, Dore's career had been a long, steady climb from actor to writer to a position as head of the most prestigious studio in Hollywood—which made his precipitous drop at the end extremely traumatic.

When, sometime in the 1960s, I ran into him on St. Pierre Road in Bel Air, it was a pleasant surprise. He was living not two blocks from Jean and me, and we hadn't known it. The moment I saw him at his curb mailbox, I braked to a stop, jumped out of my car, and crossed the street to say hello. Even as I approached him, I could see that his usual guileless, upbeat demeanor was missing. And almost immediately after our initial greetings, he looked down at the meager collection of letters in his hand.

"Eddie," he said, "I had no idea how few friends I had."

Dore's problem was that he believed those hundreds of sycophantic jobholders and job-seekers truly loved him.

"Tell me about it!" was all I could say.

A new look came into his eyes as he regarded me with some intensity. He was putting himself in my shoes.

"Yeah," he said. And perhaps for a few moments, he didn't feel quite so alone.

The memory of that scene comes back to me often. It has helped me to realize how lucky I've been. True, like Dore, I count my friends on the fingers of one hand, but even when the silver lining had turned a dirty gray, millions of people saw my films, and a few of them still write to me. They don't seem to care whether I was a communist, an excommunist, or an anticommunist. In their view, I have always been the same man, making motion pictures that delivered the same messages, which they received with apparent approval. Perhaps, I tell myself, these people, too, are my true friends and able to judge me more clearly and honestly than my enemies.

So, in spite of the dark alleys and the miserable streets through which it has sometimes led me, I feel that the decision I made at Cal Tech in 1927 was the right one after all.

Index

Academy of Motion Pictures Arts and
Sciences, 99
Actors' Lab, 6
Actors' Studio, 6, 7
Adler, Luther, 20
AFL (American Federation of Labor), 25,
162
AFTRA (American Federation of
Television and Radio Artists), 94, 95
Allen, Woody, 198
All the King's Men, 115. *See also* Rossen,
Robert
American Legion, 91, 107, 110, 154
American Legion Magazine, 179
Anhalt, Edna, 175
Anhalt, Edward, 175, 191
Argentina, 19
Arlen, Richard (Dick), 3
Arthur, Art, 173
Atheneum Court Hotel, 105
Atlas, Leopold, 22

Bacall, Lauren, 55
Back to Bataan, 17, 19, 119, 199
Balzer, 141
Barcelona, 197, 199
Barry, Don (Red), 96
Barzman, Ben, 16, 21, 99, 108, 113
Bataan, 16
Behind the Rising Sun, 17
Bells of St. Mary's, 47
Benedick, Lazlo, 175
Benjamin, Maurice, 48
Berg, James, 48
Bernstein, William, 197, 198
Berry, Jack, 162, 163, 197, 198
Bessie, Alvah, 8, 22, 64, 65, 74, 115, 183
Biberman, Herbert, 22, 66, 74, 75, 112, 115,
118, 146, 150, 151, 162, 168, 199
Bill of Rights, 66, 73
Blacklist, 105, 108, 179, 180
Blankfort, Michael, 160
Boehm, Sidney, 47
Bogart, Humphrey, 55, 76, 184, 186, 188
Bond, Ward, 34, 185
Brando, Marlon, 188, 191
Brecht, Bertholdt, 6, 69–71, 89
Breindel, Eric, 49

Brewer, Roy, 34, 62, 63, 173, 185
Brezhnev, Leonid, 203
Brick Foxhole, The, 30, 31
Bridges, Harry, 167
Bridges, Lloyd, 160
Britt, Mai, 192
Broken Lance, The, 188, 190, 191
Bromberg, Edward, 182n
Bronston, Nat, 105, 108, 110
Brooks, Richard, 30, 55
Browder, Earl, 92, 168
Brown, Phil, 105, 187
Buchman, Sidney, 11, 12
Busch, Niven, 24

Cabanatuan, 16
Caesar, 96
Caine Mutiny, The, 186–90
Cal Tech, 193, 204
Cantor, Eddie, 55
Capra, Frank, 3
Carlson, Oliver, 57
Castle, Bill, 117
Cellar, Emmanuel, 13n, 50, 52
Chadwick, I. E., 173
Chambers, Whittaker, 200
Chaplin, Charles, 93
Chelsea (London), 105
"Christ in Concrete," 97
Christ in Concrete, 101, 107, 108, 110
Citizen Kane, 154n
Clark, Colonel, 16
Clark, Tom, 107
Clift, Montgomery, 122, 189, 191, 192
Clurman, Harold, 6
Cobb, Lee, 160, 184
Cohn, Harry, 53, 91, 175, 190
Cole, Lester, 45, 47, 67–69, 75, 94
Collins, Richard, 20, 170, 171
Columbia Pictures, 150; 175, 186, 189, 194
Comintern, 22, 53, 64, 136, 144, 200
Committee for the First Amendment, 55,
57, 60
Communist Political Association, 9, 161,
168
Conference of Studio Unions, 164
Congreve, William, 115
Cooper, Gary, 11, 47

205

Index

Coppel, Alec, 105
Cornered, 11, 17, 20, 60, 115, 164, 170, 189
Corregidor, 16
Corwin, Norman, 55
counterattack, 179
Crawford, Joan, 42
Crossfire, 27, 30–32, 66, 67, 99, 179
Crowther, Bosley, 91
Crum, Bartley, 35–38, 40, 48, 50, 52, 53, 57, 58, 68, 70, 73, 75, 104, 121, 122, 144–46, 152, 153, 169
Cuernavaca, 96
Cukor, George, 7
Curtiz, Mike, 95

Dales, Jack, 173
Dassin, Jules, 163, 197–99
Daves, Delmer, 148
Davis, John, 107, 110
DeMille, Agnes, 55
DeMille, C. B., 34, 94, 95, 147–49, 151, 179, 189
Diamond, I. A. L., 55
di Donato, Pietro, 97
Dies Committee, 59n
Dieterle, William, 25
Dmytryk, Jean. See Porter (Dmytryk), Jean
Dmytryk, Michael, 4, 94, 116, 190
Dmytryk, Mike, 5
Dmytryk, Rebecca, 196
Dmytryk, Richard, 109, 146
Dmytryk, Victoria, 190, 196
Doctor Zhivago, 22, 23
Douglas, Kirk, 55
Dozier, William, 18
Duclos, Jacques, 168
Duke of Windsor, 29
Dunfee, Jack, 107
Dunne, Philip, 55

Edwards, Michael, 8
Eisenhower, D. D., 65, 95
Eisler, Gerhardt, 70
Eisler, Hans, 6, 70
Ellicott City, 103, 172, 173
Embassy Club, 106
English, Richard, 154

Famous Players Lasky Studio, 5
Farmer (prison guard), 140

Farrow, John, 148
Fast, Howard, 22, 128, 132, 133, 135–37, 146, 188, 203
FBI, 45, 95, 96, 170, 176
Federal Prison Administration, 33, 133, 141, 143
Feldman, Charles, 112, 116, 150, 151, 194
Ferrer, Jose, 160, 186
Feuchtwanger, Leon, 6
Fonda, Henry, 55
Fonda, Jane, 189
Ford, Henry, 72
Ford, John, 147, 148
Frankl, Ben, 110
Franz, Arthur, 175
Frazier, James B., 156
Fregonese, Hugo, 175
Fried, Valery, 199
Frye, Christopher, 6

Gallup Poll, 83
Gang, Martin, 148
Gardner, Ava, 55
Garfield, John, 42
Geiger, Rod, 97–100, 108, 110, 113, 183
Gerstad, Harry, 96, 111
Gide, André, 61
Give Us This Day, 139, 154. See also Christ in Concrete
Glebe Place, 105
Going My Way, 46, 47
Gold, Michael, 22
Goldwyn, Samuel, 91
Goodman, Benny, 55
Gorbachev, Mikhail, 10
Gordean, Jack, 150
Graham, Gloria, 31
Gray, Sally, 105
graylist, 179, 180, 181
Greene, Graham, 191
Gubern, Ruben, 197

Hart, Moss, 55
Harvey's Restaurant, 50
Hayden, Sterling, 111
Hecht, Ben, 18
Helms, Jessie, 201
Hepburn, Katharine, 55
HICCASP (Hollywood Citizens

Committee of the Arts, Sciences, and Professions), 7, 13
High Wall, The, 47
Hilton, James, 27, 29
Hitler, Adolph, 42, 71, 159
Hollywood Daily Variety, 197
Hollywood Ten, 1, 11, 23, 27, 39, 59, 65, 72, 76, 89–93, 106, 112–15, 118, 124, 126, 138, 143, 150, 151, 154, 160, 161, 166, 167, 172, 173, 176–79, 194, 202
Hoover, J. Edgar, 50, 170
Hopper, Hedda, 29, 34, 185
House Judiciary Committee, 13, 50
Houseman, John, 196
House of Representatives, 89, 90
Howard, Trevor, 28
Howe, James Wong, 7
HUAC, 1, 2, 4, 6, 24, 27, 33–35, 49, 52–55, 59, 62, 64–67, 73, 89, 91, 92, 94, 102, 106, 113–16, 119, 147, 152–54, 156, 159, 172, 176, 181, 182, 190, 193, 198, 202
Hughes, Howard, 29, 34, 45
Hughes, Rupert, 45, 57
Hunt, J. Roy, 31
Hurst, Fanny, 41
Huston, John, 55, 92, 93
Huston, Walter, 55
Huxley, Aldous, 6

IATSE (International Association of Theatrical and Stage Employees), 25, 62, 162, 164
Isherwood, Christopher, 6
Israel, 145

Jackson, Donald L., 156, 185
Jarrico, Paul, 164
Jeeter (prisoner), 131
Jefferson, Thomas, 48
Johnson, Eric, 43, 48, 74, 180
Johnson, Lyndon, 58
Johnson, Van, 186
Joint Anti-Fascist Refugee Committee, 132
Jurado, Katy, 190

Kahn, Gordon, 13n, 45, 55, 66, 69, 72, 74, 90
Katya, 98

Katz, Charles, 36, 37, 113
Kaufman, George, 55
Kaye, Danny, 55
Kazan, Elia, 22, 37, 38, 41, 147, 148, 188, 192
Kearney, Bernard W., 156
Keaton, Buster, 140
Keech (Judge), 118
Kelly, Gene, 55
Kempner, Alexander, 173
Kennedy, Jack, 194
Kenny, Robert, 36, 38, 40, 48, 53, 58, 70, 73
Kerr, Deborah, 189
Khruschev, Nikita, 22, 23, 92, 136
Kiley, Richard, 176
King Brothers, 173–75
King's Road (London), 105, 106
Knowles, Patrick, 174
Knox, Alexander, 55
Koch, Howard, 36, 52, 70
Koestler, Arthur, 14, 61
Kramer, Stanley, 175, 176, 178, 186, 187, 189, 190, 192
Ku Klux Klan, 63, 201

Lancaster, Burt, 55
Lang, Fritz, 6, 148
Lange, Hope, 122, 192
Lansbury, Angela, 174
Lardner, Ring, Jr., 67, 68, 75, 94, 203
Last Mile, The, 19
Lawson, John Howard, 20–22, 24, 35, 36, 38, 45, 57–60, 68, 72–74, 76, 92, 101, 114, 115, 118, 167, 168, 172
Lenin, Nicolai, 15, 90, 104
Lennert, Isobel, 160
Leone, Sergio, 195, 196
Leroy, Mervyn, 189
Levene, Sam, 31
Lewton, Val, 112
Lieber, Perry, 95
Lincoln Brigade, 8, 64, 109
London, 27, 100, 105, 106, 108, 116
Losey, Joe, 163
Loy, Myrna, 55
Lubitsch, Ernst, 10

MacArthur, Douglas, 16
Macauley Richard, 57
Madison, Guy, 24

Index

Maltz, Albert, 21–23, 35, 51, 60, 63, 64, 74,
94, 103, 104, 112, 115, 122, 124, 126,
132–37, 143–46, 164, 172, 173, 200
Maltz, Margaret, 143–45
Mankiewicz, Joe, 147, 148, 190
Mann, Thomas, 6, 92, 93
Margolis, Ben, 17, 36–38, 113, 167
Marshall, E. G., 190
Marshall, George, 34, 185
Martin, Dean, 192
Marx, Bert, 173
Maryland, 102
Matthau, Walter, 194
Mayer, Louis B., 6, 43, 44, 174
McCarey, Leo, 34, 46, 47
McCarthy, Joseph, 33, 91, 147, 179, 193
McDowell, John, 40, 42
McGrath, 146
McGuiness, James, 57
McGuire, Dorothy, 24, 55
McIntyre, O. O., 46
McMurray, Fred, 186
McNutt, Paul V., 48, 63
Murder, My Sweet, 4, 18, 20, 30, 152
Murnau, Franz, 6
Murphy, Frank, 107
Murphy, George, 48, 179
Murphy, Richard, 190
Mutiny, 174

Navasky, Victor, 76, 175, 181–83, 187
New Masses, 22
Newton, Robert, 105
New York, 89, 98, 116, 145
New York Daily Worker, 176
New York Seven, the, 167
New York Times, 91
Niblo, Fred, Jr., 45, 57
Nineteen, the, 37, 38, 48, 52–59, 65, 66,
69–71, 73, 76, 89, 171
Nixon, Richard M., 40, 58
North, Joseph, 22

Obsession, 105, 107
Odets, Clifford, 6, 41, 46, 160
O'Neal, Charles, 96, 112
Ornitz, Samuel, 65, 66, 74, 118
Oxford Street (London), 100

Painters' Union strike, 25, 164

Paisan, 97
Paramount, 5, 174, 190, 194–96
Parks, Larry, 7, 38, 68, 155, 157–60, 171
Pasternack, Boris, 22, 23
Paxton, John, 18, 19, 27, 30, 31, 55
Peck, Gregory, 55, 189, 194
People's Educational Center, 7
Peters, Jean, 190
Philadelphia, 104, 172
Pichel, Irving, 36
Platt, David, 176
Poe, E. A., 7
Popper, Marty, 155
Porter, Henry and Mrs., 104
Porter (Dmytryk), Jean, 25, 27, 29, 32, 37,
55, 75, 90, 98–111, 113, 116, 117, 119,
121, 122, 138, 139, 143–46, 151, 152,
166–69, 172, 174, 175, 181, 183, 191,
193, 194, 197–99, 202
Potter, Charles, E., 156
Powell, Richard (Dick), 17, 20, 96
Price, Vincent, 55
Pryor, Tom, 197, 199

Quinn, Anthony, 189

Raft, George, 111
Raksin, David, 160
Rand, Ayn, 44, 57
Rank, J. Arthur, 27–29, 107, 108, 110, 116,
139, 151
Rankin, John, 34, 148
Rathvon, N. Peter, 30, 31, 90
Reagan, Ronald, 14, 48, 173, 178, 179
Red Channels, 179
Reed, Carol, 105
Reed, Tom, 112
Reis, Irving, 175
Revueltas, Rosaura, 197
Reynolds, Sen. Robert R., 34
RKO, 4, 11, 18, 24, 25, 27, 29, 30, 32, 33,
46, 58, 95, 99, 169
Robeson, Paul, 13, 14, 104
Robinson, Edward G., 36
Rogers, Ginger, 4, 46
Rogers, Lela, 4, 34, 46
Rome, 97
Rose, David, 191
Rossellini, Roberto, 97
Rossen, Robert, 60, 114, 115, 160

Rush, Barbara, 192
Rushmore, Howard, 57
Rutledge, Wiley, 107
Ryan, Robert, 31, 55
Ryskind, Maurie, 45, 57

Sahl, Mort, 183
Salt to the Devil, 110n. *See also Give Us This Day*
Saturday Evening Post, 154, 172
Schary, Dore, 20, 24, 25, 31, 33, 34, 53, 57, 58, 72, 73, 90, 91, 203, 204
Schell, Maximillian, 189, 194
Schoenberg, Arnold, 6
Schulberg, Budd, 60, 160, 188
Schulman, Tom, 193
Scott, Adrian, 11, 12, 14, 15, 17, 18, 20–22, 27, 28, 30, 31, 33–35, 50–52, 60, 66, 67, 75, 90, 92, 93, 111, 118, 138, 182, 183, 203
Scott, Joan, 182, 183, 187
Scott, Martha, 28
Screen Actors Guild, 48, 162, 195
Screen Directors Guild, 48, 55, 94, 96, 147, 162, 163, 191
Screen Writers Guild, 59, 61, 62, 65, 67, 68, 74, 112, 162, 164, 195
Selsden Park Hotel, 100
Selznick, David, 24, 91, 112
Shaw, Irwin, 55
Shaw, James (Commander), 187
Shelley, Mary, 112
Shirley, Anne, 182
Siegal, Sol, 190
Signal Corps, 97
Sillen, Samuel, 22
Sinatra, Frank, 171
Slezak, Walter, 20
Smith, Gerald L. K., 63, 63n
Smith, H. A., 43, 44
Sniper, The, 175, 176, 178, 180
Sokolsky, Sidney, 76, 179
Song of Russia, 43, 44
Sorrel, Herbert, 25
Soviet Union, 178
So Well Remembered, 27, 29, 30, 101, 107
Spender, Stephen (epigraph), 61, 62
Sperling, Milton, 194, 195
Spielberg, Steven, 189
Stalin, 15, 90, 91, 95, 102, 119, 151, 160, 203

Stephens, George, 147
Stevens, Mark, 174
Stevenson, Adlai, 193
Streisand, Barbra, 189
Stripling, Robert E., 40, 43, 44, 47, 57, 62, 64–70, 74, 75

Taradash, Daniel, 197
Tavenner, Frank, 1, 156–58, 160–64, 166, 167, 170, 171
Taylor, Elizabeth, 188, 189
Taylor, Robert, 43, 47, 48
Temple, Shirley, 24, 25
Tender Comrade, 3, 4, 17, 46
Thieman, K. E., 130, 138, 139
Thomas, J. Parnell, 33, 40–42, 45, 48, 50, 57–59, 61–63, 65–71, 73–75, 106, 156, 179
Thoreau, Henry David, 24
Till the End of Time, 20, 24, 27, 150, 189
Townsend, Leo, 113
Tracy, Spencer, 188, 190
Truman, Harry S., 35, 145
Trumbo, Dalton, 4, 38, 61, 62, 74, 94, 101, 113, 118, 174, 203
Tuttle, Frank, 8, 162
Twentieth Century-Fox, 29, 41, 190–92

United Artists, 195, 196
Universal Studio, 194
U.S. Supreme Court, 52, 54, 61, 74, 89, 101, 116
Utley, Freda, 159

Vail, Richard, B., 40, 42, 43
Velde, Harold, 159
Vishinsky, 39
Vorhaus, Bernard, 162

Wagner, R. J., 190
Waldorf-Astoria Declaration, 90, 91, 94, 97, 113, 150, 179, 190
Waldorf-Astoria Hotel, 89
Walk on the Wild Side, A, 18, 188
Walter, Frances E., 156, 157, 166
Wanamaker, Sam, 108
Warner, J. L. (Jack), 41–43, 195, 196
Washington, George, 45
Watts, Bill, 147, 184
Watts, Flo, 147, 184

Index

Wayne, John, 16, 17, 34, 112, 119, 185
Wayne, Naunton, 105
Webb, Clifton, 112
Weir, Peter, 193
West Virginia, 127, 140, 149
Wexley, John, 19–21
Widmark, Richard, 189, 190, 194
Wilder, Billy, 55
Williams, Bill, 24
Williams, Robin, 193
Winchell, Walter, 138
Winston, Archer, 32
Wood, John S., 156

Wood, Sam, 34, 44, 45, 47, 57
Wright, Richard, 61, 62
Writers Mobilization, 7
Wyler, William, 55, 148

Yordan, Phil, 113
Young, Robert, 31
Young Lions, The, 188, 191

Zanuck, Darryl, 29, 190, 191
Zimmerman, Stan, 48
Zinneman, Fred, 148, 175

Edward Dmytryk directed his first film at Paramount in 1939 and reached the A bracket with *Tender Comrade* and *Murder, My Sweet* in 1943 and 1944. After *Crossfire* in 1947, he was charged with contempt of Congress and, in 1950, served a six-month sentence in a federal prison. After a second appearance before Congress in 1951, he refueled his career with films like *The Caine Mutiny, Raintree County, The Broken Lance*, and *The Young Lions*, for a career total of more than fifty films. Since 1979, he has been teaching filmmaking—first, at the University of Texas, then, from 1981, at the University of Southern California.